P9-DNK-820

GROWN AT GLEN GARDEN

*Ben Hogan, Byron Nelson, and the Little Texas Golf
Course that Propelled Them to Stardom*

JEFF MILLER

Skyhorse Publishing

To the Dirty Dozen, past and present

Copyright © 2012 by Jeff Miller

All Rights Reserved. No part of this book may be reproduced in any manner without the express written consent of the publisher, except in the case of brief excerpts in critical reviews or articles. All inquiries should be addressed to Skyhorse Publishing, 307 West 36th Street, 11th Floor, New York, NY 10018.

Skyhorse Publishing books may be purchased in bulk at special discounts for sales promotion, corporate gifts, fund-raising, or educational purposes. Special editions can also be created to specifications. For details, contact the Special Sales Department, Skyhorse Publishing, 307 West 36th Street, 11th Floor, New York, NY 10018 or info@skyhorsepublishing.com.

Skyhorse° and Skyhorse Publishing° are registered trademarks of Skyhorse Publishing, Inc.°, a Delaware corporation.

Visit our website at www.skyhorsepublishing.com.

10 9 8 7 6 5 4 3 2 1

Library of Congress Cataloging-in-Publication Data is available on file.
ISBN: 978-1-61608-841-5

Printed in the United States of America

CONTENTS

Foreword by Sandra Palmer   vii

FOREWORD

I'M TEXAN THROUGH and through, born in Fort Worth, even though I've lived in California for some time. If you want to learn how to play golf, you don't go to Palm Springs. You go where that wind's blowing, and Texas is one of those places. And Glen Garden was a great place to learn.

We moved to Maine when I was ten, and we stayed there for three years. That's actually where I started to play. We lived just south of Bangor. There was a nine-hole golf course called Lucerne where I got off the school bus, That started my fascination with golf. There was a wonderful man there named John Brown. He let me work in the shop and pay for a set of clubs – Jackie Burke Jr. clubs. I took them home, and I was worried my mother would think they cost too much and wouldn't let me keep them. But it all worked out.

I moved back to Texas when I was thirteen, to the northwest part of Fort Worth near River Oaks, to live with my grandmother because things at home weren't going so well. I used to go to Rockwood Park, and my step-granddad would drop me off in the morning and pick me up when he got off work. I got a nice reputation and started to play in some tournaments. One of those tournaments was at Glen Garden, and that's where I met the Warrens – Vida and Ed – and we hit it off. He was the president of Glen Garden at the time, and we built up a friendship. They were a wonderful couple who never had children. They never said an unkind word to each other. They took an interest in me because my background wasn't too pleasant. My mother had me when she was very young, and we were more like sisters. Going to live with the Warrens changed my life as a golfer and as a person.

I guess you could say my grandmother was my confidante. When something happened between her and my step-grandfather, she said I should go live with the Warrens because she really liked them. She knew I wanted to go to college, and she said they could provide for me more than she could. It was a big thing for her to let me go, though it wasn't *that* far away. I still kept in touch with her.

So I moved in with the Warrens on Timberline Drive, right behind the third hole at Glen Garden. I learned years later that Byron Nelson lived on Timberline years before I did, a couple of blocks over toward Mitchell Boulevard. When I first moved in, there wasn't a fence between the course and our property, and golf balls would be all over the yard. Glen Garden was a great place to learn golf. The greens were tiny; you really had to work to get your shot on the green. I got a little membership there. It had been years since Ben Hogan and Byron Nelson were there, but they were still special to the people there. You'd often hear the story that Mr. Hogan would sleep in a bunker so that he'd be the first caddie to get a bag in the morning.

A few years later, I was a pro golfer, too. It's pretty miraculous that three people who went on to become professional golfers got their starts at little Glen Garden. Then years later when I was playing professionally, I was in the Hogan factory in Fort Worth getting adjustments on my Hogan clubs from Gene Sheeley, who was Mr. Hogan's clubmaker. The phone rang, and he said Mr. Hogan wanted to see me. So off I go to his office. I know on the golf course he didn't smile much, but he was very pleasant to me that day.

I got to meet Byron Nelson, too. He was always really nice. When Marilynn Smith started a tournament in Dallas for the legends of the L.P.G.A. Tour, they both came out to a little cocktail party before the tournament began, and it was a real thrill. They were so good for the game. And to think they both started as caddies at Glen Garden.

Grown at Glen Garden takes a different look at the careers of Ben Hogan and Byron Nelson. It brings refreshing new perspective – a more local glimpse of their careers, their upbringings and the legacies they left behind – and tells a few stories that haven't previous been told. I hope you enjoy it.

—Sandra Palmer, August 2012

(Sandra Palmer was a member of Glen Garden Golf and Country Club before embarking on a career in professional golf in which she won twenty-one tournaments while playing on the L.P.G.A. Tour, including the U.S. Women's Open and the Colgate Dinah Shore major championship. She was the L.P.G.A. Player of the Year in 1975. From 1968 through 1977, she ranked in the top ten on the L.P.G.A. Tour's money winnings list.)

1

ONE FINAL HURRAH

JEFF RUDE'S PASSIONS since an early age have been golf and sportswriting. Growing up in Waukegan, Illinois, Rude caddied at Glen Flora Country Club and later attended the University of Missouri's prestigious journalism school on an Evans Scholarship awarded by the Western Golf Association. The Evans Scholars Foundation based near Chicago was founded by former pro golfer Chick Evans and has funded college scholarships for youngsters involved in caddying since 1930.

After graduation from Mizzou, Rude climbed the newspaper ladder quickly with sportswriting jobs at *The Shreveport Journal* and *Jacksonville Journal*, became sports editor and lead columnist at *Cocoa Today* on Florida's Space Coast and moved into management in markets with big-league sports at the *Pittsburgh Post-Gazette*, *The Dallas Morning News* and the *Chicago Sun-Times*. During his short time in Shreveport, Rude became well acquainted with local golf star Hal Sutton, *Golf Magazine*'s college player of the year for 1980 playing for Centenary College. A few years later, when writing in Jacksonville, Rude had preliminary talks with Sutton about becoming his caddie on the P.G.A. Tour.

But Rude stayed in journalism and returned to his first love in the business, returning to *The Dallas Morning News* in autumn 1991 as its golf writer. One of his first priorities upon returning to Dallas was to set up the cover story and photo for *The News'* 1992 golf preview section that published in February. Rude had little trouble identifying a theme. Nineteen ninety-two would mark the eightieth birthdays for north Texas' two living golf legends, Byron Nelson and Ben Hogan. Among the most dominant golfers of the mid-twentieth century, Hogan and Nelson not only were born in the same year, they were introduced to the game at the same place (Glen Garden Golf and Country Club, just outside Fort Worth at the time but part of an area annexed into the city years ago) in the same fashion (serving as caddies, earning the princely sum of fifty cents for toting a bag around the course). Both experienced success as amateurs, winning events not only in Fort Worth – also known as "Where the West Begins" or "Cowtown" – but across north Texas.

Hogan went pro in 1930 and struggled painfully for years. In the spring of 1940, like a safecracker who suddenly heard the tumblers click, he not only broke into the victory column for the first time individually but scored wins in his next two tournaments as well. He would claim sixty-four career wins, nine in official major tournaments, three Vardon Trophies, five money earnings titles plus two achievements singular in their standing in golf history. First, there was the unlikely return to tournament play less than a year after the horrific car accident of February 1949 in west Texas that nearly killed him and left him with physical issues he would cope with for the rest of his life. Just coming back to play in 1950 would have been enough. It was enough to compel Hollywood film director Sidney Lanfield to shoot the 1951 movie *Follow the Sun* starring Glenn Ford as Hogan. But Hogan left the golf world speechless by winning the 1950 U.S. Open – the "Miracle at Merion." Incredibly, fans had not yet seen Hogan at his best. That magic was displayed in 1953, when he claimed his second Masters championship, fourth U.S. Open and came home from his first and only journey to the British Open with the Claret Jug from Carnoustie, Scotland.

Along the way, Hogan was ferocious in his approach to the game that he loved: the game that consumed much of his life; the game that might have in some way helped him cope with a devastating family tragedy. A diminutive figure at about 5-foot-7 and 135–140 pounds, he was dubbed Bantam Ben early on. On occasion he liked to refer to himself as Henny Bogan. Hogan practiced at a pace and duration unseen among his peers. That was accompanied by a focus that didn't allow for frivolity to enter his workplace. (Was that what led to another nickname, the Hawk? He told Jimmy Burch of the *Fort Worth Star-Telegram* the nickname was coined by one of his closest friends on the Tour, Jimmy Demaret of Houston, on a hunting trip in south Texas.) Caddies were told to keep quiet. Playing partners heard very little from him, and he usually disdained reporters. His aversion to being the center of attention carried over to his tournament attire: muted shades – usually gray and white – with a meticulousness that included the flat linen cap that became his trademark. His hands bled from so much practice. Hogan's intensity didn't always abate when the day was over; Nelson recalled being awakened by a constant scratching noise when sharing a motel room with Hogan only to discover it was the sound of his roomie grinding his teeth in his sleep.

Famed British golf writer Pat Ward-Thomas wrote, "Hogan came as near to dehumanizing golf as anyone has even done." After Hogan's death, long-time Dallas-Fort Worth sportswriter Frank Luksa wrote in *The Dallas Morning News* that Hogan "played the game as if locked in a cocoon." Then there was the perspective of a fellow competitor like George Fazio, whose lone moment in the P.G.A. Tour spotlight was the three-man playoff at Merion in 1950 with Hogan and Lloyd Mangrum: "Hogan is the most perfect gentleman on the golf course that I ever played with." And the same man initiated the champions dinner preceding each Masters that has become a part of Augusta tradition. For decades during Hogan's ascent to the top and afterward, there grew a fascination with the "Hogan secret" for golfing success that was eventually "revealed" in magazine articles and books. The many "how-tos" though, failed to produce another Hogan. Secret or not, Hogan played with his clubface slightly open and from a slightly open stance. Various figures – including former Glen Garden pro Ted Longworth, Tour player Henry Picard and major league outfielder-turned-P.G.A. Tour pro Sam Byrd, have been credited with assisting him to overcome the dire hook that appeared to doom his early playing career.

His fellow caddie yard alum, Byron Nelson, was a contrast in both profile and personality. Nelson quickly passed six feet in height as a teen; in what is surely the first photo of them together – shot at Glen Garden in December 1927 – he towered over Hogan (even without the huge cowboy hat). While Nelson also dedicated much of his adult life to becoming the best golfer that he could be, he said late in life that he'd rather be known for how he treated people than how he played. Maybe that was an easier goal to pursue without the fruitless years of pro play that Hogan had to endure. In Nelson's first pro event – played in Texarkana, Arkansas, in November 1932 – he finished third and pocketed $75. From the time that Hogan first played in a pro event (the 1930 Texas Open in San Antonio) to the first year in which he was able to play regularly on the P.G.A. Tour (1937), he cashed only four checks. In the year in which Hogan was finally good enough to play regularly, Nelson was beginning his collection of major championships at the 1937 Masters.

Nelson was among the pros who adapted easily when golf evolved from hickory-shaft clubs to the steel shafts in the late 1920s and early 1930s. He won five majors, one Vardon Trophy (it wasn't awarded during much of his heyday), two earnings championships and put together the best statistical year in American golf history, the well-chronicled 1945 season. He won eighteen

Tour events that year, including a stretch of eleven consecutive events in which he played. That amazing streak started with the Miami Four-Ball in early March (teaming with Harold "Jug" McSpaden, probably his best friend on the Tour) and extended through the Canadian Open in early August. The makeup of the Tour roster that year was altered by Uncle Sam calling many pros off to war; Nelson was classified 4-F because of a blood condition. Hogan enlisted in the Army Air Corps. Debate has gone on for decades regarding the quality of competition that Nelson faced in running up such incredible numbers. Such debate should include the following number – his scoring average per round that year was 68.33, a Tour record until broken by Tiger Woods' 68.17 in 2000. (Woods' average was compiled playing eighty total rounds; Nelson put together a stretch of eighty consecutive rounds during his 1945 campaign in which his scoring average was 68.10.) During the eleven-tournament winning streak, Nelson's winning margin was 6.3 strokes. He played in thirty events that year. Hogan, one of the pros who returned from the service early in 1945, played in eighteen that year and won five. Sam Snead, who served in the Navy from 1942–44 before being discharged with a slipped vertebra, was a six-time winner that year. Most of the major tournaments that Nelson won took place before any pros were called away by Uncle Sam.

A year later, with all of the pros back from the battlefields, Hogan collected the second-largest amount of Tour victories in a season with thirteen and claimed his first major championship – the 1946 P.G.A. Championship. Nelson retreated from regular Tour play after the 1946 season at the age of thirty-four. He and his wife, Louise, tired of the constant travel. Nelson yearned for a different existence, centered around a homestead in the quiet pastures north of Dallas and Fort Worth that he named Fairway Ranch. In 1948, Hogan fashioned another spectacular season that saw him put together the second-longest winning streak with six. The run started in grand fashion with his second major title of the year and the first of his four U.S. Open titles, played at Riviera Country Club near Los Angeles. He collected nine official major titles in his career, a total exceeded only by Jack Nicklaus, Woods, and Walter Hagen. One of Hogan's predecessors among the golfing elite, Hagen, said of him, "Hogan is a great player because he is able to make the right decision at the moment it must be made." Many golf authorities count the 1942 Hale America Open as Hogan's tenth major since the tournament was meant as a wartime replacement for the suspended U.S. Open. Among that cluster is World Golf Hall of Fame writer Dan Jenkins, who grew up in Fort Worth and took his writing skills from Texas Christian University to the *Fort Worth Press*, *Sports Illustrated* and *Golf Digest.* (The site of the Hale America, Chicago's Ridgemoor Country Club, wasn't considered representative of Open layouts.) Jenkins also classifies Hogan's three wins at the North and South Open and two Western Open titles as well, to increase the total to fifteen.

In 2009, *Sports Illustrated* writers Gary Van Sickle and Jim Gorant chose up sides in a Hogan-Nelson debate. Van Sickle picked Hogan, arguing he proved his mettle over the greater period of time and scored many of his most impressive triumphs against all odds following the 1949 auto accident. Gorant took Nelson primarily on the basis of the 1945 superlatives but also cited a textbook form that became the model for future players (and the literal model for the "Iron Byron" mechanical swing machine, minimizing body turn and instead moving laterally with a slight dip at the knees) and continued contributions to the game long after halting regular Tour participation. With the streak and the eighteen wins in 1945 and the five majors won before he turned thirty-four, Nelson stated he was most proud of his consistency – specifically, cashing in 113 consecutive tournaments during an era when events often paid only the top fifteen or twenty participants. Jenkins has expressed his Cowtown pride that Nelson and Hogan both represented his hometown spectacularly for many years, but he has never straddled the fence when choosing his favorite.

"A man can get carried away trying to prove that Ben Hogan was the greatest golfer who ever lived," wrote Jenkins, who declined to be interviewed for this book, citing work on his own memoirs.

Coincidentally, neither the Hogans nor the Nelsons reared children. In Nelson's case, there were medical reasons related to childhood illnesses, and they decided not to adopt. In each case, the constant travel required to build up and maintain a career as a top P.G.A. Tour professional came into play. Valerie Hogan told Martin Davis for his book *The Hogan Mystique*, "We wanted to have children, but it just didn't happen. We didn't want to adopt children." Lisa Scott, a great-niece of Hogan, recalls it wasn't a topic often discussed. "Mother told me one time that Aunt Valerie thought she was pregnant and Uncle Ben was real excited, passing out cigars," she says. "It was never meant to be." The two childless wives, Louise Nelson and Valerie Hogan, shared many times together on hotel verandas and in roadside restaurants. "We became just like sisters," Valerie told Davis. "We had a much closer relationship than Byron and Ben did."

For those who contend Nelson and Hogan weren't friends, Nelson's brother, Charles, fourteen years his junior, disputes that. "I never saw any animosity between them," says Charles. He recalls Hogan dropping by the Nelsons' Fort Worth home in the 1930s to drive Byron places. And from the two summers during the 1940s when Charles lived with Byron and Louise in Ohio, he recalls frequent pleasant phone conversations between the families. "It is my opinion that a lot has been made of it because they want some conflict," he says. "Conflict is marketable. Friendship is not marketable."

So here were Nelson and Hogan, golfing legends similar yet disparate, living out their final years in the relative shadow of Glen Garden Country Club in the early 1990s. Jeff Rude decided to approach Hogan first because he feared Hogan's reputation for curt and brusque responses to reporters, and his understanding that Hogan's memory issues might cause some difficulties in an interview. Rude asked Hogan's secretary to schedule a one-on-one interview and asked if Hogan would pose for a photo with Nelson. By all indications, the most recent photo of Hogan and Nelson together to that point was shot in 1987, when they were both inducted into the initial class of the Fort Worth Sports Hall of Honor. Hogan's secretary called Rude back a few days later and, to the journalist's surprise and joy, agreed to both requests. Hogan, she said, wanted the photo shoot to take place at Shady Oaks Country Club, the luxurious club in the small municipality of Westover Hills in northwest Fort Worth that became his second home soon after its construction in the mid-1950s.

A few days later, Rude approached Nelson in person at the Four Seasons Resort and Club – home to his namesake P.G.A. Tour event since 1983 – on the day that the resort unveiled the nine-and-a-half-foot statue of its golfing icon on the main walkway through the clubhouse area leading to the golf course. Rude told Nelson that Hogan had already agreed to the photo and specified Shady Oaks as the venue. "That Hogan," Nelson blurted. "Do it on his turf … All right, I'll do it." That night, Rude was filling in for *Morning News* Dallas Mavericks basketball beat writer Mitch Lawrence, covering a home game at Reunion Arena. Rude was working on pregame notes when he received a call from his office. Nelson had called the sports department looking for him. Rude immediately phoned Nelson, who said, "Jeff, you know, I've been thinking about that Hogan picture. I'm just not really comfortable going all the way to Shady Oaks. But I'm willing to meet him sort of in between. How 'bout Colonial?" Rude said he'd call Hogan's office the following morning. Hogan's secretary ran the change past him, and he accepted.

Rude conducted his face-to-face interviews before the photo shoot took place. In Hogan's case, the meeting happened in Hogan's office with a specific time limit of fifteen minutes. Rude arrived early and with a list of written questions – and an opening icebreaker line that he played Hogan clubs. He took his seat about ten feet in front of Hogan's desk and opened by asking, "You turn eighty this year. For someone who has everything, like you, what do you want for your birthday?" Hogan stared at him for about ten seconds, shook his head and replied, "I can't answer that question." Undaunted, Rude proceeded: "For someone who's accomplished all that you've accomplished, what's your most meaningful achievement?" Hogan again stared for a bit, then said, "I can't answer that, either." Question number three: "For years you've gone out to Shady Oaks and hit balls. Do you still go out there and do that?" Hogan didn't need as much time to formulate a reply that time: "I've hit very few since the wreck." Rude was aware of only one wreck in Hogan's life. He scooted his chair in a few feet, leaned toward the desk and said, "Are you talking about the wreck in 1949, or is there one that I missed recently?" "No, the one in '49."

Rude was quietly consumed by panic. He recalls, "Sands of the hour glass are flying by. I've got nothing! I'd written not a word!" Rude abandoned the rest of the questions on his list and instead grasped for his next attempt from thin air: "Do you miss hitting balls?" Suddenly, the gentleman who seemingly couldn't speak couldn't stop: "Oh, yes, I miss hitting balls! I love golf and swinging a golf club and hitting balls. That's been my life for a long time." They talked for the full fifteen minutes. And for another fifteen, days later over the phone in a follow-up session that Hogan gladly agreed to. The subject matter focused primarily on how Hogan had dealt with retirement. The headline for Rude's piece was: *Ben Hogan: Private man is mellowing*. The subsequent interview with Nelson didn't feature any such drama. They met at Fairway Ranch and talked for hours, Rude later describing him in print as a "jukebox waiting for a quarter." The headline for that story borrowed from a quote within, that Nelson's preference was to be remembered as friendly and a good, Christian man rather than as being a good golfer: *'Friendly man' as vibrant as ever*. The interview marked the beginning of a close relationship between the former golfer whose tournament in nearby Irving was considered Dallas' P.G.A. Tour event and the new *Dallas Morning News* golf writer who would move on to *Golfweek* in 1995 and continue to chronicle the sport for decades.

All that remained for *The News*' cover display and main inside package was to shoot the all-important photos. The shoot took place at Colonial Country Club in southwest Fort Worth on Monday morning, February 10, only days before the golf preview section running the following Sunday would go to print. (Section editor Don McMullen was prepared to fall back on file shots lest the scheduled shoot be scrubbed for some reason.) The shooting assignment went to veteran photojournalist David Woo, a two-time Pulitzer Prize finalist out of the University of Texas who'd joined *The News* in 1975. Rude explained to Woo that Hogan and Nelson had not been shot together in years, that an attempt by *Golf Digest* to shoot Hogan, Nelson and their contemporary, Sam Snead, together in the late 1980s – paying each man $50,000 – was scuttled by Hogan. "You don't get many chances to earn $50,000 in a day," Snead told Rude, "but I guess with his [golf club] company, he didn't need the money."

The morning of the shoot was cool but not cold for February in Fort Worth, temperatures in the 50s. It was cloudy, which delighted Woo; he wouldn't have to contend with changing light and shadows. Woo loaded his equipment into one golf cart while Hogan and Nelson climbed into another (Nelson at the wheel) and headed to the eighteenth green. That's the closest part of the course to the clubhouse, minimizing the inconvenience for the two elderly subjects. That was particularly appreciated by Nelson, who was still somewhat hobbled as a result of hip replacement surgeries in July 1990 and October 1991. Before one of the hip operations, Nelson's surgeon spelled out the extreme range of possible outcomes just before the procedure began. If all went well, Nelson would regain range of motion in the hip that he hadn't enjoyed in years. But there was the possibility, be it ever so slight, of complications related to his age and anesthesia that could mean he wouldn't regain consciousness. The surgeon felt it was his duty to convey that even though the chance was remote. "Let me get this straight," Nelson replied. "If this works, I'll be able to play golf again. If it doesn't, I'll be going to heaven . . . Well, what are we waiting for? Seems like a win-win to me!"

Woo didn't instruct Hogan and Nelson what to wear that morning, but each conveniently arrived wearing a fedora, jacket and tie. Hogan wore a gray suit, the fedora matching. Nelson's beige hat matched his sport jacket. With an unofficial time limit of ten minutes to shoot, Woo posed them and began clicking away. He was confident early on that one of his first frames provided an image that was worthy of the cover (the shoot took place well before digital photography

Ben Hogan [left] and Byron Nelson pose on the eighteenth green at Colonial Country Club for *The Dallas Morning News'* golf preview section for 1992, the year in which each turned eighty years old. The February 10, 1992 photo shoot is believed to be the last time that Hogan and Nelson were photographed together. (*The Dallas Morning News: David Woo*)

allowed shooters to instantly review what was just shot). Woo realized after only a few minutes that his subjects were already tiring of the session and said, "Done."

Hogan and Nelson turned and headed back toward their cart. That's when Woo noticed Hogan extend his right arm and offer help to the pained Nelson. Woo immediately grabbed one of his cameras and captured the duo, six decades after they'd initially met as caddies on the other side of southern Fort Worth, as they slowly ambled together for most likely the last time.

2

EVENTS OF 1912

AN UNSINKABLE OCEAN liner, a baseball park wedged into Boston's Back Bay, a sandwich cookie, two new states, and the achievements of America's most decorated athlete were among the most significant mileposts to enter the country's consciousness during the year 1912. The *Titanic*, built at a cost of $7.5 million, set sail from Southampton, England on April 10, 1912 headed for New York City. The 46,000-ton ocean liner struck an iceberg at 11:40 p.m. on April 14, about halfway through her transatlantic maiden voyage, and soon began to plunge bow first into the frigid waters of the North Atlantic. At 2:20 a.m. the following day, the mighty ship's stern was the last to disappear from sight. Of the 2,228 passengers and crew members, 705 were rescued. The longest to live among those was Millvina Dean, an infant lowered into a lifeboat in a canvas mail sack that fateful night. She was ninety-seven years old when she passed away in May 2009.

The contiguous forty-eight states of the continental United States took form when New Mexico and Arizona were admitted to the Union during a five-week period in January and February 1912. They'd been together as one territory until 1863, when the western portion became Arizona. And they were nearly brought in as one state in a process called jointure – the bill to do so was signed by President William Howard Taft – but the idea was ultimately spurned by Arizonans. While Arizona is about three times as populous as New Mexico now, New Mexico was the larger territory at the time.

Nabisco (originally the National Biscuit Company) began producing Oreos in March 1912. At seventy-one percent cookie and twenty-nine crème filling, the Oreo actually mimicked the Hydrox cookie that was created by the Sunshine bakery in 1909. Oreo soon proved to be more popular and was able to market itself as the original sandwich cookie. The elaborate design on each of the Oreo facings has changed only twice through the years, the current pattern adopted in 1952. It's not known when the Oreo might have first been unhinged and eaten as separate pieces. Or first dipped in a glass of milk.

On April 20, 1912, Fenway Park opened in Boston. The hometown Red Sox welcomed 24,000 fans that day for their game against the New York Highlanders, so many that some needed to stand in parts of the outfield grass that were roped off from play. The Sox didn't disappoint, though they were forced to extra innings after grabbing an early 5-1 lead. A two-out hit by Boston star hitter Tris Speaker skidded beyond the reach of New York short-stop Roy Hartzell and scored Steve Yerkes to give the Red Sox a 7-6 victory. The time of the game was three hours and twenty minutes, which might get you to the seventh-inning stretch of a Boston-New York game these days. The Sox went on to win 105 games, a record then in the twelve-year-old American League, and claim their third pennant and win the World Series over New York's National League representative, the Giants, four games to three. Seventy-four years before Bill Buckner's infamous botched grounder, Boston won the deciding game after Giants outfielder Fred Snodgrass dropped a routine fly ball. (The New York Highlanders who helped open Fenway officially became the Yankees in 1913.)

The college football season of 1912 ended with no playoffs, no bowls, no *SportsCenter* bleating for a better system. Five teams went undefeated: Harvard, Notre Dame, Penn State, Washington, and Wisconsin. The first awarding of the Heisman Trophy was still decades away, but a running back at Carlisle Indian Industrial School named Jim Thorpe gained a fair measure of national acclaim for his play. Not a bad finish to a calendar year in which Thorpe also won Olympic gold medals in the pentathlon and decathlon at the Summer Games staged in Stockholm, Sweden. Thorpe was ordered in 1913 to surrender those medals as well as the one that he won following the Olympics at the popular All-Around Games in New York after it was revealed that he'd previously earned a couple hundred dollars playing baseball before the Stockholm Games. The Olympic pentathlon gold was awarded to Norway's Ferdinand Bie, the Olympic decathlon gold to Sweden's Hugo Wieslander, and the first-place medal at the All-Around Games to Princeton graduate John Bredemus. The debate over Thorpe's amateurism raged for decades, and the two Olympic medals were reinstated to him posthumously in 1982 after a successful and extended campaign by his descendents. By then, the medals had been stolen from the museum where they'd been stored and would never be presented to Thorpe's family.

Claudia Alta Taylor was born on December 22, 1912, in the little east Texas town of Karnack. *Who?* When Claudia was an infant, her nurse, Alice Tittle, declared the baby girl was "purty as a ladybird," and the nickname stuck. Lady Bird Johnson might be best remembered for her stoic pose in November 1963 as her husband, Lyndon Baines Johnson, was sworn in as the nation's thirty-sixth president aboard Air Force One at Love Field in Dallas soon after John F. Kennedy was declared dead as a result of the shooting in front of the School Book Depository Building at the corner of Elm and Houston Street.

On a bright, cool Saturday morning in autumn 2011, Charles Nelson is seated in his motorized scooter in the living room of his home in Abilene, Texas, identifying the fortunate circumstances that took place in his life and that of his older brother Byron early in their lives. When Charles turned fourteen in 1940, the family moved from Fort Worth up to Denton, Texas, and practically onto the doorstep of North Texas State Teachers College and its renowned music program. He went on to become nationally known as an operatic performer and a distinguished vocal instructor. Earlier, when Byron turned ten in 1922, the Nelsons moved southeast of downtown Fort Worth to 3109 Timberline Drive, within walking distance of Glen Garden Country Club – a course that would launch a future career as one of the greatest American golfers of the twentieth century. Charles lets out a belly laugh and says, "Einstein said coincidence was when God was anonymous."

John Byron Nelson Sr. and his wife, Madge, settled in on Timberline when Margaret Ellen was three years old and Charles Wade four years away from joining the family. When Byron was born, the Nelsons lived on a 160-acre cotton farm about thirty miles south of Dallas in Ellis County. They lived just west of the town of Waxahachie in a hamlet called Long Branch, named for the Long Branch Creek that flowed through it. His birth at the family farm endangered the life of his eighteen-year-old mother, due greatly to his size (twelve pounds, eight ounces). The doctor who assisted Madge actually assumed Byron couldn't have survived such a tumultuous delivery and had all but left him for dead and concentrated on saving Madge. It was Byron's maternal Grandmother Allen who alerted the others in the room that the baby boy was indeed alive.

Byron Nelson poses at age fifteen with his toddler brother Charles on their one-acre lot on Timberline Drive in Fort Worth only blocks away from Glen Garden Country Club. (Courtesy of Charles Nelson)

GROWN AT GLEN GARDEN

John Byron Nelson Sr., a native of Ellis County, was named after the British Romantic poet Lord Byron. O.B. Keeler, a golf writer for *The Atlanta Journal* decades later, was the first sportswriter to attach the nickname "Lord" to the regular golfer in the family. John Byron was a man of the land and wasn't one for idle chitchat. This could be because he dealt with serious life issues early on, childhood being a luxury that he wasn't truly afforded. His mother died when he was seven months old, his father when he was nine. He and his older sister, May, were raised by their aunt, Delilah (known as Dillie). They grew up on a farm, and John Byron decided third grade was enough schooling for running a farm. His farm experience led to a love of horses and a prowess in trick riding. That became such a driving force in his life that he planned to run away from home to go live on the Midwest farm that developed the day's popular stunt rider, Dan Patch. (One of John Byron's cousins blabbed his secret plan to Aunt Dillie and May, and he acquiesced to their pleas to stay.)

As a fifteen-year-old showing off his horse and buggy at the Ellis County Fair, John Byron and a cousin took notice of ten-year-old Madge Allen. John Byron proclaimed, "I'm going to marry ol' man Allen's daughter when she's old enough." The cousin asked why, and John Byron explained, "She'll produce good sons." The courtship began five years later, and they were married two years afterward. Charles Nelson, the younger of those two "good sons," recalls his mother asking his father about his reluctance to make conversation: "Coming home from a Sunday visit with neighbors in a buggy, Mother would ask, 'Why don't you talk? They're going to think you're dumb.' He'd say, 'I listen, but I have nothing to contribute. I'd rather keep quiet.' He was at ease with himself as much as anyone I ever knew." Years later, when teenage Charles helped his father plant peanuts on their farm in Denton, Charles noticed the farmer across the road was getting his hoeing done a lot faster than the Nelsons. Charles mentioned that to his father. "He said, 'Son, just wait three weeks,'" Charles recalls. "In three weeks, they were redoing their field. Turns out they hadn't gotten all the weeds the first time."

Whereas John Byron had his fill of formal education after the third grade, Madge Allen Nelson couldn't wait to get to school and started a year early. She read voraciously and would read aloud to her children for years. That included regular exposure to the Bible. She grew up a Baptist, John Byron a Presbyterian; soon after their wedding, they converted to the Church of Christ. Had the times allowed for her to become formally involved in ministerial matters, she would have. Instead, she hoped her sons would become preachers. Charles says their mother was the parent who defined the family's values and priorities through constant reinforcement: "When we were little and put to a task – sweep the floor or dig a flower bed – if it wasn't done correctly after they showed us how to do it, she had a poem that became a mantra. 'If a task is once begun, do not leave it 'til it's done.' We got tired of repeating that."

Byron was known throughout his life and career for his gregarious, giving nature. Charles offers an example of that from Byron's early childhood: "When Byron was five, he and Daddy went to town on a Saturday morning like people did then, rode the wagon into town. Dad bought Byron a little sack of hard candy. Byron didn't want to have any until he got home and could share it with Mother. They got home, and some neighbors were visiting with several children. Byron walked over to Mother and offered her the candy. She said, 'Son, offer it to your guests first.' The kids all reached in. When they were through, there was only one piece left. He gave it to Mother."

When Byron was in the first or second grade, Charles was told, a bigger boy in his class named Truman began picking on him after school. Byron would often come home crying, and his mother would counsel him. "Mother wasn't one to take abuse lightly," Charles says. "She told him, 'Son, you're going to have to fight back. You're going to have to whip Truman. Go after him and get him.' Next day, she was real anxious to see what happened because it always happened on his way home. He came in, and he was covered with blood. 'Don't worry, Mother!' Byron said. 'It's Truman's blood!' Byron was getting the best of Truman, and Truman ran. Byron picked up a rock and hit him in the head. So Truman didn't bother him anymore."

Charles recalls another episode in the life of young Byron that exhibited his older brother's keen aim: "There was another man who worked with Dad. He had a son who was a teen when Byron was just a little boy. They went out rabbit hunting. The older boy had a .22. Byron carried rocks. They jumped a rabbit. The other boy was firing away and missing it. Byron threw a rock and hit the rabbit in the head and killed it. He knew exactly how far it was from point A to point B. He knew if it was 112 yards instead of 110. Some musicians have perfect pitch; he always had an eye for that." Nelson had large, sensitive hands, even as a youngster, which Charles says he inherited from their father: "At the feed store, Dad could tell you what something weighed just by holding it. Feed was sold in 100-pound sacks. He could pick up a sack of feed and tell you if it weighed 100 pounds or ninety-nine pounds."

The Nelsons began a sojourn across the Lone Star State as John Byron sought various avenues for providing for his family. They left Ellis County for San Saba down in the Hill Country, then out to San Angelo in west Texas, to Alvarado south of Fort Worth and then relocation into Cowtown itself in 1922. Ellen was born in 1919, seven years after Byron and seven years before Charles, when the family lived in San Saba. She suffered from multiple illnesses as a child – rheumatic fever, polio, tuberculosis, kidney issues. She often was too sick to attend school, her mother providing instruction at home. Ellen took after Byron in that she stood 6-foot-2 at age twelve, though her many health problems left her uncommonly skinny for that height. That prompted a visit from a local health official; a piqued Madge bluntly pointed out Ellen ate at the same table as her chubby younger brother.

When Byron's maternal grandmother was dying in Waxahachie around 1929, she said she had no remorse and was proud that she'd raised what she considered a fine family. According to Charles, she did express regret that certain events would occur after her passing. "A lot of extraordinary things would happen in the world," Charles was told she said, "and Byron [seventeen years old at that time] would become a great man." Byron was already a young man when Charles, born in 1926, was a toddler. Given the family philosophy of looking out for each other, Byron often assumed the role of Charles' caretaker. Charles recalls Byron assuming that responsibility gladly. "He played with me, gave me attention," Charles says. "When Byron went to practice at Glen Garden – at dusk, working on his pitching and putting – I went with him and rolled down the hills." Byron was his brother's hero. All Madge needed to say to keep Charles in line was, "I'm going to tell 'Brother.' "

Soon after the Nelsons moved to Fort Worth, ten-year-old Byron had to undergo a series of painful shots after he and other neighborhood children had played with a neighbor's rabid dog. Byron and the others were sent to Austin for three weeks to receive the shots since state medical personnel there would do it free of charge. During the treatment, Byron developed typhoid fever, his weight dropping from 124 pounds to sixty-five (he stood five-foot-eight). His temperature soared to 106 degrees, and he was packed in ice. About the time that a doctor had given up hope for his survival for the second time in his relatively short life, a woman who attended the same Church of Christ as the Nelsons identified a course of action – administering a colon cleansing – that gradually pulled Byron back to health after a matter of weeks. He wrote in his autobiography that the high fever left him with memory loss: "I have very little recollection of my childhood, other than what my family and friends have told me."

In 1922, William Ben Hogan had not moved to various corners of Texas like Byron Nelson. There had been only one relocation, but it played a critical role in the family's fortunes. The Hogans lived in the small town of Dublin in Erath County, about eighty miles southwest of Fort Worth. Ben Hogan's grandparents first arrived in Dublin in the early 1880s following a journey from Choctaw County, Mississippi, and Ben's father, Chester, was born in Dublin in 1885. He became a blacksmith, following in the line of work of his father, which happened to be the profession of about forty percent of the male population of Choctaw County then. Chester also spent a short amount of time in the first years of the 1900s as a bottle washer under the employ of Sam Houston Prim, owner of the town's Dr. Pepper bottling plant. Chester married Clara Williams and began to start a family in 1908 with the arrival of a daughter, Chester, known by her middle name, Princess. She was followed by Royal a year later and finally Ben in 1912.

A young Ben Hogan sits on his father Chester's lap, flanked by Royal [left] and Princess [right]. (Ben Hogan estate)

Life in Dublin began to change when Sam Prim moved there in 1891 from east Texas along with his wife, Ella, and brought along an Arctic Soda Water Apparatus – a bottling machine. They spent the first night in their new hometown in the Traweek Hotel at the intersection of Patrick and Elm Street, affectionately called Rats Row in honor of the preponderance of both gamblers and rodents. Prim's father was a farmer who died at the age of thirty-six. Prim, a teenager then, most likely linked his father's early death to his choice of occupations and decided not to follow the same career path. He bought the bookstore in Sulphur Springs, but his business plan grew far beyond the bound volume. His list of wares for sale included candy, tobacco, and stationery. Almost ten years before arriving in Dublin, he bought the bottling machine – and bottles. Prim learned of the growing American interest in carbonated soda, particularly of the new concoction produced down in Waco by a pharmacist named Charles Alderton. When Prim first ordered a sample of the soda syrup, the mix was simply called "Waco." Wade Morrison, a Waco drug store owner involved in the shipping of the new product, was the first to call it Dr. Pepper. Karen Wright, a Dublin resident who wrote a book about the soft drink's history in the little town, wrote the name was derived either from the father of a girl whom Morrison once loved or from his initial employer.

Prim enjoyed Dr. Pepper and apparently was thinking one step ahead of the growing soda fountain industry. His intent was to take soda, specifically Dr. Pepper, and bottle it – fizz and all – for delivery to out-of-town customers. In 1902, Prim bought the lease for the lot at the corner of Patrick and Elm – where the Traweek burned to the ground shortly after the Prims stayed there – and constructed a two-story building to house Dublin Bottling Works. For the buying public who were unaware of Dr. Pepper, he'd gladly include a bottle or two *gratis* along with the other products that had been ordered. What began as a handshake agreement between Prim and the makers of Dr. Pepper syrup finally developed into a formal contract in 1925, when the originating operation expanded and shifted from Waco to Dallas. On the back of the contract, Prim sketched out a square to represent an area of exclusivity that included everything within a forty-five mile radius of Dublin. The Prims' only child, Grace, years later said her father assumed Dublin would grow to be larger than Fort Worth. "He was never a good businessman," she told Wright. "He was conservative and had good judgment, so he just took what he knew he could cover." Prim's younger brother, Jim, moved to Dublin in 1894 and joined him in the bottling business. They formed Prim Brothers, whose varied products included food for people and farm animals, cotton seed, and coal. They advertised Dr. Pepper nationally as a source of "vim, vigor, and vitality." Early ads pointed out the drink contained neither caffeine nor cocaine, the latter not illegal at the time. The 1904 World's Fair in St. Louis proved to be a boon to the soft drink.

Jon Anthony Awbrey, current publisher of the nearby *DeLeon Free Press* and a local historian, reported young Ben Hogan was teased by his older brother because he was small and quiet and was forced to chase down errant baseballs during Royal's games. Princess and Royal turned at least some of their attention to the arts; Princess competed in theater talent contests and sang small parts at the Dublin Opera House, while Royal performed violin solos for Dublin's Baptist worshipers. One of Ben's most fervent interests was the silent movies that played at the theater on Patrick Street. Awbrey also found a possible early local link between the game of golf and young Ben. One of the Hogans' prominent neighbors, Charles Foust, was a trustee at the Dublin-DeLeon Country Club based at the nine-hole course located only a few miles northwest of town on the road between Dublin and DeLeon.

With Sam Prim's soft drink sales increasing, his zeal to expand his financial portfolio led him to build another bottling plant out in the west Texas town of Sweetwater and then erect an opera house nearby. While the opera house was initially very popular, it quickly lost favor. It was one of multiple ventures that began to drain Sam's resources. That led to a shocking disclosure that the good people of Dublin learned when they read the January 2, 1920, edition of the weekly *Dublin Progress*: Prim sold the Dublin Bottling Works a few weeks earlier to a competing entity, Coca-Cola. The arrangement was actually for only one year. But the folks from Coca-Cola quickly installed their own equipment and were bottling Coke and several other brands of soda. While the Dublin Bottling Works and the specific bottling of Dr. Pepper might have devolved into only one of Sam Prim's business interests, it had become the day in, day out job for twenty-five years of plant manager Jim Prim, forty-seven years old when Coke displaced Dr. Pepper at the corner of Patrick and Elm. He was already somewhat depressed over Prim Brothers' fiscal challenges when he left town in mid-December for a period of weeks, during which Sam signed the contract to hand over the bottling company. Jim returned to Dublin on a Saturday in mid-January mostly in much greater spirits. On the following Monday morning, Sam and some family friends visited with Jim and left convinced he was on the road to recovery. Instead, Jim walked out the back door later that day, entered a smaller building in the backyard, and took his own life with a .38-caliber pistol aimed at his left temple. Ironically, as stated in the written agreement, Coke handed the Dublin bottling company back to Sam Prim after only one year to produce Dr. Pepper and a wide array of other drinks, and the company prospered.

Chester Hogan's blacksmith business in Dublin was hurt by the growing popularity of the automobile as the 1920s dawned, and he spiraled from quiet to withdrawn. Clara Hogan took the bold step of moving the family up to Fort Worth in August 1921 for two apparent reasons. She could better seek employment herself in an effort to improve the family's increasingly dire financial situation, and Fort Worth was home to one of the area's few mental hospitals at the time, where Chester could seek help. Chester, however, was unable to land a job in Fort Worth, and after visiting the hospital for a matter of months, he abruptly left the family in late 1921 to return to Dublin with the intent of reopening his blacksmith shop. He traveled back to Fort Worth on Saturday, February 11, 1922, with local people who saw him at the train station in Dublin later attesting he was in a good mood; he reported his business was doing fine. He visited his family with the idea of convincing Clara that he was of sound mind and the family should be reunited back in Dublin. Instead, the result of the exchange the following Monday night in the front room of their home on Hemphill Street was Chester shooting himself in the upper chest with a .38-caliber revolver.

The report of the shooting in the February 14 *Fort Worth Record* stated Chester shot himself in front of his six-year-old son; there was no six-year-old boy in the family then, though nine-year-old Ben was admittedly small for his age. Chester was rushed by ambulance to Protestant Hospital, where a doctor assessed his chance of recovery as good according to the *Record*. But he died the following morning, on Valentine's Day. The story that appeared in the weekly *Dublin Progress* three days later stated Chester was alone in the front room when Royal walked in, saw his father holding a gun, and asked, "Daddy, what are you going to do?" The *Progress* story also quoted the critically injured Chester as saying, "I wish I hadn't done it." The body was returned by train to Dublin and claimed by Chester's brother-in-law, Willie Williams, before burial in the Old Dublin Cemetery. "He was an active and industrious man and had many friends," was the last line of the *Progress* story. Awbrey, the Dublin-area historian, has wondered for years whether there was a link between the suicides of Jim Prim in January 1920 and Chester Hogan in February 1922 since Chester had worked at the bottling plant and might have related to Prim's frustrations to his own plight.

Sometime between the birth of Byron Nelson in February 1912 and the birth of Ben Hogan six months later, a Fort Worth rancher named H.H. Cobb was pushed into making a business decision that would have at least an indirectly profound effect on American golf. Cobb wanted to join the city's only country club at the time, River Crest, which opened on Fort Worth's well-heeled north side in 1911. River Crest's gala opening included an outdoor barbeque attended by 500 guests and the sale of surrounding residential lots; it was the first club in the state to offer housing on its property. Cobb, though, was denied membership and then did what anyone owning hundreds of acres of pasture land might do under the same circumstances: He decided to build his own country club.

Glen Garden Golf and Country Club was chartered in 1912, and a two-story clubhouse that included living quarters upstairs and a spacious ballroom downstairs was soon built. Cobb began somewhat conservatively by building only nine holes, occupying the east side of the property beginning in 1914. The golf holes featured oiled sand greens. Accounts vary on when the other nine holes were laid out on the western fork of land that today comprises Glen Garden's back nine. The club history states the second nine were added only a few years later, and the overall length was barely in the range of 3,000 yards. It also credits the design of the course to a man who apparently didn't live in Texas until 1919. That was John Bredemus, the same John Bredemus who was awarded the first-place trophy in the 1912 All-Around athletic competition initially won by Jim Thorpe. Research by the noted Texas golf historian Frances Trimble indicates Bredemus, a native Northeasterner, moved to Texas when he left his job as the athletic director at Connecticut's Stamford Preparatory School to become principal of a high school in San Antonio. The first course designed and constructed by Bredemus, according to Trimble, was San Felipe Springs Country Club in the Texas-Mexico border town of Del Rio in 1921.

GROWN AT GLEN GARDEN

Other sources credit Glen Garden's layout to Tom Bendelow (who designed River Crest) or, according to Trimble, a gentleman from New York named Nieman. No matter the identity of the person who designed the eighteen holes of Glen Garden, it was accomplished with disregard for the traditional golf course layout. The front nine is a par-37, the back nine a par-34. The front nine features one par-3, the back nine four – all located within the final five holes. As Dan Jenkins told *Fort Worth Weekly* almost a decade ago, "It's about the funkiest golf course in the world. I loved that course." When the film version of Jenkins' best selling golf novel *Dead Solid Perfect* was shot in the 1980s, scenes were shot both at Colonial and Glen Garden. (Jenkins, like Alfred Hitchcock, made a cameo appearance.)

3

ROOKIE CADDIES

ALMOST MYSTICALLY, Ben Hogan and Byron Nelson arrived at Glen Garden Country Club only weeks apart in 1924. Nelson learned of the opportunity to earn some money by caddying there from classmates. Hogan, having hawked newspapers at Fort Worth's train depot for more than two years, heard about caddying at Glen Garden from his brother. He was intrigued by the prospect of being paid simply to carry a bag of golf clubs. That sure seemed to beat the territorial battles that came with trying to sell papers in the most advantageous positions of the city's transportation hub. For Nelson, Glen Garden was less than a mile from his home on Timberline Drive; most of his "commute" to the golf shop could actually take place on the club's grounds since Glen Garden's southern boundary borders Timberline. For Hogan, getting to Glen Garden meant a walk of almost six miles round trip from the family's home on East Allen Street on the city's east side.

Nelson and Hogan years later described the hierarchy of caddie life, which included an initiation that at times could border on physical hazing. Hey, new caddies meant competition for the veterans for work. So the rookie had to run a gauntlet with the vets whacking him with wooden paddles or belts. The newbie might also be stuffed into a barrel and rolled downhill near the clubhouse. Nelson said he wasn't afforded the experience of the barrel roll. And after he was accepted into the order, he wasn't one to dish out punishments to the newcomers. Nelson was already a Glen Garden caddie when Hogan sought membership in the bag-toting fraternity and, years later, said he was out on the course hard at work when Hogan was put through his initiation paces. Hogan recalled he was also required to participate in a fistfight with a large caddie in which he handled his opponent sufficiently.

Becoming a caddie naturally created an interest in playing golf. Caddies were forbidden from playing while on the clock, and doing so would incur the wrath of caddiemaster Harold Akey or the club manager James Kidd – known as "Captain Kidd." But many of the boys were resourceful enough to figure out ways to sneak in the occasional hole or two, usually with borrowed clubs. Hogan said he was naturally left-handed and only resorted to playing golf right-handed at his brother Royal's urging. The caddies made a competition out of hitting balls on the practice range. The boy whose drive carried the shortest distance had to trudge out and pick up all the golf balls. Hogan, usually smaller than most or all of his adversaries, was frequently relegated to pickup duty. He soon gained distance on his shots by turning over his left hand, though that also created a consistent hook. Nelson played his first full round of golf later in 1924 and claimed a score of 118.

Hogan's gruff personality fit in with most of the boys. Nelson didn't share the same hard edges. Coincidentally or not, Nelson was invited by Glen Garden club pro Ted Longworth to spend time in the shop helping with the cleaning and reshafting of clubs. In the fall of 1927, Longworth asked Nelson to come along to watch the Friday afternoon semifinal between Walter Hagen and Al Espinosa in the match play P.G.A. Championship played over in Dallas at Cedar Crest Country Club. Hagen was then the game's most successful and glamorous player. Known as "The Haig," he captured eleven major titles (ten of them in an eleven-year period, 1919–29) and commanded attention much like Babe Ruth of the New York Yankees did then in baseball. His bombastic presence paved the way for (this will seem odd these days) professional golfers to be granted access to clubhouses during tournaments. The congenial Nelson even allowed Hagen to borrow his cap for one shot facing into the western sun late in the afternoon when it was apparent Hagen was struggling to see.

Glen Garden held an annual Christmas tournament for its caddies, a nine-hole affair followed by a holiday feast in the clubhouse ballroom. Club members reversed roles with the kids, caddying and then serving the meal. Nelson's caddie was Judge J.B. Wade, whom Nelson caddied for regularly. On one previous occasion, Nelson snuck in a phantom swing with one of the judge's clubs and was mortified when the club head sailed right off the shaft. Their relationship survived the club-head calamity to the extent that, when Nelson was allowed to pick the middle name of his baby brother Charles, he chose Wade. Hogan also developed rapport with regular "clients" such as talented amateur Ed Stewart, fellow teen Dan Greenwood and, in particular, a successful Fort Worth retailer named Marvin Leonard.

Fourteen- to sixteen-hour workdays helped Leonard and his brother, Obie, establish something of a department store empire downtown; the Leonard Brothers' complex would eventually envelop seven city blocks. Leonard initially joined Glen Garden in 1922 to take up golf, but found the experience of playing eighteen holes to be ponderous, too slow of an activity that required far too much time away from work. But five years later when he was feeling bad enough to visit his doctor, Leonard was advised that regular exercise was probably the best medicine for him to avoid serious health problems. Leonard decided he would play regularly like it or not, and even took a few lessons from Ted Longworth. After paying his back dues, he developed a routine of playing nine holes at least four times a week before breakfast at either Glen Garden or River Crest, which resulted in him eating a good breakfast and actually enjoying it. Soon after Leonard established that routine at Glen Garden, Kidd regularly assigned young Hogan to carry Leonard's bag.

It appeared Hogan would claim first place in the 1927 Christmas tournament until Nelson sank a thirty-foot putt on no. 9 to tie him and force a playoff. Hogan won the tenth hole and figured he won the sudden death playoff. He was informed the playoff was for another nine holes, leading to debate decades later of

The Fort Worth Record-Telegram published a story on the Glen Garden Christmas caddie tournament of 1927 plus a group photo that included Ben Hogan [second from right] and Byron Nelson [far right], believed to be the first time that they were photographed together. (Ben Hogan estate)

whether the members wanted to see the more popular Nelson win and changed the rules of the playoff on the fly. Play continued, and Nelson holed another long putt on the final hole to win by one shot. The two boys were awarded irons, Nelson a 5-iron and Hogan a 2-iron. Since each already owned the club that he won and lacked the other's, they swapped. A few months later, Hogan's situation at the club improved when Longworth also brought him into the shop to work on clubs. Nelson's status changed, too; he was the one Glen Garden caddie selected that year to receive a junior membership with complete playing privileges.

Golf was fast becoming the consuming passion for both boys, certainly a much higher priority than formal education. Nelson attended Poly High School, located on the east side of Fort Worth. Hogan attended Central High School though he lived between Central and Poly, about the same distance from each. Poly's 1927-28 yearbook staff exhibited no restraint in trumpeting the potential of one of the school's rising seniors and did so in rhyme: "Johnny Vaught is now our president, but we think some day he'll be the White House resident." Vaught not only became class president in 1928-29 but was also the valedictorian. Politics, though, weren't in his future. Vaught went across town to play college football and became an All-American guard for Texas Christian University (TCU). He's best known as the head football coach at the University of Mississippi, where his 1960 Rebels won a share of the national championship.

Poly's athletic teams are called the Parrots, but the most clever name for a campus organization might have been the label for the club associated with math and geometry – the Polygons. Decades after Nelson ended his stay at Poly, well short of graduation, he told a Dallas sportswriter about an experience from his days as a high school baseball player. He said Poly's principal was umpiring a game when Nelson came to bat and asked if anyone had ever sent a home run flying into one of the principal's office windows just beyond the fence. No, the principal replied. "Wouldn't be long," Nelson predicted. The next day at practice, Nelson said, he did just that. The principal said nothing to him but had heavy screens erected that would prevent a repeat episode.

Hogan also left school shortly after Nelson. But not before building a relationship with a girl a year ahead of him at Central who would become his wife of 62 years. Valerie Fox was the older of two sisters who moved to Fort Worth from Mineral Wells, a town about fifty miles to the west. Their first formal date as teens was a trip to the movies and subsequent pit stop for a lemonade on the walk home. While Hogan felt the need to leave high school before receiving a diploma, Valerie not only graduated from Central but started college at TCU. Decades later, Hogan would emphasize the importance of education to younger generations of the family. That included great-niece Lisa Scott, who is now the executive director of the Ben Hogan Foundation. She grew up in southern California but often spent summers in Fort Worth along with her brother, Sean, visiting their grandmother, Sarah (Valerie's sister), and their Uncle Ben and Aunt Valerie. "When I was a sophomore in high school," Scott recalls, "he told me, 'You do your part. And when it's time for college, I'll pay for it.' He never talked about the fact that he didn't go to school. I could just tell it really mattered to him."

4

TURNING HEADS

ONE DAY IN 1928, Fort Worth pro golfers "Smiley" Rowland and Bennie Adams teamed to easily pilfer a significant amount of cash from their opponents at the city nine-hole municipal course named Z Boaz (pronounced *ZEE-Boze*). One of the members of the losing pair wasn't prepared to accept defeat and insisted Rowland and Adams return to the course the following day for another match. That losing player brought a different playing partner the next day, sixteen-year-old Ben Hogan. The match was tied going to the par-4 sixteenth hole when Hogan blasted his tee shot onto the green and one-putted for an eagle-2. The last two holes were halved, and Hogan shared in the victory — not to mention shooting a 64 to break the course record by two shots. For all the evidence that Hogan struggled throughout the 1930s before seeing the results of his labors, this anecdote from Z Boaz proves he had something early to build on.

Byron Nelson's play also began to turn heads in March 1928 with a victory at Katy Lake Golf Course in south Fort Worth. Back at Katy Lake in April 1929, he earned medalist honors in the annual spring match play tournament by shooting par-70 in qualifying. He opened with a 1-up victory over Madison Reed, ousted favorite Ned Baugh along the way, and defeated Lansing Williamson in the 36-hole final 5-and-4. And during an off day between the semis and final, Nelson broke Baugh's course record with a 66.

Other golfers in Fort Worth set their sights on different, more unusual goals, possibly a natural concession to the mindset of the Roaring Twenties. Take Clarence "Skeet" Fincher, for instance. On August 8, 1928, the 23-year-old Fincher took dead aim at the record – ninety-nine – for golf holes played from dawn to dusk. "I'm going to try to play fourteen nines or 126 holes," he told the *Fort Worth Press*. He began his "training" in late July something like a runner preparing for a 26.2-mile marathon. Fincher played every day for a full week, starting with eighteen holes and adding nine each day for a couple of days and then tapering back to eighteen. On the big day, Fincher teed off at municipal Worth Hills at 5 a.m., a good forty-seven minutes before the sun rose – apparently not a violation of the golfing marathon rules. He played the equivalent of a four-round tournament by noon and hit a record 100 holes around 3 p.m. Fincher bulled onward for twenty-seven more, striking his final putt at 7:20 p.m. (Sunset was 7:22; it might have looked like the end of *Bagger Vance*.) The next morning, "Skeet" said he was feeling fine. That night at the Majestic Theater, he was presented a loving cup by the Association of Commerce. Let's hope no one spent much money on the engraving, at least the part that read "record for holes played in one day." His mark was broken again twice in the next eight days.

At the match play Southwestern Championships played at River Crest in early September 1928, Hogan was eliminated in the early going but still managed to impress in both the formal tournament and the preliminary long drive competition. Said Glen Garden's Ed Stewart of the 130-pound Hogan: "It's a good thing that kid don't weigh about 170." Hogan was paired against defending champion and heavily favored M.L. "Happy" Massingill of the host club and was defeated in nineteen holes, after evening things on no. 18 with an eagle putt. *Press* sports editor "Pop" Boone was watching: "Ben Hogan made his bid for glory yesterday. It was a magnificent gesture that failed by a hair's breadth … If he works hard and avoids the pitfalls that lurk to trip the youths of today, if he is the right sort, he'll be heard from and maybe beyond the confines of the city, the state, or the nation."

At sixteen years old, Hogan was playing out of Meadowbrook Golf Course on the east side of Fort Worth as the 1929 golfing season began. At the 72-hole state municipal championship held in Waco during the final weekend in May, he placed eighth. Moving directly to the match play state amateur the following week at Dallas' Brook Hollow, Hogan reached the round of sixteen. And there was barely a break before he competed in the first invitational tournament hosted by Cleburne Country Club, located about thirty miles south of Fort Worth in the town of the same name. He marched into the final to face a fifty-two-year-old opponent, John Douglas of Galveston. Hogan showed no signs of intimidation, jumping to an early lead and winning 3-and-2, a victory far more significant than helping to win an informal four-ball against "Smiley" Rowland and Bennie Adams at Z Boaz. Honest-to-goodness victory in a real tournament was his. Leroy Menzing, golf writer for the *Star-Telegram*, lamented that Hogan and former Central High classmate Charles Ramsel had departed from the local municipal ranks. But, Menzing noted, "a new young threat appears there. He is Byron Nelson."

Those who keenly followed golf in Fort Worth didn't have to wait long for Nelson and Hogan to again display their prowess. Both Hogan and Nelson played in the 1929 city championship in July with three rounds of medal play qualifying – eighteen holes each at River Crest, Glen Garden and Meadowbrook – followed by match play at Meadowbrook. Nelson led the qualifying through two rounds but closed with an 86 at Meadowbrook for a 233 that placed him second to Rowland by two shots. But such a performance didn't provide him with a break in drawing his first-round foe; he

Not yet adorned with the familiar cap, sixteen-year-old Ben Hogan did sport some fancy argyle socks. (Ben Hogan estate)

was matched against River Crest's Joe Ballard, the defending champion, who struggled through qualifying with a 250. Ballard, a student at the University of Wisconsin, played to his previous form and ousted Nelson in the opening round 6-and-4. Hogan suffered no such fate, winning his opener over the young man whom he'd caddied for at Glen Garden, Dan Greenwood, 1-up. As was the case at Cleburne, Hogan methodically advanced to the championship final. Standing between him and another title was Ballard. The *Star-Telegram*'s Menzing compared the finalists before the match: "Hogan, stocky, tanned lad of the fairways, is a cool, steady player. A bad shot is forgotten as he prepares for his next effort. Ballard may become riled over a missed shot, but it has never affected his play. He goes into his next with more vim."

There apparently was little in the 36-hole championship match to rankle Ballard. He won 6-and-5 to repeat as Fort Worth city champion. Well, maybe early there was something to upset him. Ballard bogeyed the first two holes and immediately trailed by two. But he soon came charging back and led 6-up after the first eighteen holes. The consolation final turned out to be a matchup of the top two qualifiers; Nelson beat Rowland 5-and-4. The winner of the second flight was Royal Hogan. And there was something different for the repeat champion following the final. The city awarded a new trophy, a loving cup standing two-and-a-half-feet tall including a small statuette of a golfer at the top of his backswing. Maybe the folks at the city's three country clubs couldn't agree on a name for the new bauble. The rather bland name given to it was the Three-Club Trophy.

Hogan traveled to Shreveport, Louisiana for another shot at the Southwestern amateur crown in July 1929. He and other contenders were probably pleased when the qualifying medalist, eighteen-year-old hometown star Edwin McClure, was knocked off in the first round of match play by Gordon Howard of New Orleans. Howard provided another public service – at least for Hogan – in the second round by upsetting the usually difficult Ballard.

Hogan reached yet another final, where he faced Dallas' Gus Moreland. But Hogan couldn't command his tee shots, often putting himself in drastic trouble on his approaches, and lost the 36-hole final to Moreland 4-and-3.

If Hogan could reach the finals of the Fort Worth city championship and the Southwestern amateur, surely he would dominate a lesser field in the third annual Dublin-DeLeon tournament on the outskirts of his former hometown. He actually rated only the no. 2 choice in the pretournament Calcutta betting, behind sixteen-year-old Dubliner J. Dixon White.

Hogan arrived in town a few days before competition began and, according to the *Dublin Progress*, was visiting relatives in addition to getting familiar with the course. But these were no walkovers for Hogan. His second-round match against Rouse Baxter of Dublin went twenty-one holes before Baxter succumbed. In the semifinals against Bob Scott of Colorado, Hogan needed to set the course record of 68 to advance. Then in the final against sixteen-year-old George Meredith from nearby Eastland, Hogan trailed by three holes early and rallied to clinch victory on the seventeenth hole. It appears the victory at Dublin-DeLeon in August 1929 was Hogan's last triumph as an amateur before he decided to turn pro at the Texas Open in San Antonio in February 1930. The trophy he was awarded is displayed in the Hogan Room established in 1999 at Golf House at U.S.G.A. headquarters in Far Hills, New Jersey.

But Fort Worth's most visible sports figure in the summer 1929 wasn't Hogan or Nelson or Ballard. It was a Central High grad, Class of 1925, named Wilmer Allison. He was a top-notch baseball player at Central who intended to pursue of career in pro ball until his father prohibited him from signing with the Beaumont Exporters of the Texas League. Plan B was to enroll at the University of Texas, where his athletic career continued in tennis and he won the N.C.A.A. singles championship in 1927. Soon after leaving the Forty Acres, Allison found success mostly in doubles. He and John Van

Ryn of Orange, New Jersey won the Wimbledon gentlemen's doubles title early in July 1929 over the British duo of Ian Collins and Colin Gregory. The score of the marathon five-set match was 6-4, 5-7, 6-3, 10-12, and finally 6-4.

A few weeks later, Allison and Van Ryn did their part on the United States Davis Cup team playing against France at Roland Garros stadium in the challenge round. The American team was on the verge of elimination in the best-of-five competition after "Big Bill" Tilden and George Lott lost their singles matches. Allison and Van Ryn swept the heavily favored French pairing of Henri Cochet and Jean Borotra 6-1, 8-6, 6-4 in the only doubles play of the competition. The Yanks hung in with Tilden beating Borotra in the fourth match, but France bid the Americans *au revoir* when Cochet defeated Lott.

Allison and Van Ryn repeated as Wimbledon champions in 1930, and Allison also reached the gentlemen's singles finals. He shocked the top-seeded Cochet in straight sets in the quarterfinals and eventually reached a championship matchup with Tilden, who was something of the Babe Ruth of tennis and seemingly always performing, whether in the arena or out. (During an amazing stretch during which he won fifty-seven consecutive tournament games in 1925, he deadpanned: "When I missed, I was surprised.") Tilden downed Allison 6-3, 9-7, 6-4 to claim his third Wimbledon singles crown to go with seven U.S. Open championships and one French Open crown. Allison claimed the men's singles title at the U.S. Open in 1935, sweeping fellow American Sidney Wood. He returned to Texas following his playing days and coached his alma mater to four Southwest Conference championships.

5

TURNING PRO

JOHN BREDEMUS' CAREER took him in 1919 to San Antonio, where A.W. Tillinghast had opened Texas' first public course, Brackenridge Park, just east of downtown three years earlier. Brackenridge was relatively short and featured an oddity: rubber mats in the tee boxes. It became Bredemus' second home, and he soon became assistant pro and apparently continued to hone his knowledge regarding courses. But he was also interested in bringing pro play to Texas, which at the time hosted no tournaments. Bredemus and Jack O'Brien, the sports editor of the *San Antonio Evening News*, decided that needed to change, specifically with an event at Brackenridge. There was one way to make the top pros – many of whom lived in the Northeast – come play in a tournament in south Texas – offer an extravagant purse. The first Texas Open was played in February 1922 with total prize money of $5,000, more than twice what was awarded at that year's U.S. Open. It also helped that Bredemus held sway with many pros from his years in the Northeast. Bob MacDonald, "the Silver Scot," captured the first installment of the state's longest-running professional golf tournament and happily accepted a check for $1,633.33.

In February 1930, much of the nation's sporting attention was focused on Babe Ruth's threat to stay home while the rest of the New York Yankees traveled to Florida for spring training. The "Bambino" demanded a raise from $70,000 annually to $85,000 for the next three seasons while the Yankees drew the line at $75,000 for two years. "I'm worth it," crowed the Babe, who was about to celebrate his thirty-sixth birthday. In his favor was the fact that he led the majors in home runs in 1929 (with forty-six) for the tenth time in twelve years; but the 1929 Yankees not only failed to reach the World Series for the first time in four years, their second-place finish was a distant eighteen games behind the Philadelphia Athletics. That most likely convinced management there was rationale for holding the financial line. Stating the Yanks' case was Ed Barrow, the team's tight-fisted general manager: "We are not interested, and we have nothing to say." Ruth warned he was prepared to sit out the season and live that year on $25,000 of investment income: "There's enough bread and butter in our house." But compromise was arrived before the Yanks headed north at $80,000 for the next two campaigns. And while the Babe again led the American League home run parade in 1930 with forty-nine, the Yankees slipped into third place.

Ben Hogan first registered as a pro in February 1930 at Brackenridge, having a caught a ride to San Antonio from Glen Garden's pro Ted Longworth. Byron Nelson also played that week at Brackenridge but in the pro-am portion of the ninth Texas Open. In the two-man format, he was paired with Bobby Cruickshank. They placed second, and a somewhat proud Nelson was disappointed to hear Cruickshank forego congratulations in favor of blunt criticism of his grip. Nelson, in his autobiography, depicted Cruickshank's half of the one-sided conversation thusly: "Laddie, if ye don't larn to grip the club right, ye'll niver make a good player."

Nelson and Hogan benefitted from thoughtful instruction and introduction to out-of-town tournament play from Longworth and others at

Glen Garden. Hogan was fifteen, working in Longworth's shop, when he began copying his boss' overlapping grip. When Longworth left Fort Worth for Texarkana Country Club in 1930, Glen Garden brought in the Grout brothers – Dick and Jack – from Oklahoma City. They continued to hone the skills of the young protégés. Jack played on Tour from the early 1930s into the mid-1940s, leaving Fort Worth in 1937 for Hershey Country Club to work for Henry Picard. That led him to a job in 1950 at Scioto Country Club in Columbus, Ohio, when he began schooling ten-year-old Jack Nicklaus.

The original clubhouse at Glen Garden included second-story living quarters. Some of the bases of the stone columns remain in front of the current clubhouse. (Glen Garden Country Club)

Hogan's first round as a pro that Friday was a 7-over-par 78. He followed that with a 4-over 75 on Saturday during which he equaled par on the back nine. He was scheduled to go off in the third group for Sunday's concluding 36 holes at 8:10 a.m. with By Chamberlain of Chicago and Larry Nabholtz from Houston. But Hogan never reported for his tee time, electing instead to halt his first pro attempt short of a full schedule of play. Years later, he acknowledged overwhelming disappointment with his performance, particularly with the uncontrollable hooks that exited the course. He left San Antonio questioning whether he belonged in the pro game, only to relive the agony a week later in the Houston Open played at par-72 Rio Rico with another early withdrawal from play. Hogan shot a 5-over-par 77 followed by a 76, his 9-over 153 leaving him fourteen strokes off the lead. He was scheduled to play Sunday with Eddie Gayer of Chicago and Tom Lally of San Antonio but again couldn't bring himself to complete play.

Nelson left San Antonio with a less paralyzing amount of self-doubt following Crickshank's well-meaning review of his game and was eager to accept help. He later consulted with Longworth, whose suggestions helped form the swing that essentially carried Nelson through his Hall of Fame career. The relationship between Longworth and Nelson would continue though Longworth left Glen Garden soon after to become head pro at Texarkana Country Club in Texarkana, Arkansas. In August 1930, Nelson earned the distinction of winning the first Glen Garden Invitational with a 9-and-7 triumph in the 36-hole final over River Crest's "Happy" Massingill. Coverage of the tournament, which featured a field of 212 entrants, described the eighteen-year-old Nelson as "the genial Glen Garden ace" and a "likable chap." Said Massingill afterward: "I haven't seen a player putt like that since I've been playing." Adam Dubb wrote in the *Fort Worth Press*: "Nelson, in copping the Glen Garden invitation, dispelled a suspicion among certain persons that he didn't have enough staying qualities to ever become a good golfer. He had several severe tests in this tourney and came thru them in great style."

In 1931, the field for the U.S. Amateur was first opened to sectional qualifying at twenty locations around the country involving a total of almost 600 aspirants. Nelson, at age nineteen, shot his way into the group of 132 invited to Chicago's Beverly Country Club, southwest of downtown. He was making his first trip out of the great state of Texas on a travel budget that accounted for train fare but not a hotel room. Luckily for him, acquaintance Edwin McClure from Louisiana also qualified. McClure and his father stayed at the Morrison Hotel in Chicago and invited Nelson to stay in their room. Another north

Texan venturing from the state for the first time to play was twenty-year-old Gus Moreland, defending champion of both the Dallas city tournament and the Texas state event.

The golfers would play thirty-six holes over two days to whittle the field to thirty-two for match play. Beverly's layout was initially designed in 1908 by the club's first pro, George O'Neil, but redone beginning in 1918 by Donald Ross. His handiwork required about ten years to complete, after which no two consecutive holes played in the same direction. Among the tournament favorites was thirty-eight-year-old Francis Ouimet, who won the 1913 U.S. Open at The Country Club in Brookline, Massachusetts, as an amateur and added the 1914 U.S. Amateur title won at Ekawnok Country Club in Manchester, Vermont. But the most excitement might have been directed initially toward a member of the gallery. The incomparable Bobby Jones, recently retired at age twenty-eight, decided to take in play from the other side of the ropes. Others amid the Beverly gathering were Chicago Cubs president Bill Veeck Sr. (father of the man who amused and annoyed baseball fans years later) and the future Baseball Hall of Famer Tris Speaker.

The first two rounds were played Monday and Tuesday, August 31 and September 1. Nelson arrived in Chicago late that Sunday afternoon with no chance to play a practice round. He went out that opening day in 40 and shot 37 on the back nine for a 6-over-par 77 that left him in promising position, tied for twenty-second place. Moreland had an even better first round. His 2-over 73 left him only one shot off the pace set by Jack Westland, a local player based out of Sunset Ridge Country Club in suburban Winnetka. On the following day, September came in like a lion near Lake Michigan. A heavy rain fell overnight and continued throughout the following day, drenching the field. Only fifty-one golfers were fortunate enough to break 9-over 80 that second day. Nelson wasn't among them. He trudged in with a 10-over-par 81 and a two-day total of 16-over 158. Given the miserable conditions, a 157 was good enough for fourteen players to move into sudden-elimination competition to fill the last five match play berths. Moreland made it through, negotiating the muddy layout with a 5-over 76 for a 7-over 149 that was one shot off the best score. But his good fortune didn't last long; he was beaten 3-and-1 in the opening round of match play by Frank Connelly of Mount Pleasant, Michigan. The tournament winner was Ouimet, beating Westland 6-and-5.

A couple of months after Longworth sent Nelson to Chicago, he invited Hogan to take another stab at a pro tournament. Hogan and Dallas youngster Ralph Guldahl joined Longworth on a trip to play in an event in St. Louis. Hogan completed the tournament, an improvement on his ventures in San Antonio and Houston in February 1930, but didn't finish in the money. Another difference from the dreadful Texas two-step of the previous year was his willingness to keep trying, specifically to accompany Longworth to more tournaments out west.

Nelson was out of work in November 1932, recently let go from his office job at the Fort Worth-Denver City Railroad, when he received a note in the mail from Ted Longworth now at Texarkana Country Club. (The two Texarkanas are separate cities that share the Texas-Arkansas border with State Line Drive shared by both; southbound traffic is in Texas, northbound in Arkansas. The country club, founded in 1914, is located on the southern edge of Texarkana, Arkansas.) Longworth was inaugurating an event in late November open to pros and amateurs and invited Nelson to participate. Nelson decided he'd play and, while riding the bus across northeast Texas, also determined he'd register as a pro – which meant plunking down $5. He'd played well in the months preceding the tournament. In early September, he won the fifth annual Wichita Falls match play championship with some impressive winning margins. In the quarterfinals, he beat Dudley Raines of Abilene 7-and-6. In the semifinals, he downed hometown talent Morris Norton 4-and-3. In the 36-hole final, Nelson put away Bob Burns of

Wichita Falls 5-and-3. That was the same Bob Burns whom Nelson defeated 11-and-10 in the River Crest final the previous spring.

The event carried a purse of $600 in prize money and merchandise, paying the first five places with the winner earning $140. The format was thirty-six holes each on Tuesday and Wednesday, November 29-30, preceded by an 18-hole pro-am. The pretournament write-up in the *Texarkana Press* identified Longworth and Hogan among the contenders for the championship along with Louisiana standout McClure. But sports columnist Jim Montgomery devoted a significant amount of space to a player who had yet to play in a professional event: "Dressed in flashy black-and-white, Byron Nelson stepped up to the first tee at the Country club yesterday and proceeded to sock a long straight one, officially ending his brilliant amateur career. The Fort Worth champion entered Texarkana Country club's pro-amateur contest, initial feature of the open tourney, as a pro, making his debut outside amateur ranks here." (For what it's worth, Nelson and pro-am partner W.B. Walsh of Texarkana shot a 1-under-par 72 to finish four shots off the pace. First-place honors with 5-under 68s were shared by Hogan with Texarkana's E.C. Brown and Tyler pro Ray Garrett with J.D. Lambeth from Shreveport, Louisiana.)

Glen Garden's "Smiley" Rowland wasn't thrilled with the Texarkana Country Club layout: "A magician planned this course." And his sentiments were likely shared by a field that couldn't break par for the opening day's first two rounds. Topping the field with 2-over 148s were Longworth and Houston's Jimmy Demaret. The latter would in later years serve as something of a yin to Hogan's yang, gladly satisfying reporters' appetite for entertaining comments in the clubhouse while also dressing like a human kaleidoscope. Demaret was the definition of the happy-go-lucky pro, though not simply a clown. He scored thirty-one Tour wins and became the first golfer to win the Masters three times. Early in his career, he abandoned traditional golfing garb in favor of lighter fabrics and garish hues. He cited family genes; his father was a housepainter and apparently passed along an affinity for a colorful work environment. Green was an excellent color for Demaret in 1947; he was the Tour's leading money winner while also claiming the Vardon Trophy.

One shot behind Longworth and Demaret was Hogan, alone in third place. Nelson's debut round was a 5-over 78 followed by a 3-over 76, leaving him six strokes off the pace and tied for eleventh place. (The perplexed Rowland scored 85-86 for a 25-over 171, well beyond the twenty-five golfers who advanced to Wednesday's play.) In particular, the players struggled with the course's large, sloping greens. "Dutch" Harrison from Little Rock, Arkansas was the only competitor to as much as match par during the afternoon round. During Wednesday's concluding rounds, Longworth started with a par 73 to build a lead of five shots that wasn't compromised by his finishing 3-over 76. His 5-over 297 was good for a three-shot margin over Denver's colorful Ky Laffoon and two amateurs – McClure and Dallas' David "Spec" Goldman. Nelson was only one shot behind them, at 9-over 301, and officially finished third to claim $75 in winnings. Hogan's score skied nine strokes above his Tuesday total, a 15-over 307, relegating him to tenth place among the pros.

Nelson wasn't sure how his parents would react to his newfound line of work, but the first week's pay surely couldn't hurt his cause. "Mother was real proud of me," he wrote in his autobiography, "and though my father didn't say much, they told me, 'Whatever you do, do it the best you can and be a good man.' They always supported me, even though they didn't get much of a chance to come see me play." Nelson set off in January 1933 seeking his fortune in P.G.A. Tour events – helped by a stipend of $500 from some optimistic friends – on the western swing that began the year. With most tournaments paying only the top fifteen or so players, the young rookie only brought home experience, which he shared in letters to Longworth in Texarkana. Two months later, Longworth wrote back with more than his thoughts on Nelson's golfing baptism in California. Longworth was changing jobs again, headed to Waverley

Country Club in Portland, Oregon. He advised Nelson to apply for the position that he was vacating in Texarkana. It didn't hurt matters that the president of the Texarkana club was Finis Pharr, whose wife, Pearl, had played golf with Nelson at an amateur event in Fort Worth the previous year. Mere weeks after Longworth's letter arrived, Nelson was the new head professional at Texarkana Country Club. *The Texarkana Press* reported the news on its first sports page beneath the headline: "Ft. Worth Star Is Signed For Longworth Job." The story quoted Nelson detailing the quality of play on his California foray as being "so close yet so far." The club's secretary spoke for the board, saying he had no doubt in Nelson's ability to ably succeed Longworth: "He has been recommended highly as an instructor and should be an excellent man for the job."

Nelson immediately collected his belongings, which consisted of his clubs and clothes, and headed to Texarkana. He rented a room in a house close to the club from a couple who also threw in two meals a day for the combined price of $7 a week. Nelson then located a local Church of Christ, which happened to be the Walnut Church of Christ on the Texas side of the twin cities. It was at the church, in a Sunday Bible study session, that he met Louise Shofner. Nelson was immediately smitten, but Louise was dating someone else at the time. Displaying the same persistence that he used in mastering the golf swing, Nelson called Louise every day nonetheless. At one of their casual meetings, when Louise was able to convince her young sister to behave, Nelson boldly asked, "Are you going to make our children behave like you do your sister?" Louise might have been slightly dumbstruck by the question, looked at Nelson for a minute, and said, "I guess so." They never dated anyone else and married in June 1934. Charles Nelson reports the new couple's first houseguest upon returning from their honeymoon was none other than he. "I was seven," he says. "How many twenty-one-year-old boys do that? My parents put me on a train in Fort Worth; I'd never been on a train. The conductor would call each town. My parents said, 'When they call Texarkana, you get off.' "

Nelson's stay at Texarkana Country Club was relatively brief; in the spring of 1935, he was hired to become the assistant pro at Ridgewood Country Club in northeast New Jersey by George Jacobus, the head pro of the club and the president of the Professional Golfers Association of America for seven years beginning in 1932. But Nelson's time in Texarkana was most significant for beginning a fifty-year relationship with Louise – married at the Shofners' home since he couldn't afford a church wedding – not to mention shooting the only double eagle of his career. It took place later that summer, when Nelson and Pearl Pharr were playing the 560-yard, par-5 sixteenth hole. Nelson's drive downwind carried about 300 yards. Choosing a 2-wood, he took dead aim at the pin – and sent the ball rolling right into the hole. Current Texarkana head pro Art Romero recently honored the event by installing a bronze marker in the sixteenth fairway at the spot where it's believed Nelson hit his second shot.

Nelson was prepared to head to California late in 1934 thanks to a financial arrangement that he made with a Texarkana member who took a liking to him. J. K. Wadley, who owned a local lumber business, would loan Nelson money and accept fifty percent of Nelson's earnings. When Nelson's new father-in-law got wind of that plan, he offered to make a straight loan and keep all of the money in the family. Soon after the exchange of funds, Nelson bought a Ford Model A convertible for the newlyweds' upcoming trip to California. The roadster lacked roll-up windows and a heater, so the resourceful couple often heated bricks to place beneath Louise's feet. Jack Grout made part of the trip until Louise stated the obvious; there wasn't enough room for the three of them, luggage, and two sets of golf clubs. Grout was left to find alternate transportation.

6

TASTE OF VICTORY

SOON AFTER GETTING settled at the Ridgewood Country Club, Byron Nelson took his second run at the U.S. Open. He'd missed the cut at the 1934 Open at Merion Golf Club near Philadelphia and was hoping for a much better fate a year later at Oakmont Country Club near Pittsburgh. With money tight, the Nelsons found accommodations that week in the basement of a local parsonage. His week got off to a poor start when he struggled with his driver during a practice round. That night after dinner, Nelson bemoaned his lack of luck with the four drivers he'd purchased that year to Louise. She kept at her knitting and didn't immediately respond, then quietly noted she had not even bought a dress or a pair of shoes during that time. "Either you don't know what kind of driver you want," Louise said, "or you don't know how to drive." The little lady from Texarkana got her message across. Nelson worked on one of his drivers the next day in the pro shop at Oakmont and later said he never had extensive troubles with that club again. He managed to make the cut but was never in contention, staggering in with a 31-over 315. The winner at 15-over 299 was Sam Parks Jr., a local pro who was relatively unknown nationally and not really one of the boys among Tour pros. Parks was an outlier, born into a wealthy family. His father belonged to Pittsburgh's Highland Country Club, and young Sam took lessons from Highland's head pro – namely Gene Sarazen, the dazzling talent who would claim seven major championships during the 1920s and 1930s and thirty-nine career P.G.A. Tour titles. Parks was also a rare college grad among Tour players, owning a degree from the University of Pittsburgh. With his father's assistance, Parks was hired locally as the pro at Short Hills Country Club. It was about a twenty-five-mile drive from Short Hills to Oakmont Country Club, site of the 1935 Open. Parks finished second at the 1934 state open, played there, and was able to practice at Oakmont about two dozen times, jotting down detailed notes upon each trip. With all of that going for him, Parks doubled his list of career victories that previously included only the Western Pennsylvania Junior Championship.

Two months later, Ridgewood's new assistant was one of sixty-one entrants in the $1,500 New Jersey Open, a non-Tour event, played at Monmouth Country Club. The 6,700-yard, par-71 layout was located in Eatontown, only about five miles inland from the northern tip of the Jersey Shore. Described by William D. Richardson of *The New York Times* as one of the East's most exacting courses, Monmouth featured a par-34 on the front nine and par-37 on the back. The tournament's seventy-two holes would be played over a Thursday, Friday, and Saturday in early August.

The field included a couple of current or future P.G.A. Tour notables. The defending champion was thirty-four-year-old Craig Wood, the pro at Hollywood Country Club in the shore town of Deal, just north of Asbury Park. Wood's golden coiffure and penchant for booming drives earned him the nickname "Blond Bomber." A pro since the 1920s, Wood had absorbed a number of agonizing losses on some of pro golf's grandest stages. At the 1933

British Open at St. Andrews, he advanced to a 36-hole playoff with Denny Shute and lost by five shots. In Bobby Jones' initial Masters staged in 1934, Wood finished second to Horton Smith. At the 1934 P.G.A. Championship at The Park Country Club in Williamsville, New York, he dropped a sudden-death playoff to Paul Runyan on the fourth hole. And only four months before defending his title at Monmouth Country Club, Wood appeared to have won the Masters only to have the championship virtually yanked from him by Sarazen's mythical 4-wood on Augusta National's No. 15 that holed the double-eagle to erase a three-shot deficit. Wood lost the 36-hole playoff the next day, also by five strokes.

There was also twenty-five-year-old Vic Gheezi, in his fourth season of professional competition. He was another son of the shore, born in Rumson, and in his first year as head pro at Deal Country Club. Ten-year pro Jimmy Thomson from Ridgewood shared the lead at the 1935 U.S. Open at Oakmont going into the final round, four-putted no. 17 and lost by two strokes to Parks. Johnny Farrell of Baltusrol Country Club in Springfield, New Jersey, won the 1928 U.S. Open at Olympia Fields Country Club near Chicago, making up five shots on Jones in the final round and then edging the legend by one shot in a 36-hole playoff. Farrell also placed second in the 1929 British Open and P.G.A. Championship.

The tournament was preceded by a 36-hole pro-am event in which Nelson was paired with S. Ashton Clark from Ridgewood Country Club. Clark was a 1931 graduate of the prestigious Peddie School and then played and coached golf at Wesleyan University in Middletown, Connecticut. Nelson and Clark won on the fourth hole of a playoff over Gheezi and H.V. Garrity following a curious turn of events. Both teams finished the two-day event three shots behind the Branch Brook Country Club duo of pro Dominick Morano and amateur Jerry Volpe. But the executive committee of the New Jersey Golf

Association announced that team was disqualified after determining Morano was neither the head pro nor the assistant pro at Branch Brook. Nelson's winnings for the pro-am triumph came to $40.

Wood wasted little time moving up the opening day leaderboard, following his par-4 on the first hole with a birdie on a par-3 second. But he double-bogeyed no. 3, went out in 4-over 38, and settled for an opening round of 4-over 75. Nelson struggled on the front nine even more, opening with 39 but rallying with a 1-under 36 to join Wood at 75. The day's honors went to Alec Ternyei, the 25-year-old pro at Saddle River Country Club in northern New Jersey, not far from the New York state line, who was playing in only his third pro tournament. On a day when no one even equaled par, Ternyei's 1-over 72 was good for a one-shot lead. And that came after he double-bogeyed the par-5 closing hole.

Nelson shot par on the second day, leaving him tied for fourth place and three shots behind the leader, Jack Forrester, a Scot representing Hackensack Country Club, who shot a 1-under 70. Between Forrester and Nelson were Bert McDougall of Essex Falls Country Club and George Sullivan of Long Branch Country Club. They were two strokes behind at 3-over 145, McDougall getting there by tying the course record of 68. Ternyei followed his opening 72 with a 4-over 75 and was a shot behind Nelson and the field was cut to fifty-two.

Nelson put together his best round of the tournament during the morning run of Saturday's closing thirty-six holes, a 1-under 70, but it wasn't enough to put him in the lead. Forrester matched that, Sullivan shot 71, and McDougall struggled to a 3-over 74 to set up the afternoon finale with Forrester leading at even-par 213, Nelson and Sullivan at 216, and McDougall at 219. Monmouth Country Club's par-4 sixth hole began to determine the victor. Nelson parred the hole while Forrester and Sullivan couldn't recover from poor approaches to the green, which featured water in front and on the left and a massive sand

55

trap to the right. Forrester and Sullivan each hooked into the drink. Forrester scored a 6, Sullivan a 7. That pulled Nelson even with Forrester, his final-round playing partner, and pushed Sullivan two shots behind them. Nelson grabbed a one-shot lead on no. 8, bogeyed no. 9 to return the favor, then fired birdies on the first three closing holes thanks to deadeye approach shots that allowed him to one-putt each green.

Nelson signed to a 4-over 288 for a three-shot margin over Forrester, earning him the first-place check of $400 – and more important, his first professional victory, though not in an official P.G.A. Tour event. Farrell, while never in the hunt, grabbed a measure of glory. His finishing 4-over 67 established a course record for the second consecutive day. Gheezi tied for sixth with Sullivan and Ternyei. Wood never cracked par in any round, a 17-over 301 leaving him mired in fourteenth place. Afterward, Nelson asked George Jacobus if he thought he had what it took to be a championship player, and Jacobus said yes. Nelson then set a curious goal for someone who had yet to win a P.G.A. Tour event: "If I don't win the Open by 1939, I'll never win it at all. I think, though, that'll be my year."

Nelson closed out the 1935 season with some promising results. He tied for sixth place at Hershey and tied for fourth at Louisville. Turning the calendar into 1936, he tied for third at Riverside and finished third a few weeks later at Sacramento. His return to a second Masters resulted in a tie for thirteen, after which his next start was back in the New York area at the Metropolitan Open at Quaker Ridge in suburban Mamaroneck. Nelson fought off a poor start to finish the first round in 1-over 71, tying him for third place with Paul Runyan and Craig Wood. They were two shots behind leader Gene Sarazen – who'd first won the event twenty years earlier – whose 69 tied the course record. Henry Picard, the defending champion, stood two shots behind. Nelson bogeyed the par-5 first and par-4 second but rallied to pull even at the turn. Similarly on the back nine, he balanced two bogeys with two birdies before bogeying the par-4 eighteenth. Nelson equaled Sarazen's first-round feat on day two with a 69, but another former Met Open champion shattered the course record later in the day. Runyan, the 1934 tournament winner, fired a 3-under 67 on the strength of a powerful driver. His course mark would have been even more impressive had he been able to sink more short putts. He and Sarazen tied atop the leaderboard with 2-under 138s at the midpoint of the event. Nelson's even-par 140 gave him third place, one shot ahead of Wood and two in front of Picard.

On the final day, traversing Quaker Ridge twice, Nelson opened with a 2-over 72 that gave him a tournament total of 2-over 212 and inched him within one shot of the lead. That belonged to Runyan, following a morning round of 3-over 73. Beginning the fourth round, Runyan was 3-over for the first six holes. A birdie on the par-4 eighth only temporarily slowed his slide. He shot 3-over on the back nine for a closing 5-over 75 for a final score of 6-over 286. Nelson, conversely, was the picture of consistency during the final round. He parred every hole on the front nine. A bogey on the par-4 eleventh was offset by a birdie on the par-5 fourteenth. Nelson nearly caved in on the par-4 sixteenth when he held a two-shot lead over Runyan. His drive hooked into a bunker, and his escape shot nearly sailed over the green. Nelson then chipped, the ball coming to a stop about five feet from the hole and leaving him with an onerous downhill putt. He sank the putt for a bogey, cutting his lead to a single stroke. Runyan was within that one shot heading to the par-4 eighteenth hole and promptly contributed his sixth bogey over his final sixteen holes.

Sarazen went from swaggering to staggering. He shot a 6-over 76 in the morning that virtually took him out of contention and followed with an 11-over 81. Wood finished second with a 5-over 285 that trailed Nelson by

Byron Nelson takes a snack break en route to his first victory in a national event, the 1936 Metropolitan Open at Quaker Ridge Golf Club in Mamaroneck, New York. (Byron Nelson estate)

two. His final schizophrenic round included five birdies and six bogeys. His two tours across the front nine on the final Saturday took him five more shots than Nelson, costing him the title. Nelson collected $750, appropriately the largest paycheck of his career to that point. While he didn't win again that year, he did earn more – a check for $975 for finishing in a tie for second place at the Vancouver Jubilee Open in late July. That purse was $4,994, nearly equal to the Met Open's $5,000. But the winner was an amateur, Canadian Ken Black, whose earnings went back into the pool.

Aside from the valuable experience provided for young Ben Hogan beginning in the 1920s, the love affair that merchant Marvin Leonard developed with golf at Glen Garden would uplift the entire sport in Texas. Leonard's ever-active entrepreneurial mind melded with his zeal for golf. He acquired 140 acres along the Trinity River just north of TCU to build a golf course – Colonial Country Club – that would be worthy of national championship competition. That was a radical concept for the day. The U.S. Open had never been played outside the Northeast or the upper Midwest, homes to courses that were more mature than those elsewhere – not to mention greater portions of the country's population. The P.G.A. Championship occasionally ventured from beyond those unofficial confines. It came to Dallas' Cedar Crest in 1927, was played in Los Angeles two years later, and would come to Oklahoma City's Twin Hills Country Club later in 1936.

Leonard teamed the man who had become Texas' most prolific course designer, John Bredemus, with Perry Maxwell from Oklahoma to build a course that would earn national acclaim. He also was intent on employing bentgrass greens, uncommon on courses in the Southwest given the region's extreme temperatures and occasionally relentless winds. The alternative was Bermuda greens, which were less consistent than bentgrass. Leonard spared no expense in keeping the bentgrass sufficiently watered and protected from diseases. In the early 1930s when serving on Glen Garden's board of directors, Leonard persuaded the club to experiment with bentgrass greens, which were used on most of the most prominent golf courses in other regions of the country. He had Glen Garden's eighteenth green planted with bentgrass and provided with a healthy amount of moisture. The result was a lush surface, possibly the best in the state. Glen Garden didn't have the means to do more than run the brief experiment on one hole, but Leonard was convinced bentgrass would work in Texas. Colonial would provide him the opportunity to put his theory to a larger test.

7

TRIUMPH AND TRIBULATION

A S THIRTY-EIGHT P.G.A. Tour pros, seven amateurs, and the legendary Bobby Jones prepared to attack Augusta National for the fourth Masters in 1937, the odds-on favorite to capture the first-place slice of the $5,000 jackpot was "Lighthorse" Harry Cooper at 9-to-1. Cooper, a native of England who honed his game in Texas after his father became the head pro at Dallas' Cedar Crest Golf Course during the 1920s, was the leading money winner of the early season Tour and was the 1936 Masters runner-up to Horton Smith. Smith and Augusta pro Ed Dudley followed close behind at 10-to-1 with Jones, Dallas native Ralph Guldahl (then playing out of St. Louis), Sam Snead, Paul Runyan, and Byron Nelson next at 14-to-1.

Nelson arrived in Georgia having secured a more lucrative situation only two weeks earlier. He landed the head pro job at Reading Country Club in Pennsylvania following two years as the assistant pro at Ridgewood in New Jersey. His guaranteed annual salary at age twenty-five was $3,750 plus proceeds from the pro shop and lessons. As he put it in his autobiography, "It certainly looked as if we wouldn't have to borrow any more money from Louise's folks." Thus they were able to stay at the ornate Bon-Air Hotel. The morning of the opening round, the Nelsons ate breakfast in the main dining room while a woman played *The Blue Danube* on an organ just down the hallway. Nelson almost unconsciously fell in synch with the waltz's rhythm and carried that feeling with him out to the course.

There, Nelson made beautiful music with a 6-under-par 66 on a warm, breezy afternoon that gave him a three-shot bulge over Guldahl, a round that would stand as the tournament's 18-hole standard until 1976. The artistry featured six one-putt greens. Asked what he could possibly do for an encore on Friday, Nelson smiled and said, "This is one of the best rounds I've ever played but not the best." He then proceeded to put away a sandwich and some milk. The second round saw Nelson paired with his chum, "Jug" McSpaden, in one of the last groups of the day. Nelson could manage only par-72, but his overall 6-under 138 was good enough to maintain the three-stroke lead over Guldahl and Dudley.

Putting at the Dublin-DeLeon golf course in the 1930s meant using a roller to smooth out a portion of the sand greens. (Courtesy of Candace Bibby and *DeLeon Free Press*)

On Saturday, Nelson recorded a 3-over 75 for a 3-under 213 to fall behind both Guldahl (at 7-under 209 following a 68) and Dudley (at 4-under 212). In the words of *Augusta Chronicle* sports editor Tom Wall, he "cracked up." O.B. Keeler of *The Atlanta Journal* served a warning for Nelson in his assessment that "the third round of a medal play golf tournament is the Big One, and pretty frequently it seems to be the truth." That didn't prove to be the case on this occasion. Playing thirty minutes behind Guldahl, Nelson matched the tournament leader through Augusta's front nine and then pinned him down coming back in. As he walked down the tenth fairway following his tee shot, Nelson heard someone from the gallery say Guldahl had birdied the par-4 no. 10. So Nelson, realizing par would leave him four behind with eight remaining, got his second shot not only on the green but within fifteen feet of the hole. He sank the putt, to which playing partner Wiffy Cox concluded, "Kid, I think that's the one we needed."

Nelson headed to Amen Corner, also birdied no. 12 and shot an eagle-3 on no. 13. He told himself, "The Lord hates a coward" before chipping in with a hooded 8-iron from about twenty feet off the green. He parred out the rest of the way to play his final eleven holes in 4-under; he played nos. 12 and 13 in a combined 3-under while Guldahl played them in 3-over, going into Rae's Creek at no. 12 and shooting back into the water at no. 13. Nelson's Sunday 2-under 70 gave him a final score of 5-under 283 and a two-stroke margin over Guldahl. He was a major champion in his eighth attempt; his previous best showing in a Masters, National Open or P.G.A. Championship was his tie for ninth place at Augusta in 1935. "I never thought about my chances," a smiling Nelson told reporters late Sunday afternoon. "I just kept plugging away and hoping. It seemed that everything I did was right and the ball was rolling for me." It was a dozen years before the green jacket became emblematic of Masters victory; Nelson was presented the championship gold medal by Jones and the $1,500 winner's check by famed sportswriter Grantland Rice, a founding member of Augusta National. Nelson later called the '37 Masters the most significant victory of his career, the one that provided him with overwhelming confidence. The *Atlanta Journal*'s O.B. Keeler wrote: "Byron, I watched you play the back nine today, and it reminded me of a piece of poetry that was written by Lord Byron when Napoleon was defeated at the battle of Waterloo." Nelson didn't mention to Keeler how his father got his name.

Late in 1931, Ben Hogan ran out of money while playing in California. Marvin Leonard wired him funds that not only kept him going while on the road but also allowed him to buy a Christmas present for his girlfriend, Valerie Fox. Many of those who followed golf in Fort Worth were convinced that the Hogan boy, whose game displayed the better promise, was Royal, who often fared well in tournaments at Glen Garden and elsewhere around the city. Royal, who was becoming successful in the office supply business in Cowtown, would also see to it that Ben's coffers didn't run completely dry. The younger Hogan boy was working part-time at a small Fort Worth course called Oakhurst and performing a number of duties at the downtown Blackstone Hotel, including serving as a poker dealer at night. As the calendar turned to 1932, Hogan's next attempt at regular Tour play lasted only a few weeks into the winter tour but did include his first check from a P.G.A. Tour event – $200 for finishing in a tie for fifth place at the Agua Caliente Open played in Tijuana, Mexico.

But a promising business opportunity presented itself. Valerie's father, Claude Fox, informed him that a small course in Cleburne, Nolan River Country Club, was desperately seeking a new professional. Hogan jumped at the chance; while he wasn't bringing home regular money from tournament competition, he now had a steady golf income of another kind. It wasn't long before the romance between Ben and Valerie led to marriage, their wedding taking place in April 1935 in the Foxes' home. The newlyweds settled in Fort Worth, initially staying with Hogan's mother and then getting a two-bedroom apartment in the same complex where the Leonards lived. Their second bedroom was rented to Valerie's sister, Sarah, who for years had been extremely close to Valerie and Ben.

While Hogan was able to compete in only a handful of Tour events before gaining a measure of good footing in 1937, he managed to gain entry through regional qualifying to the U.S. Opens of 1934 (at Merion Golf Club) and 1936 (at Baltusrol) – though he failed to survive the cut each time. With Byron Nelson serving as assistant pro at Ridgewood Country Club in New Jersey, the Hogans came calling before play at the '36 Open began. Louise took Valerie to see the sights in nearby New York City. The 1937 season saw Hogan participate in ten tournaments, which nearly equaled all of his previous play. He scored a career-high, third-place finish at Lake Placid and closed out the year with earnings of $1,164.

During the waning days of 1937, Henry Picard and Jack Grout were traveling west through Texas on their way to California for the resumption of Tour play in a few weeks when they stopped for dinner at Fort Worth's Blackstone Hotel. Across the room, Picard spied Hogan and his wife eating, and apparently quarreling. Though Picard didn't know Hogan very well at the time, he approached the couple and asked what was wrong. Valerie volunteered that she was pushing Ben to head off for Tour play without her, fearing their bank account couldn't support both of them on the road. Picard's reply: "I'm not the richest man in the world. But if you need money, I've got it. You go to the coast with her." Hogan never had to call upon Picard's generosity but later said it meant the world to him knowing that financial safety net was available.

Hogan's 1938 season got off to a rocky start. He finished a distant fifty-second in the opening Los Angeles Open, far out of the money, and followed that with a $75 payday at the Bing Crosby Pro-Am. Tying for tenth place at the Pasadena Open was good for only another $67. They drove back up the Golden State for the Oakland Open at Sequoia Country Club with only about $100. As Valerie Hogan told Dave Anderson during a series of interviews in the late 1990s, Ben told her that if he didn't earn anything in Oakland he would sell their Buick right there in California to pay for their trip home and give up his dream of being a professional golfer. They agreed to give it a try at Sequoia and proceeded to check into an inexpensive hotel, which was usually their practice.

When it appeared things couldn't get worse, they did. As Hogan left the hotel for the course the day of the first round, he was jolted by the sight of the rear of the couple's car propped up on cinder blocks where the back tires had been. Hogan caught a ride to the club with Nelson and somehow kept enough concentration to shoot a first-round 70. He followed that up with 71 and 72, faltering in the final round with a 74 to drop into a tie for sixth place. But that finish paid off with a check for $285. That was the second-largest payoff of his career to date, behind only the $375 for the third-place finish at Lake Placid the previous year. But because of the circumstances at play, Hogan called it "the biggest check I'd ever seen in my life," in a television interview with Ken Venturi almost fifty years later. That "biggest check" was topped the following week at the Sacramento Open, where Hogan finished third and pocketed $350. He finished the year making another quantum leap in earnings ($4,794, thirteenth on the P.G.A. Tour list) and finally broke into the win column, albeit in a four-ball event. He was invited in September to fill a last-minute vacancy in the field of the Hershey Four-Ball through the efforts of Hershey Country Club's pro, Picard. Hogan and Vic Gheezi teamed to dominate play from start to finish. Were that not enough, Hogan that year landed the job as assistant pro at the Century Country Club in the Westchester County, New York town of Purchase – again, with the assistance of Picard.

GROWN AT GLEN GARDEN

Glen Garden's membership decreased annually through the late 1930s, from 325 members in 1935 to 251 in 1939. The club filed for bankruptcy in 1936. In October 1938, T.J. Brown, club president from 1935 until his death in 1949, and a man considered by many as a leading influence in its history, wrote to the club's stockholders. Tom Brown was often referred to as "Coke" since his sizable fortune came courtesy of his relationship to the Coca-Cola Bottling Company. "First, we wish to report that the Club is in better financial condition than at any other time in its existence. Fortunately, our membership is made up of good folk – loyal and interested in all of the Club activities." Brown pointed out the condition of the golf course will determine the size of the membership, and he zeroed in on the fact that Glen Garden's water supply covered only watering of the greens and not the fairways. He further mentioned the club's competition in Fort Worth, Colonial, and River Crest, were spending considerable money in keeping their fairways watered and in top condition.

Brown proposed spending $9,000 to create a lake on the property that would serve as a reservoir from which the course could be adequately watered. The lake that currently runs down the right side of the 344-yard, par-4 seventh hole and rests between the tee area and green of the 432-yard, par-4 eighth hole is the result of Brown's efforts to provide Glen Garden with a secure water supply. Years later, Jackie Towery, one of Ben Hogan's nieces, explained how her father, Royal, one day early in his golfing career, placed shot after shot into the lake. That provoked him to toss his driver into the lake and then command his young caddie to wade into the briny deep and retrieve the club. The young man politely declined, noting he was deathly afraid of snakes. Hogan asked his caddie again but received the same refusal. So, Hogan said the caddie should simply return to the clubhouse. "I don't know the end of this story," Towery says, "but I can assure you that club was back in my dad's bag before he left the course that day." And the caddie? His name was Robert Towery and became Jackie's husband.

Wendell Waddle has been associated with Glen Garden for most of his life. A 1948 graduate of Byron Nelson's alma mater, Poly High, Waddle worked in the club's pro shop while still in high school. He says Brown would walk into the office of general manager Bill Overton after the monthly bills went out and ask, "How are we doing this month?" Overton might say, "Tom we're down about $200. I don't think we can handle it."

"Whatever they were down," Waddle recalls, "he'd make it up. In many cases, he'd donate it to them. In fact, he put up the cash for the [P.G.A. Tour] tournament in 1946 – $3,500. I knew him real well. I was in the pro shop when I was fifteen, and I couldn't close the shop until dark. Nobody was on the course, but I couldn't leave. He'd come out in the evening and say, 'Let's play 1 and 9.' Such a nice guy. He was never married. The club was all he had."

8

SPRING MILL MARATHON

BYRON NELSON HEADED to the Spring Mill course of the Philadel-phia Country Club in June 1939 with every reason to believe he could win his first U.S. Open championship and his second major title. He'd won in three of his previous five tournament starts; granted, the wins at the Seminole Invitational and St. Augustine Open weren't official P.G.A. Tour events. He won at Phoenix the first weekend of February by twelve shots despite playing only fifty-four holes, the result of play being snowed out on Friday and Saturday (yes, snowed out in Phoenix). In winning the North and South Open at Pinehurst, North Carolina in late March, his two-shot victory margin was accomplished despite consistent putting problems. At the Masters, a promising start (opening rounds of 71-69) faded (72-75) into what was relatively disappointing to date that year, a seventh-place finish. He then skipped the next three events while negotiating to leave his job as the pro at Reading Country Club in Pennsylvania for Inverness Country Club in Toledo, Ohio, starting in April 1940.

The U.S.G.A. decided to convert two of Spring Mill's par-5s into par-4s for the National Open, shaving the overall par score down to 69. Nelson didn't break from the gate on day one like one of the hottest golfers on the Tour. On the front nine, he struggled to a 4-over 38 and finished with a 3-over 72 that lodged him amid a half-dozen players tied for twelfth place; in his autobiography, Nelson stated he was nervous in that opening round. The first-day leader was Sam Snead, whose 1-under 68 was the only round to sneak below par. Talk about reversals – ten days earlier, Snead was so dissatisfied with his practice round at Spring Mill that he concluded he had little chance to claim his first U.S. Open. Following with a 2-over 71 in Friday's second round amid blistering heat, Snead marched toward Saturday's final thirty-six holes with a two-shot cushion over Craig Wood. Nelson's 4-over 73 placed him at 7-over 145 and six shots behind.

In Saturday's morning round, Nelson began to make his move with a 2-over 71 but still had a five-shot deficit to make up, and sharing ninth place, with a lot of folks to catch. He was still four strokes behind Snead, Wood, and Denny Shute. He was paired with Olin Dutra, and between rounds they had lunch along with J.K. Wadley, the Texarkana businessman who got to know Nelson during his time there and had remained close. When Nelson went to repeat Dutra's lunch order of roast beef, gravy, mashed potatoes, and vegetables, Wadley put the kibosh on that. On Nelson's behalf, Wadley instead ordered him a chicken sandwich on toast with no mayonnaise, vegetables, iced tea, and half a slice of apple pie.

The final eighteen holes at Spring Mill that steamy, summer day live in golf lore, probably infamy in Snead's home state of Virginia. Nelson continued his improved play by closing with a 1-under 68. He was one stroke behind Snead as Snead prepared to cap his day on the 558-yard, par-5 eighteenth from an elevated tee box. There were no scoreboards on the course, and judging one's place in the field could sometimes be difficult. When Snead heard cheers from the pairing playing behind him, he assumed that meant one of the golfers chasing him – Wood or Shute – had birdied. As he took his stance, Snead erroneously thought he needed a birdie-4 on the final hole to win the National Open.

Snead's situation wasn't helped by a throng of fans who spilled out into the eighteenth fairway because of their desire to catch a glimpse of a fellow spectator – one Bobby Jones. The marshals needed almost half an hour to return the hole to playable condition, with Snead fretting the entire time. His drive covered 260 yards, but it sailed to the left and came to rest in rough. Instead of concentrating on simply getting back into the fairway with a reasonable third shot, Snead pulled out a 2-wood and aimed toward the flag stick. He didn't make good contact, and the ball plopped into a fairway bunker more than 100 yards from the pin. A sand wedge would give him the best chance of escape but would probably leave him short of the green hitting four. Snead selected his 8-iron, but the shot was low and didn't make it out of the trap. His second try made it out but only to find another bunker to the left of the putting surface.

At that point, word-of-mouth information made its way to Snead. He overheard a fan say Nelson had finished at 284. He was stunned, realizing he must get down in two shots merely to earn a tie with Nelson and anyone else at that same score. "Why the hell didn't someone tell me earlier?" he growled. His sixth shot reached the green, some forty feet from the hole. He pondered the putt for a good while and then sent the ball on direct line to the cup. As it appeared headed right in, the ball slid slightly to the left about three feet ahead of the pin and missed by three feet. Already at 284, Snead missed on the three-footer coming back and finished the par-5 with an 8 that banished him two strokes behind Nelson. The gallery gave him an empathetic round of applause after which he tried to speak but couldn't.

Though Snead didn't know it, Shute and Wood also finished Saturday's grueling test at 284 to send the U.S. Open into a three-way playoff on Sunday. Another day's play merely sliced the field of championship contenders from three to two. Shute bogeyed three holes on the front nine that left him four strokes behind Nelson and Wood, and he was essentially finished. Wood owned an early two-shot advantage over Nelson, but Nelson rallied to lead by one with two to play thanks to a birdie on the par-4 sixteenth hole. But suddenly the tables were turned when Nelson three-putted no. 17 and Wood birdied to gain a one-shot edge. Yet Wood's drive on no. 18 was almost as bad as Snead's. He hooked a wood into the gallery, where the ball ricocheted off the face of a man named Bob Mossman – knocking him down – and sending the ball back into the fairway. Mossman lost consciousness and was carried off in front of Wood. ("That didn't bother me," Wood told reporters later. He more regretted hitting with a wood on that shot instead of a 2-iron.)

Wood managed to save par and nearly birdied for the win with a five-foot putt that just missed. When his ball missed the cup, Louise Nelson fainted in the press tent to become the second individual to lose consciousness as a result of Wood's play on that single hole (surely a P.G.A. Tour record). Meanwhile, Nelson's third shot was a chip close to the green that put the ball seven feet from the flag stick. He sank the putt and forced yet another 18-hole playoff, then one-on-one, for Monday. In the locker room, Nelson told Wood, "Well, we got one out of there." To which Wood replied, "Yes, and if you throw another round like that at me tomorrow, I'll be out of it." To the gaggle of newsmen, the competitive side of the usually amiable Nelson was on full display: "I merely said to myself that Wood's putts had been dropping for him all afternoon, and it was high time one didn't find that hole. I was telling myself that I had missed a couple, and my opponent was due for one break against him. I kept telling myself over and over Wood would miss. Sure enough, he shot and failed to hit the bucket." As for his own putt, he later said he was thinking of all the times back at Glen Garden when caddies would play and dream out loud, "This putt is for the U.S. Open." "That steadied me enough," he said.

On Monday following an evening of rain in the Philadelphia area, Nelson hustled to save par on the first two holes. He then birdied no. 3 to grab a one-shot advantage. On the par-4 fourth, he followed a solid drive with a 1-iron for an eagle for a three-stroke lead only four holes in – "Straight in the hole like a rat," Nelson wrote in his autobiography. He couldn't keep up that pace, but Wood couldn't gain any ground. With both carding multiple bogeys the rest of the way – could they have resembled Rocky Balboa and Apollo Creed in the fifteenth round somewhere else in Philadelphia? – Nelson shot a 1-over 70, Wood a 4-over 73. A giddy George Jacobus who doubled as president of the P.G.A. in addition to being the head pro at Ridgewood, greeted Nelson afterward and reminded him of their conversation of four years earlier, when Nelson cited 1939 as the year that he would win the National Open. Wood, a New Jersey resident who had also been close to Jacobus through the years, wasn't enamored with Jacobus pulling for Nelson to win – even saying so in a radio interview. "Things can never be the same between us after this," Wood told him. "As president of our association, I think you spoke out of turn regardless of your affection for Nelson. That washes us up."

Snead – like Nelson and Hogan, born in 1912 – would become the Tour leader in career victories with eighty-two including three Masters, two P.G.A. Championships, and one British Open – but would never hoist the U.S. Open trophy. While Hogan was often tight-lipped and Nelson usually polite, Snead was apt to say almost anything without attempting to be brash or colorful. He was raised in rural Virginia, the youngest of five brothers. After winning the Oakland Open in 1937, he was legitimately surprised upon learning his picture appeared in a New York newspaper because, as he put it, "I ain't never been there." He played five holes during a practice round before the 1941 Canadian Open barefoot and later won the tournament. P.G.A. tournament manager Fred Corcoran reminded Snead of that the following spring at Augusta, suggesting he abandon the shoes again. He happily complied (though he also didn't win that week). To save a buck one year at the Los Angeles Open, he and Johnny Bulla shared a room at the home of Snead's uncle. Shared a bed, even. When he won the 1965 Greensboro Open at age fifty-two (plus ten months), he became the oldest player to win on the P.G.A. Tour.

One day after Nelson's marathon six-round effort, the new National Open champion again referenced his golfing roots: "Thirteen years ago when I was a caddie at the Glen Garden Country Club back in Fort Worth, Texas, I dreamed of three things – winning the National Open and the P.G.A. titles and going to England to play on the Ryder Cup team. I realized one when I went to England with the Ryder Cup team. The second came true yesterday afternoon at Spring Mill. Naturally, I'm tickled pink."

Back in the Handley section of Fort Worth, John Byron Nelson told an inquiring photographer that he'd begrudgingly stand and pose for a newspaper photo. "It's so seldom we have a national champion in the family that I guess I will." Ellen, twenty years old, said, "I nearly wore that place on the sofa out." Added Madge Nelson: "I couldn't stand the strain. I went out in the yard and walked up and down." Nelson returned to Reading Country Club a conquering hero. Only a few days later, they were joined by Ben and Valerie Hogan, who came over from Purchase, New York, where Hogan recently became the assistant pro at the Century Country Club. The men played golf – maybe sharing some flashbacks to Glen Garden – while the women shopped. The club party at Reading proved to be a bittersweet bash for the Nelsons since Byron would soon leave for Inverness. "I hate to leave Reading and my friends," he told the gathering at the club. "My wife feels the same way. I have been lucky ever since coming to this town. We will leave here this fall with a deep feeling in our hearts for all our friends. And you may rest assured that we will be back to see you all."

Nelson won four more times in P.G.A. Tour events that year (and a couple of lesser tournaments) and nearly won consecutive majors. The 1939 P.G.A. Championship was staged at Pomonok Country Club on Long Island. The field of sixty-four competitors was set through thirty-six holes of qualifying play on Sunday and Monday to determine the final four entrants before match play began. Hogan snagged one of those four spots to join the others, which naturally included the new National Open champion. Hogan breezed through his first-round morning match, disposing of Steve Zappe 7-and-6 but was taken out that afternoon by Paul Runyan 4-and-3. Nelson toppled Chuck Garringer 4-and-2, William Francis 3-and-1 and Johnny Revolta 6-and-4 during the 18-hole rounds. With the format shifting to 36-hole matches beginning with the quarterfinals, Nelson vanquished Emerick Kocsis 10-and-9 and "Dutch" Harrison 9-and-8. His opponent in the final was Henry Picard whose 20-plus P.G.A. Tour victories to date during the 1930s most notably included the '38 Masters.

Nelson spent much of the match staying close to Picard, alternating between being a stroke down or even. He dramatically birdied no. 11 during the afternoon session; under stymie rules with no marking of a ball on the greens, Nelson's shot at the hole jumped Picard's ball in its route and went into the cup. That put Nelson in the lead for the first time all day. Picard was in danger of falling two behind on the thirty-fourth hole before nailing a 25-foot putt to remain one down. Back on the 300-yard, par-4 no. 18, each player was on in two with Nelson twelve feet from the flag stick and Picard only four. Nelson missed his putt while Picard made his, forcing extra play for the fourth time in tournament history. The "overtime" didn't last long; Picard one-putted for a birdie, and Nelson couldn't match. That took place after Picard sailed his tee shot into rough, and the ball was driven over by a truck carrying a couple of radio announcers. Picard was awarded a free drop and put his second shot only seven feet from the pin, setting up the birdie.

The most anomalous episode of Nelson's season – maybe of his entire pro career – took place over Labor Day weekend at the Hershey Open in his then-adopted home state. Nelson was cruising along with a healthy lead with four holes to play and sent his tee shot on no. 15 straight down the fairway and over a ridge. When he cleared the crest and tried to locate his ball, it wasn't there. No member of the gallery volunteered what happened to the AWOL ball, and Nelson had no choice but to return to the tee box and re-hit with a two-stroke penalty. The penalty was the difference in him winning and finishing fourth, and the subsequent headlines across the country dealt less with winner Felix Serafin than with the mystery of the Nelson golf ball.

A few weeks later, Nelson received a letter dated September 11, post-marked in New York City and addressed to "Mr. Byron Nelson, Open Golf Champion of 1939."

Mr. Byron Nelson –
Reading, Pa.
Dear Sir:-

On Sunday, Sept. 3rd, at Hershey, as we were leaving the match, and did not know we were walking in the line of play, a lady in my party and who was my guest, unwittingly picked up your ball and that fact was not known until too late. She knew practically nothing about the game and thought she had found a ball someone had unknowingly dropped in the rough. It seems quite unnecessary to go into detail now – but I thank the Almighty it was only a money game and that your resulting loss can be restored. As she was my guest I feel responsible and she has suffered sufficiently because of the unfortunate incident.

Therefore it is best that her identity be undisclosed – as well as mine. I learn from the newspaper account that your loss was $300 and therefore I am enclosing that amount in Postal Money Orders, so mailed I feel sure it will reach you.

I wish there could be an acknowledgment but I prefer to remain
Anonymous
Regret – delayed remittance – could not be avoided

The account in Nelson's autobiography indicated he was confident the ball was in the fairway and didn't mention any attempt to search through the rough. Why no spectator couldn't have helped is another head-scratcher.

9

BRACKENRIDGE BATTLE

THE ARRIVAL OF February in 1940 meant hope for a new start for a unique baseball hero who had fallen on hard times. Cincinnati left-handed pitcher Johnny Vander Meer was the toast of the nation in 1938 when he became the first big leaguer to throw consecutive no-hitters. (The second of those no-hitters took place during the first night game played at Brooklyn's Ebbets Field, and some of the frustrated Dodgers claimed hitters that night were at a disadvantage. Didn't hurt the Reds' hitters as much; Cincinnati won 6-0). Vander Meer compiled fifteen wins against ten losses that season but couldn't nearly duplicate that success in 1939, going 5-9 with his earned run average rising from 3.12 per nine innings to 4.67. He later admitted all the publicity that engulfed him following the double no-hitters adversely affected him.

As the Reds prepared to report to Tampa, Florida for their 1940 spring training camp, Vander Meer prepared as if he were a rookie again. "I'm going down there as a 'busher,' " he said. "I'm sure I can make the grade." But he couldn't, at least not immediately. Vander Meer appeared in only ten games for a Reds team that would win the World Series, banished instead to the minor leagues for most of the season. But he was far from finished in the majors. Vander Meer earned a spot on Cincinnati's roster again in 1941 and led the National League in strikeouts each of the next three seasons while averaging a solid sixteen victories. He pitched thirteen years in the majors in all, winning 119 games. As his pro career concluded back in the minors in the early 1950s, Vander Meer threw a third no-hitter – as a member of the Texas League's Tulsa Oilers against the Beaumont Roughnecks in 1952.

During the first weekend of February 1940, the steady and occasionally drenching rains that seemed to hover over south central Texas were probably welcomed by the area's farmers and even by the organizers of the fourteenth annual Texas Open, scheduled for San Antonio's Brackenridge Park Golf Course the following weekend. The weather did play havoc with amateur qualifying at nearby Riverside Country Club for the tournament's Thursday pro-am event and caused Brackenridge to be closed for play on Sunday. But the overall dry and windy winter had left the course's fairways hard and harmed the winter grass on the greens. The rainy weekend left the tournament staff hopeful that playing conditions would be excellent come Thursday, certainly by Friday's opening round.

Almost a thousand miles to the west that Sunday, the only natural phenomenon affecting play on the final day of the Phoenix Open was a twenty-three-year-old Tour golfer from a sleepy little town in western New York State. His name was Ed Oliver, but, by carrying almost 250 pounds on his 5-foot-9 frame, he was known to most Tour competitors and golf fans as "Porky." Oliver finished his third and final tour around the Phoenix Country Club layout in 7-under-par 64, a course record, 5-under on the back nine, to finish at 8-under 205 and erase a five-shot gap between him and Ben Hogan after Sunday's morning round.

Needing a par-5 on the finishing hole, Oliver rallied from a second shot that died in a greenside bunker, managing to save par and maintain his one-stroke advantage over Hogan. For Oliver, the eleventh-hour victory worth $700 extended the second-year pro's good fortunes. For Hogan, the $450 runner-up reward represented only extended disappointment. Oliver scored his second consecutive Tour victory, having won at Bing Crosby's popular tournament in Rancho Santa Fe, California the previous week. Hogan's almost Ahab-like pursuit of an elusive first tour victory – excluding the team event that he won in 1938 with Vic Gheezi – would continue the following week in his home state of Texas.

Byron Nelson arrived in the Alamo City with nothing to show for his time in Phoenix, at least financially. He finished ten shots off Oliver's pace and out of the money. But his recent history at Brackenridge gave him and his many fans reason for optimism. In 1939, Nelson was headed toward the clubhouse on Sunday afternoon in apparent possession of the championship trophy. Then his tee shot on the 375-yard, par-4 sixteenth hole struck a fan and came to rest at the base of a tree. He finished third, the '39 Texas Open title going to "Dutch" Harrison, though the colorful Arkansan hardly backed in; his four-round total of 271 broke the course record.

The drive from Phoenix to San Antonio was one of many that the Hogans and Nelsons made together in separate cars. In fact, a little motor-driven wagon train was formed on this occasion when Oliver and "Jug" McSpaden decided to tail along since their wives weren't on the trip. The caravan stopped just beyond the halfway mark at an unassuming restaurant in Las Cruces, New Mexico, a regular stop for the Hogans and Nelsons where they were particularly enamored with the tamales and chili. So much so, that they asked their waitress this time to have some prepared to take on the rest of the trip, still more than 450 miles through barren west Texas. To the diners' dismay, they were informed the tamales weren't homemade: produced and canned at the Armour

Meat Company in Fort Worth. The foursome from north Texas never again stopped at the little Mexican restaurant in Las Cruces, New Mexico.

McSpaden and Oliver nearly had much more to regret than canned tamales. Oliver was usually a conservative driver, especially on unfamiliar open roads. McSpaden didn't share that same caution and often bellowed that he knew the stretch of roadway in question. On a two-lane road just east of El Paso, Texas, McSpaden whizzed through a tunnel; in those days, the lanes in a tunnel often were decidedly narrower than on regular roads. As their car about reached the midpoint of the tunnel, McSpaden still gunning at high speed, he suddenly noticed a wagon being pulled by two mules. He barely had enough room to avoid hitting the wagon and avoiding disaster. After which an exasperated Oliver exclaimed: "Don't tell me you knew that wagon and those mules were going to be there, too!" Upon arriving in San Antonio, Oliver ended the pair's brief carpooling arrangement.

McSpaden, no worse for wear, recorded the best score among the pros who arrived by train or automobile in time to play a practice round on Tuesday, shooting a 2-under 69 despite a significant wind that blustered across most of the fairways. But the biggest attraction for locals who came out to the course was the chance to watch Sam Snead, entered in his first Texas Open. Slammin' Sammy, having never previously seen the Brackenridge Park layout, shot 1-under-par. Mother Nature rudely reminded San Antonio during Friday's opening round that mid-February was still winter, even in south Texas. Rain and cold returned to the area, but dozens of players were still able to shoot par or better. The day's three leaders included none other than Oliver, seeking a third consecutive victory. He recorded five birdies on Brackenridge's first dozen holes and six overall to shoot a 5-under 66. Also at 66 was Toney Penna, a 32-year-old native of Naples, Italy who grew up in the suburbs north of New York City. He struggled early, bogeying two of the first four holes but more than compensated with seven birdies. Joining Oliver and Penna was Hogan. He opened by bogeying the 390-yard, par-4 first hole, but his six birdies included two of Brackenridge's four par-3 holes. Nelson finished the opening day with a 3-under 68, two shots off the lead.

The original tournament format called for the top 120 pros and fifteen amateurs to continue on to Saturday's second round. (The amateur field included Royal Hogan.) But because of Friday's weather conditions, eleven golfers were unable to finish the opening round on Friday. Saturday's starting time was moved up from 9 a.m. to 8 a.m. with the final threesome scheduled off at 1 p.m. Nelson was placed in the group teeing off at 10:36 a.m. with Clayton Heafner and amateur John Barnum. Hogan was next up, at 10:42, with Penna and Sam Byrd, who was an outfielder for the New York Yankees and Cincinnati Reds from the late 1920s into the mid-1930s. (Upon his exit from baseball, Byrd noted anyone who hit only .250 with those great Yankee teams should find another line of work.) With more pleasant playing conditions for Saturday's second round, Nelson followed with a 4-under 67, stung again by misadventures on no. 16. Instead of hitting a spectator this time, his tee shot splashed into a river to cost him a stroke. Hogan struggled to a 2-over-par round leaving him with a two-day score of 139, seven shots off the pace. The leader going into Sunday's last two rounds was Lawson Little, a promising 29-year-old who'd swept the U.S. and British Amateur titles in 1935 and '36. Little's 6-under in Saturday's round, combined with his 4-under performance on Friday, gave him an overall score of 132 and a three-shot lead. The group tied for second place consisted of Nelson, central Texas' own Lefty Stackhouse and Dallas native Lloyd Mangrum. Stackhouse's infamous temper made him worth following around the course no matter his place in the standings. He was known to punish himself for missing easy putts by slamming his head with his putter, or against a tree if the latter was readily available. Stackhouse actually knocked himself out once during one such outburst. On another occasion, he tossed all of his clubs into a water hazard and then threw his caddie in, too.

Hogan would need a mammoth Sunday effort over the final thirty-six holes to contend, needing to lap eleven competitors and make up seven shots on Little simply to pull into a tie. He was grouped with Snead (while attracting large galleries, also struggling at 138) and Leonard Dodson. Nelson drew placement in the final threesome, scheduled to tee off for the third round at 10:18 a.m. and for the final round at 2:18 p.m. He was joined by Little and "Dutch" Harrison, who was four shots off the lead. Little wasted no time in giving hope to the golfers just behind him on the leaderboard. He shot a 2-over 73 in the morning round. Making up the most ground were Mangrum (a 4-under 67 put him at 9-under 202 after three, in first place) and Horton Smith (a 5-under 66 put him at 8-under 203, one stroke behind Mangrum). Nelson's 2-under 69 gave him a three-round score of 7-under 204, tying him for third place within two shots of the lead. One other golfer shot a 66 to match Smith for the best third-round total; that was Hogan, who shaved the seven-shot deficit to only three heading into the afternoon finale. He pulled himself into contention with a burst on the morning round's back nine, at 5-under par 30.

Smith's charge was blunted early in the fourth round when he bogeyed nos. 7 and 8. His 2-under 69 gave him a final score of 12-under 272, the target for all of the other contenders still out on the course. Hogan was the first to better Smith's total. He shot another 66, closing strong again with one stretch of three consecutive birdies coming in, and dramatically saved par on no. 17 despite sending his tee shot into the river. Hogan headed to the Brackenridge clubhouse with a 13-under 271. Mangrum ballooned to a 2-over 73 for a total of 9-under 275, which left him tied for sixth place. Little followed his morning 2-over 73 with a 3-under 68. He stood at 11-under 273 and two shots behind Hogan – a nine-stroke swing between them that day.

Only the round's final threesome still had no. 18 to play, Hogan clinging to the one-shot lead. With the final group about ten minutes away from finishing, Hogan cordially agreed to sign autographs for anyone who asked before he retired to the locker room to await the finish. Colleagues came by to offer their congratulations. That was more than simply a pat on the back to that week's winner; it appeared to finally be Hogan's breakthrough triumph after so many years of practice balls and tournament events that somehow didn't go his way. Smith expressed the sentiment of the group, though stating the obvious, when he told a local reporter that Hogan's victory was a long time in coming. Hogan politely shook each man's hand but also reminded them the verdict had not yet been rendered.

Among the final threesome of Little, Harrison, and Nelson, one had matched Hogan's 11-under heading into no. 18. That was Nelson, who reached that with a birdie on the par-4 no. 17 by driving the green on his tee shot. When Hogan was informed of Nelson's status with one hole to play, he told a reporter: "Then I hope he either gets a 66 and wins or takes 68 and second so there will be no playoff. But if he wins, there's no one I'd rather lose to than Byron, for he's one of the best friends I'll ever have." Nelson, it turned out, indeed nearly shot 66 to win in regulation. His 20-foot putt for birdie on no. 18 reached the cup but rimmed out. The partisan Texas audience initially groaned when Nelson's putt to win barely missed, then applauded his effort. The tie between Nelson and Hogan meant a playoff, just like in the 1927 caddie tournament at Glen Garden. It would be Hogan's first "overtime" play as a pro.

It turned out Hogan and Nelson weren't finished with their Texas Open obligations that Sunday even after playing thirty-six holes. They were invited, though participation likely wasn't optional, to ride to the outskirts of town to take part in a live interview for radio station WOAI, a 50,000-watt blowtorch that could be heard through about a dozen nearby states and into Mexico. Nelson spoke first and was gracious: "Just happy to be here. Anytime you can tie Ben, it's a feather in your cap because he's such a fine player." Next up was Hogan. Just minutes earlier in the locker room, he'd lavished praise upon his former caddying colleague. But when asked on live radio to assess his playoff opponent, he replied bluntly: "Byron's got a good game, but it'd be a lot better if he'd practice. Byron's too lazy to practice."

Years later, Hogan explained he said that simply in fun, to break the tension of the moment. Taken at face value, the statement extrapolated Hogan's values of life and golf onto Nelson. Hogan couldn't imagine using anything less than a practice day's last available light to hit another shot that he might face in tournament play; Nelson wasn't as consumed by his game. Hogan might have viewed Nelson as lazy, but their tour brethren didn't share that opinion. Jimmy Demaret would later write that he considered Hogan *and* Nelson above the curve of pro golfers of the era when it came to time spent on the practice range, a rare activity of that period.

Nelson said nothing in response to Hogan's statement. The interview continued without further issue, the main goal being to drive ticket sales for Monday's round starting at 1 p.m. The day's ticket would cost $1.10 to watch the one pairing, as had daily tickets for play on Friday and Saturday. (For Sunday's double dip, the cost rose to $1.65.) If Nelson and Hogan remained tied after the eighteen holes, another nine would be tacked on. If that still couldn't determine the winner of the $1,500 first-place prize, among the largest on tour that year, they'd return Tuesday for another eighteen.

Between 2,000 and 2,500 fans made it out to Brackenridge for the early-afternoon first shot. Tournament organizers had the luxury of locally-based Army troops serving as marshals on the course. Utmost attention was given to the players' convenience; for instance, the gallery was kept a good distance away from each green instead of allowing spectators to creep right up to the edge. With the weather cooperating again, they each parred the opening four holes. Nelson nearly birdied the 175-yard, par-3 second, but his putt rolled an inch wide and six inches past the cup. They each scrambled following poor tee shots on the 515-yard, par-5 no. 3, then each missed makeable birdie putts. Hogan took the first lead of the playoff on no. 5, a 375-yard par 4. He ripped a 300-yard drive down the middle of the fairway, a good twenty-five yards beyond Nelson's tee shot, but each reached the green in two. Hogan was eighteen feet from the pin and two-putted for his fifth consecutive par. Nelson's long lag putt rolled three feet beyond the cup, and his effort coming back rimmed out to leave him with a bogey.

Hogan survived one of his dreaded hooks teeing off the par-4 no. 6, and they each parred the 350-yard hole. But another hook on no. 7, a 430-yard par 4, helped even the match. Hogan's tee shot flew into the trees that lined the left side of the fairway. While the ball bounced back onto the edge of the fairway, his path toward the pin was impeded by some branches and required a low second shot that reached the back of the green. A long putt for birdie ran three feet beyond the hole, and his return rimmed the cup to leave him with a bogey-5. Nelson parred the hole, his second putt nearly sliding out before dropping. Nelson took his first lead of the playoff with the round's first birdie, on the 485-yard, par-5 ninth hole. He nearly reached the green in two, his second shot resting just off the putting surface. He rolled his third shot to two feet of the pin, where he converted a birdie putt. Hogan was on in three, but his chip to the green left him twenty feet beyond the hole. His first putt passed the pin by three feet, relegating him to par. Midway through the playoff round, Nelson was one shot ahead.

Brackenridge's back nine had been Hogan's playground through much of the tournament, and that didn't initially change in the playoff. He collected birdies at no. 11 (a 365-yard par 4) and no. 13 (a 520-yard par 5) to regain the lead. On no. 11, Hogan sank a 15-foot birdie putt; on no. 13, he nearly rammed home a 40-foot putt for an eagle-2 before recording another birdie. Nelson nearly birdied the hole. At the fifteenth, an inconvenient divot contributed to Hogan giving up his lead. His tee shot on the 385-yard, par-4 plunked into the divot, giving him a bad lie and costing him distance. He couldn't hit his approach wedge cleanly, and the ball landed in a branch of the San Antonio River. The penalty stroke cost him the lead as Nelson parred the hole, nearly sinking a three-foot birdie putt that would have resulted in a two-shot swing. He didn't have to wait long to take advantage of another opportunity to regain the lead. On no. 16, Nelson drove thirty yards farther on the 375-yard par 4, and he deftly placed his second shot only eight feet from the flag stick near the back of the green. The ensuing putt put him 1-under for the first time in the playoff. Hogan was also on in two but was forty feet short of the hole and two-putted, par for the hole and par for the round.

On the remaining two holes, Hogan had recorded three birdies, three pars and two bogeys during the regulation tournament. Nelson had been spotless, with three birdies and five pars. On no. 17, they each hooked their tee shots but escaped trouble. Nelson went into the trees but had a clear path to reach the green in two. Hogan's drive struck a tree hard enough to send the ball back into the fairway, and his approach landed twelve feet from the flag. His birdie attempt, to tie for the lead, began to break about six inches from the hole and stopped rolling about a foot from the pin. Nelson was on in two, twenty-five feet from the hole, and two-putted for par to maintain his recently acquired advantage of one shot. His tee shot on the par-3 closing hole landed only five feet from the pin while Hogan's was about eighteen feet away. With Hogan probably needing to sink the birdie putt to force another eighteen holes, the ball rimmed the cup leaving him with a three-footer for par. Nelson needed only to two-putt for the win, his first attempt nearly going in before he easily dropped in the short comeback. Thirteen years after the Christmas caddie tournament at Glen Garden, Nelson had beaten Hogan by one stroke in a playoff again.

The extra day's play resulted in about $200 more awarded to Nelson on top of the original $1,500 winner's share, Hogan receiving $750. During the post-round session for the benefit of reporters and photographers, Nelson appeared more relieved than excited. It could have been he was simply in a hurry; as a member of the United States Ryder Cup team for that fall's scheduled matches against Great Britain and Ireland, Nelson was scheduled to catch a flight that afternoon to join his teammates for a tune-up the following day in Dallas against a group of top local amateurs. He'd catch up with the other pros the following weekend in Houston. Hogan wasn't a member of the Ryder Cup team and agreed to take some gear that Nelson wouldn't need in Dallas and carry it in his car to Houston. A reporter who had followed Hogan into the Brackenridge locker room heard that he would do Nelson the favor of taking his belongings to Houston. "That's awful decent of you, Ben," the reporter said. "Not every guy would do that for the guy who just beat him out of an important golf tournament." Hogan looked up at the scribe with an expression that carried surprise and probably some indignation. "Really?" he replied. "Well, we're friends. It's just a golf tournament. There will be others."

10

CAROLINA CONQUESTS

CARRYING ALL OF $36, Ben Hogan and wife Valerie arrived in Pinehurst, North Carolina more than a week before the prestigious North and South Open was scheduled to begin on Tuesday, March 19, 1940. Hogan decided to skip a couple of smaller pro-am events in Florida following the Tour stop in Thomasville, Georgia won by Lloyd Mangrum to take "dead aim," his brother Royal said a few weeks later, at Pinehurst. And to be at his best at Augusta during the first week of April. The Hogans were joined a few days later by the Nelsons, and Byron – the North and South defending champion – had something to show Ben. Both golfers were under contract to MacGregor, and the manufacturer had just sent two custom-made drivers to Nelson, who was one of the company's most high-profile clients. Nelson selected the one that he preferred and offered the other – at fourteen ounces, slightly heavier than the one Hogan was using – to his compatriot. Hogan gladly accepted, immediately headed to the practice range and decided the new club would indeed go in his bag. Before play began, Hogan also spent some quality time with Henry Picard. During a practice round, Picard told

Hogan to turn his left hand more to the left, to the so-called weak position. "If you return that thing [club] at full impact to the ball," Picard said, "the clubhead will true itself up at impact." To which Hogan replied, "Up to that statement, I thought you were smart. But now you're the most ignorant man I ever saw." Picard absorbed the criticism in stride and simply advised Hogan to try his plan.

Hogan birdied Pinehurst no. 2's first two holes, birdied the fourth hole, and was setting a course for personal history. His opening round of 6-under-par 66 tied the course record and gave him a three-shot lead over Paul Runyan. Afterward, Hogan hailed the new driver that Nelson had given him: "Heck, I've never hit tee shots like that before. Clothesline drives, every one of them. And not a hook in the lot." Hogan followed with a second-round 5-under 67, the highlight being an eagle-3 on the 473-yard sixteenth hole. He managed to reach the green using driver (the new MacGregor) and 3-iron, then sank a 15-foot putt. The two-day total of 133 also set records for the course and the tournament and provided Hogan a seven-shot lead over Sam Snead and Johnny Revolta.

With Thursday's final thirty-six holes lying ahead, Valerie was approached in the clubhouse to describe her feelings. "Don't pinch me; I'm afraid I'll wake up," she offered. "Ben's always said that the only way he'd win his first title would be to get so far out in front of the field that nobody could catch him. That seems to have come true now, but I don't believe it." Gene Sarazen didn't share the same confidence in Hogan's finish: "He has never won before; he won't win this time. Hogan's been out front before. Someone will catch him." The Nelsons and Hogans ate dinner together that night, when Nelson confirmed that the driver that Hogan had fallen in love with over the course of thirty-six glorious holes was his to keep.

Hogan's morning round saw him hitting short on his irons, resulting in a 2-over 74. But his closest pursuers didn't respond with any dramatic charges;

the lead remained healthy, at six strokes. Hogan closed with a 2-under 70 for a three-shot margin over runner-up Snead. Nelson moved up into third, his 286 nine shots behind. Hogan's 11-under masterpiece knocked two strokes off the tournament record, held ironically by his partner in the Hershey Four-Ball of 1938 that represented his only pro victory to date, Vic Gheezi.

The victory presentation was made on the clubhouse steps. Hogan received the winner's trophy from Donald Ross, who designed the no. 2 layout, and the $1,000 winner's check from U.S.G.A. official Edward L. Cheyney as Valerie stood quietly to the side. Hogan smiled genuinely during the ceremony but later balked at the idea of breaking into what he considered a scripted smile afterward for the sake of photographers seeking a posed shot. Likewise, he declined another request of the photographers, to give Valerie a smooch, explaining quietly that he didn't "believe in doing that in public." Not that there was denying the joy and exhilaration that resulted from the victory. "Just winning this North and South title is going to do wonders for my golf game and ease my mind," he told reporters afterward. "It's not the $1,000 check that I was so glad to have. That doesn't matter so much, yet you can't laugh off winning $1,000. The most important thing was to win a major P.G.A. title … the finest thing … the thing that I've gotten the biggest kick of my whole life is this title. For eight years, I've come so close. But somehow, I didn't come through with the titles. This title tickles me. But my wife, Valerie, is even happier, believe it or not."

The Hogans had long suffered in relative silence. Ben's multiple close calls occasionally prompted interest from the Fourth Estate, particularly after his hard-luck, runner-up finish at the Phoenix Open that January to "Porky" Oliver. A year earlier at Phoenix, the tournament crown eluded Hogan despite a two-stroke lead after thirty-six holes when he lost by two after Nelson finished with a 65 to his 71. At Pinehurst, the occasion of Hogan's first individual triumph put him in the spotlight for a much more positive reason, making him and his wife the main target of eager notepads and microphones. "I'd just about lost all faith in myself," he said. "I'd get out there and play the best I could, and then I'd practice some more. And every time, someone would come around at the last minute and walk off with the championship." Valerie recounted Ben's warnings to her as he embarked on his golfing career: "He told me things might be very tough right at the start, that it might be a long time before he'd win checks of any account. But I told him that was all right, that we'd manage somehow."

Hogan's breakthrough victory was naturally hailed back home. An optimistic but prescient headline in the March 22 *Fort Worth Press* proclaimed "Now That Bennie Has Broken Ice He May Reach Pro Golfing Peak." *Press* sportswriter Adam Dubb noted he had become acquainted with Hogan when Hogan and Nelson caddied at Glen Garden. "He has carried my clubs many a time and always was intent on only one thing – being a pro," Dubb wrote. "It wasn't easy for either of the kids. Ben did not have the success which came to Byron as an amateur. Byron is a big guy with a lot of beef behind his clubs including large hands and forearms. Ben is a Davey O'Brien [the diminutive TCU quarterback who won the 1937 Heisman Trophy] in a way, except a bit taller and much slimmer. I imagine he hits as long a ball as any man of his height who ever swung a club, and this distance was achieved in a locker room. Bennie, as folks call him, spent many weary hours of a long succession of days on the practice field. He was not a natural putter and has had to achieve a putting touch by long hours on the practice greens. Had he been a natural putter, he would have arrived much sooner. Like Nelson, he stuck with the game regardless of tough sledding for long periods.

"While Ben was scrapping his way to a career as a pro golfer, his brother, Royal, did as noble a job of scrapping toward a business career. Royal plays golf, yes, a typical weekend golfer with an occasional sneak out from his successful office fixture business for an hour's practice. He was good enough and consistent enough to do a Jack the Giant Killer act last summer to capture the Fort Worth amateur golfing crown. Royal expects a great battle in the Masters tourney at Augusta, Georgia early in April between Bennie and Byron, who scrap each other to a standstill yet remain good friends. Byron has a lead-pipe on the Masters in golfing language. It's his tourney, but now that Hogan has busted his jinx and has his sights set on the rich prize money offered by the Bobby Jones tourney – well, if Byron doesn't win it, Bennie may – and if he doesn't, Jimmy Demaret is about due again. So it'll stay in the hands of Texas golfers."

One intrepid radio announcer mistakenly referred to Hogan as being from Dallas. While folks living in Oregon or Indiana might consider Dallas and neighboring Fort Worth to be essentially the same place – and a good many Dallasites consider Fort Worth simply an outlying part of the Dallas metropolitan area – this was an unforgivable social *faux pas* of major proportions to a good many Cowtown residents. Among those aghast was Royal Hogan. As chronicled by Frank Tolbert of the *Fort Worth Star-Telegram*: "When we last heard, Royal was controlling his temper admirably. He had not sought out the offending announcer and wrapped an iron around the commentating neck with French pastry swirls. Royal, the Fort Worth city champion, just laughed and said, 'Why, Ben has never stayed in Dallas more than one night at a time, and then the Trinity [River] was up or something. When we were kids, Mother never used any of the boogeyman stuff to scare us. She'd just warn us if we didn't do so-and-so, she would make us go over and spend the weekend in Dallas.'" Adding parochial emphasis, Tolbert also mentioned that none of the 600 congratulatory phone calls fielded by *Star-Telegram* operators after Hogan's victory came from Big D.

Hogan's payday increased his winnings for the year by about a third, to $4,038, moving him into second place behind Demaret. In the P.G.A. Tour of 1940, there was almost no time to breathe before commencing the next event, the Greensboro Open. Friday, March 22 was for "travel" (Pinehurst and Greensboro are separated by about seventy-five miles) and practice. Associated Press sportswriter Bill Boni wasn't prepared to predict that Hogan's lightning would strike again, but he didn't foresee a letdown by the first-time tournament winner, either: "It may not be Hogan again this time . . . but Hogan won't be far behind." As it turned out, Boni had sold Hogan short.

Competition began on Saturday, March 23 at Starmount Country Club, where the first two rounds would be played before finishing with the final thirty-six holes scheduled nearby on Ross' Sedgefield Country Club layout the following Monday. Hogan essentially picked up where he left off at Pinehurst despite an unforgiving, chilly wind. He shot a 2-under-69 that was equaled only by local favorite Clayton Heafner. (His name was pronounced "HEFF-ner," and if a tournament starter erred at the outset of an event and called him "HEEF-ner," ol' Clayton was apt to excuse himself right there and call it a tournament without hitting a shot.) That placed them three strokes ahead of another Carolina product, Tony Manero, who was the pro at Sedgefield when he won the 1936 U.S. Open. Hogan's round featured three birdies and one bogey. Had he made half of the six putts that he missed from five feet or less, he would have equaled his wire-to-wire lead at Pinehurst. Heafner, meanwhile, gamely battled back after suffering a double-bogey on the par-4 second hole. Nelson was part of the group that opened with 73s. On Sunday, March 24, a freak early spring snowstorm dumped three inches on central North Carolina in the morning after only a few players made it onto the course – cheered on by a chattering gallery of 1,500 hearty souls – before competition was halted for the day. When the starter told Sarazen it was time for him to tee up, he incredulously replied, "You mean ski jump, don't you?" Play didn't resume until Wednesday, March 27, a three-day postponement that pushed back the start of the next event, the Land of the Sky Open up in the Smoky Mountains in Asheville, North Carolina.

As the pros waited for the snow to melt, they were asked by AP writer Boni to identify the most clutch golfer in the game. They rattled off the names of legends Walter Hagen and Bobby Jones. Then Henry Picard offered up someone who went into 1940 as one of the Tour's hottest stars yet hadn't claimed a victory in the year's early going – Dallas' Ralph Guldahl, who turned pro at the 1930 Texas Open like Hogan. "Nerve control," Picard cited as Hogan and others gathering around Boni nodded in agreement. "That's what he has better than anybody." Picard's assessment echoed what Snead previously said of Guldahl: "If Guldahl gave someone a blood transfusion, the patient would freeze to death." Born only months before Hogan and Nelson, the graduate of Woodrow Wilson High School (alma mater of Davey O'Brien) beat them into the victory column with wins in 1931 and '32. With three victories in his first four years on Tour, Guldahl actually abandoned Tour competition in 1935 and worked as a carpenter on the Warner Brothers lot in Hollywood. He returned full-time the following year, in part because of the financial backing of some actors and directors. Guldahl went on a blistering four-year run that saw him finish second on the money list in 1936, claim U.S. Opens in 1937 (by two shots at Oakland Hills) and '38 (by six at Cherry Hills) and win the '39 Masters. Later that year, he painstakingly dissected his swing for an instructional book and, coincidentally or not, was never the same in tournament play.

Snow wasn't a factor down in New Orleans during the Greensboro delay, where Royal Hogan shot a 73 to win the low gross division of the tournament being held in conjunction with a national stationers' convention. Up in Carolina, the delay didn't prove to be much of a distraction to brother Ben. He followed the opening 69 with a bogey-free round of 3-under-68 that gave him a lead of three strokes over Sarazen and Guldahl at the tournament's midpoint as play closed out at Starmount. Heafner was no longer a factor, a second-round 76 pushing him eight shots off the pace. For the event's first two rounds, Hogan missed only three greens – two coming during the second round's final nine holes, and he managed to save par on each. The following day at Sedgefield, Hogan only improved his scores – 66 in the third round and 67 at the finish for a 14-under-270 to break the tournament record like he had done at the North and South. (In terms of all-time records, it's worth noting many of these events were only a few years old; this was the third Greensboro Open.) Playing with Guldahl and Craig Wood, Hogan consistently outdrove his playing partners and was again deadly on reaching greens. The margin of victory this time was nine shots over Wood, with Nelson among the four golfers tied for third place another shot behind. The championship check for $1,200 continued to close the earnings gap between Demaret ($6,152) and Hogan ($5,238). Nelson stood in third with $3,683.

Then it was on to Asheville, where Hogan completed his trifecta in the Carolina pines. But for the first time in three starts, he didn't at least share the lead at the close of a round. Hogan opened with a respectable 4-under-67 that left him three shots behind the trio of Guldahl, Lloyd Mangrum and Dick Metz. Metz came back to the field after firing a 6-under-30 on the front nine that included four birdies and an eagle-3 on the 484-yard eighth hole. The tournament's second round was played amid occasional showers, and Hogan's 4-under-68 was the best round of the day. That left him tied for second place with Mangrum, one stroke behind Guldahl's 10-under-144.

Before the assembled writers could gather pertinent details of the end of the Guldahl victory drought for print, Hogan grabbed the tournament by the horns during the thirty-six finishing holes on Sunday, March 31 on the

Biltmore Forest course. He finished with two rounds of 3-under-69 to lap Guldahl and win with a 15-under-273. He still trailed Guldahl by one shot after three rounds and played aggressively over the final eighteen holes while Guldahl struggled on the greens. Another deposit of $1,200 vaulted Hogan into first place on the year's money list with $6,438, more than half of which was earned within the three most recent events. And Hogan's victory streak was a result of more than just replacing his driver. Playing 216 holes in the three North Carolina events, he three-putted only twice – both during the final half of the Asheville tournament. That contributed greatly to the combined 34-under play in the three tournaments during which he broke par in eleven of twelve rounds. "I've just been keeping the head of the putter dead upright and headed straight for the hole," Hogan told reporters afterward. "That's why, like you've probably noticed, some of my short putts for birdies have stopped short or gone over the hole." And Hogan, while never one to brag publicly, took advantage of the newly available forum to tout the work ethic that was so foreign to his brethren and sometimes ridiculed: "They used to kid me about practicing so much. I'd get out before a round and practice and practice some more when I was through. Now they can kid me all they like. It didn't pay off then, but I know that's what finally got me in the groove."

The events of Pinehurst, Greensboro and Asheville naturally made Hogan a prime pick to win the next tournament, the seventh Masters, an event just reaching the point where it was held in higher esteem than the North and South that Hogan had just conquered. He was rated the co-favorite, odds of 6-to-1 along with defending champion Guldahl. Hogan played two practice rounds at Augusta National before the four-day event began on Thursday, April 4, shooting 4-under-68 on Tuesday and a 5-under-67 on Wednesday. The opening round belonged to a Texan but not Hogan. Twenty-four-year-old Mangrum, who had only qualified for the tournament three weeks earlier with the victory at Thomasville, roared out of the gate with an 8-under-64 that broke the course record. Hogan shot a 1-over-73, his first round above par since the third round at Pinehurst fourteen days earlier. Things didn't get any better for him on Friday, a 2-over-74 leaving him eight strokes behind Mangrum and Demaret. Hogan rallied with a 3-under 69 in the third round, but his deficit remained significant at seven shots. With another 74 to close, Hogan's amazing run ended with a tenth-place finish and a check for $100 as Demaret won by four shots (not sure the *Fort Worth Press'* Adam Dubb should be credited for picking Demeret … if Nelson didn't win … if Hogan didn't win). The affable Houstonian pocketed $1,500 and moved back into the money lead.

Hogan scored yet another victory in mid-May, the third annual Goodall Round Robin tournament at Fresh Meadow Country Club in New York City. The event featured an elite field of only fifteen pros and resembled a miniature version of a season schedule in any of the team sports. Each pro would play an 18-hole match against everyone else entered, and the player with the best win-loss record was the winner. And that was Hogan, edging out Snead. He was still in great demand by the press on the eve of the U.S. Open at Canterbury Golf Club in Cleveland. Reporters and announcers were still eager to learn more about the man who suddenly burst into the win column a few months earlier. He was willing to comply with requests to tell his story but wasn't about to provide details of his father's death. "My dad was a blacksmith, but he died when I was nine," he said, then explaining that he and his older brother had to immediately provide income at their relatively tender ages. He noted one of the results of his tournament success was that it no longer seemed proper for Valerie and him to frequent many of the "thrifty" eateries and lodgings that were all they could afford a few years earlier: "Once you get in the public eye, you can't go around stopping at tourist camps and eating at one-arm stands. So you see, the more you earn, the more you have to spend."

The 1940 P.G.A. Championship was contested at the course where Nelson's ball was absconded from play on the fifteenth hole the previous year, the Hershey Country Club. Nelson and Hogan both captured their first two matches to advance to the round of sixteen during a week that saw northeast Pennsylvania at the mercy of intermittent showers that sometimes became storms. Hogan opened with a 3-and-2 decision over Leland Gibson and then defeated Frank Champ 5-and-4. Nelson, who hadn't played a tournament in the previous two and a half months, reached that point with a 4-and-3 victory over Dick Shoemaker and a 1-up win over Frank Walsh that required two extra holes. Nelson trailed Walsh by two holes at one point and struggled much of the match with his putting. He birdied no. 17 to pull even, then won when Walsh's second shot on the twentieth hole found a bunker and led to him three-putt. Nelson's foe in the 36-hole third round was the medalist heading into match play, Dick Metz. They traded jabs back and forth much of the day with Nelson earning the lead for good on the twenty-sixth hole. The victor remained in doubt until Nelson sank a birdie putt on No. 16 to increase his lead to two strokes.

Hogan was playing in his second P.G.A. Championship, eliminated in the second round the previous year. He passed that milestone with a 5-and-4 win over Harry Nettlebladt, sending him forward for a date with Guldahl. Hogan birdied the par-4 first hole with a 12-foot putt and held that one-hole lead until bogeying no. 14 to match. Guldahl picked up two more holes in the morning and maintained at least that margin the rest of the way for a 3-and-2 victory as Hogan struggled with his putting for the rest of the afternoon. The semifinals that pitted Nelson against Guldahl and Sam Snead against "Jug" McSpaden gave way to Mother Nature. The players were enjoying their lunch break following the day's first eighteen holes – Nelson ahead by one hole, Snead by three – when rain began to fall in torrents. The Swatira Creek that runs through the course took over the no. 2 fairway. Before the semifinals began, a friend of Nelson's came to the locker room to extend good wishes only to discover Nelson unable to keep his breakfast down. The friend dutifully reported the development to Louise, who was actually buoyed by the revelation. She considered her husband's agitated state a precursor for him faring well that day.

Play resumed the following day, Nelson increasing his lead through four holes and holding a 2-up margin over Guldahl with three holes to play. On the par-4 sixteenth, Nelson's approach instead landed well to the right of the putting surface. He was still in position to par after placing his third shot within six feet of the cup, but his putt ran out of gas short of the hole. Guldahl parred, and Nelson's advantage was one with two to play. Guldahl had a chance to birdie the par-4 seventeenth after his second shot came to rest five feet from the pin. But it was his turn to miss a makeable putt, and he remained one behind heading to the par-3 eighteenth. Nelson's tee shot landed just right of the green and nearly in a sand trap. Guldahl was on the green but was thirty-five feet from the hole, and the remnants of the week's weather affixed a glob of mud to his ball. Most likely needing to hole out to send the match to a thirty-seventh hole, his putt stopped three feet short of the cup. Nelson's second shot was a pitch that put his ball two feet from the pin. Each made par putts, and Nelson gained entry to the championship match. Snead advanced with less drama than Nelson, building on his three-hole margin from the previous day to eliminate McSpaden 5-and-4.

In the final, Nelson owned a three-hole lead at one juncture of morning play and stood 2-up at the break, including sinking a stymie putt over Snead's ball on no. 3. But within five holes of the afternoon session, Snead rallied to lead by one. That's where the margin stood with three holes remaining. Nelson made quick work of that by birdieing no. 16 with a one-putt of less than five feet and birdieing no. 17 with a one-putt about a foot longer. Nelson pulled out a 3-iron for attacking the par-3 eighteenth and put his tee shot six feet behind the flag stick. Snead chose a 4-iron and missed the green to the right. Nelson took aim at ending play on his first putt, and it lipped out. The hole was halved, and Nelson's third major championship and first in the P.G.A. Championship was won by a 1-up margin.

The major champions for 1940 were Nelson, Demaret at the Masters, and Lawson Little at the National Open (besting 38-year-old Sarazen in a playoff). But the leading money for the year was none other than a golfer who came into the year without an individual victory to his credit. Hogan collected $10,343; Nelson wasn't terribly far behind with $9,671. Hogan would lead the list again in 1941 with $18,358 and in '42 with $13,143. It's also worth noting the improved play that year of another Texan: Demaret. He had only two career P.G.A. Tour victories going into the year and won six times in 1940.

One former Glen Garden caddie had affirmed his standing as one of the nation's elite golfers by claiming his third major title in four years. The other had finally enjoyed the fruits of seemingly endless hours of practice and concentration, the early tournament withdrawals, the awkward necessity to seek out additional funding simply to make it from event to event. The golf world at long last had reason to appreciate Ben Hogan and eagerly await what was to come from him. He was polite in accepting congratulations of sorts from a visiting writer following the season but added a disclaimer that revealed his hunger apparently was hardly satisfied: "Until I manage to win a major tournament, I really won't be happy."

11

LEONARD'S GOLF GALA

THE FORT WORTH golf community was certainly happy – ecstatic, even – upon receiving word in May 1940 from the United States Golf Association that the efforts of Marvin Leonard among others convinced the sport's body to stage the 1941 U.S. Open at Colonial Country Club. Part of Leonard's lobbying efforts was a long-distance call of about twenty minutes to U.S.G.A. president Harold Pierce in Boston. It wasn't lost on Pierce that anyone who was willing to spend that kind of money on a phone call could finance the tournament. It must have helped that the Fort Worth group also guaranteed to pay the U.S.G.A. $15,000. Following the momentous announcement, *Fort Worth Press* sports editor "Pop" Boone recalled a conversation that he had with Leonard at Colonial a few years earlier in which the club's patriarch insisted either the National Open or the National Amateur would be coming to southwest Fort Worth some day. "I don't know how long it'll take, but it can be swung," Leonard said, lying in the grass while a tournament was in progress. At the time of the announcement, there was justified anticipation that local standout Byron Nelson could come to Colonial in June 1941 as the two-time Open champion, building on his dramatic "double overtime" win at Spring Mill in the '39 event. But the 1940 edition of the National Open at Canterbury was claimed by Lawson Little.

The most anticipated week in the history of Cowtown golf got off to an inauspicious beginning when Monday dawned with standing water clogging many areas of the course following heavy overnight rains that ended in the early morning hours, causing the course to be closed. A front-page photo in that afternoon's *Fort Worth Press* showed entrant Andy Gaspar standing next to what appeared to be a lake, but it was actually the eighteenth fairway. Conditions improved enough later in the day and workers feverishly manned hand pumps to allow play that afternoon. Glen Garden's own Henry Ransom was among the golfers who were able to get in a round, shooting a 2-over-par 72. Jimmy Demaret played an erratic round that was expected given that his father died the night before in Houston, and he was expected to travel down there later that day for the funeral.

Press sportswriter Delbert Willis happened upon Ben Hogan in Colonial's golf shop, where the man who'd won twice in Tour events so far that season was taking a two-by-four to his 5-iron in an effort to bend the club head slightly farther from the shaft. Hogan was soon joined by Colonial's assistant pro, Tez Davis, and Hogan requested that additional brass be soldered onto the back of his 9-iron to improve its power. Another visitor was George Barclay, a Colonial caddie who'd caddied at Glen Garden alongside Hogan and Nelson. Hogan laughed and asked Barclay, "Is the swing like it was in the old days?" Barclay replied, "No, I'd say it has improved quite a bit." Almost on cue, the welding truck pulled up next to the golf shop. A welder by the name of L.J. Boggs added the requested brass on Hogan's 9-iron and told him the service was on the house. Hogan wouldn't accept Boggs' offer; he handed him a bill, and said, "This welding job may mean a thousand dollars to me."

Valerie Hogan [left] and Louise Nelson visit during the 1941 U.S. Open at Colonial Country Club in Fort Worth. The wives became very close through years of crisscrossing the country together with their golfing husbands. (Courtesy, *Fort Worth Star-Telegram* Collection, Special Collections, The University of Texas at Arlington Library, Arlington, Texas)

The betting commissioner at the Blackstone Hotel, Jerry Roth, established Hogan and Nelson as tournament co-favorites at 5-1. They were followed by Sam Snead at 6-1. Roth listed 1-under 279 for bets on the winning score. Tuesday's schedule was highlighted by an exhibition match on behalf of the British Relief war fund with Nelson and Little, the two most recent U.S. Open winners, vying against old-timers Gene Sarazen and Tommy Armour. The vast majority of 6,000 spectators who dropped by Colonial that day – believed to be a National Open practice round record – followed the foursome as the old champs managed to play all square with the young guns. Nelson carded the best individual score of the group, 2-over-72. His second shot on the seventh hole landed on the green before all of the members of the practice group playing ahead of the exhibition players had moved on – namely, Olin Dutra. A somewhat miffed Dutra grabbed a nearby soda bottle and propped Nelson's ball atop it. Nelson played along with the gag and played the ball where it had "landed."

June Texas heat wasn't yet a major topic of course-side conversation, but a number of players and spectators new to the region became acquainted against their will with chigger bugs. Lawson Little was adorned with a fresh set of chigger bites around his ankles. There also was criticism from some players regarding the sand found in the bunkers. It wasn't as fine and as white as they'd wanted, making escape from the hazards more hazardous than they desired. Nor were all of them enamored with the narrow, par-4 no. 5 dogleg right that was lengthened to 469 yards just for the Open. While newsmen chronicled the various complaints, the *Press'* Willis was participating in the time honored journalistic pursuit of polling pros in the clubhouse. He asked a dozen top players, including Nelson and Hogan, to select the best Tour pro in playing six golf clubs or general range of club. Voted best with the driver was Sam Snead. Brassie: Lawson Little. Long irons: Nelson. Short irons: Sarazen. Short pitch: Paul Runyan. "Scrambler" or escaping rough: Johnny Revolta. Putter: Horton Smith. Those polled, by the way, were allowed to pick themselves, which Nelson and Hogan both did when identifying the best long-iron player.

The honor of playing the first shot ever in a U.S. Open played in Texas – and in the first P.G.A. Tour event hosted by Colonial Country Club – went to a young amateur from Glen Garden named Iverson Martin. "Ivey" beat the regional qualifying cutoff by four strokes in Dallas and drew the opening assignment by mere luck of the draw. "Who can tell? I may birdie the first hole and lead the National Open field for at least five minutes," he said. "Just think of that distinction." Asked about potential jitters, Martin shrugged and said, "I don't care if I hit the ball or miss it. In fact, I believe that being the first will remove the pressure. That is, if there is any pressure so far as I am concerned." Martin then picked Ralph Guldahl, the National Open champion in 1937 and 1938, as the tournament winner.

Glen Garden's Ransom roared out of the gate with birdies on the first two holes thanks to approach shots that left him short putts. His 4-under-par 31 on Colonial's front nine established a U.S. Open record. It was estimated that almost half of the 7,000 paying customers were following Ransom and his playing partners, Sarazen and Billy Burke. But on the back nine with the wind picking up, Ransom underclubbed his way to a 6-over 41 for a first-round total of 2-over 72. He bogeyed nos. 10 and 11, putting his tee shot on no. 10 in a trap and requiring four strokes to reach the green on the 593-yard, par-5 no. 11. Thursday's leader was Denny Shute at 1-under 69, with "Dutch" Harrison and Vic Gheezi only a stroke behind. Nelson stood four back of Shute at 3-over 73, Hogan five behind at 4-over 74. Hogan's work Monday on his irons proved to be doubly helpful when his woods abandoned him in the first round. He resorted to playing irons in woods situations on the later holes. In an apparent expression to his relief in not scoring any higher, Hogan followed his 20-foot putt on no. 18 by giving the ball a smooch. Topping both Nelson and Hogan was an amateur from Dallas, Harry Todd, at 2-over 72.

Friday's second round was disrupted by two hour-long weather delays, one each in the morning and afternoon, prohibiting a handful of players from finishing. The rain delays included lightning, which convinced Demaret to walk off the course after playing twelve holes and call it a tournament. In fairness to Demaret, he was playing in the 1939 Western Open when three persons were struck and killed by lightning on a nearby fairway. "Jimmy just couldn't stand out there with the lightning rod [the steel-shafted club] and be happy," he said. (Could it be Demaret was the inspiration for the Jimmy character on a 1995 episode of *Seinfeld* who constantly referred to himself in the third person?) Scores went up, and there was a log jam atop the leaderboard at 4-over 144 with Shute joined by Little, Clayton Heafner, and Craig Wood. Wood had been playing for weeks in constant back pain, the result of a strained ligament suffered when he sneezed while shaving. His back had given him problems for years, a result of an auto accident, and would keep him from being accepted for military service during World War II. Nelson and Ransom were in a pack tied for sixth place at 6-over 146. Hogan followed his troublesome Thursday with even more conflicts on Friday, a 7-over 77 leaving him at 11-over 151 and eleven strokes off the pace. Dallas' Todd stood gamely between Nelson and Hogan, a 7-over 77 putting him at 9-over 149. "Ivey" Martin's Open experience ended before Saturday's 36-hole finale; he shot 80-79 and failed to make the cut at 19-over 159.

The pairings for the third and fourth rounds placed Nelson with Shute and Todd teeing off at 9:39 a.m. and 1:54 p.m. Hogan and Snead went off at 10:43 a.m. and 2:57 p.m. Ransom took himself out of contention on the same first half of the front nine that had proved to be his ally in Thursday's opening round. He was 5-over on the first five holes, suffering a triple-bogey on the imposing no. 5 when his tee shot nipped a limb and tumbled down a river bank. Ransom finished with a 5-over 75 in the morning round and followed with a same score in the afternoon. His 16-over 296 put him in a tie for thirteenth place with the local amateur, Todd. Hogan's morning round was not only his best round of the tournament, it was the best eighteen holes scored at Colonial that weekend. He shot 33-35 for a 2-under 68 that left him five shots behind leader Wood at the lunch break. Hogan was particularly deadly with his iron play. On the par-3 no. 16, his tee shot struck the pin. On the par-4 no. 17, he hit behind the ball for a tee shot that carried about 160. But instead of using a wood to carry the subsequent 240 yards, he again turned to an iron. His approach – the "dadgumdest shot you'll see" according to *Fort Worth Star-Telegram* sports columnist Flem Hall – almost struck the pin. Hogan managed par on his final tour of the course, his overall 9-over 289 placing him tied for third with Revolta.

Nelson's scores consistently climbed throughout the tournament. He followed his Thursday and Friday 73s with a 4-over 74 on Saturday morning and a 7-over 77 in the afternoon. The 17-over 297 left the 1939 National Open champion tied in seventeenth place along with the '40 Open champ, Little. And the new champion was Craig Wood, who had also won at Augusta only two months earlier (becoming the first to win the Masters and the Open in the same year). His 4-over 284 provided a three-shot cushion over Shute. Wood's tenuous back made it through the tournament thanks to the combination of a corset that was heavily taped plus Vitamin B1 shots prescribed by his personal physician. Wood's attempt to "triple" a month later at the P.G.A. Championship at Cherry Hills Country Club near Denver ended in the second round. The winner was Gheezi, whose path to the title included a 2-and-1 quarterfinal win over Hogan and a championship victory over Nelson that required two extra holes to settle.

12

AUGUSTA DUEL

FOUR MONTHS INTO the United States' involvement in World War II, the ninth annual Masters attracted its smallest field with only forty-two players prepared to compete at Augusta National despite eighty-eight players qualifying. Vic Gheezi, for instance, was otherwise occupied at Fort Dix, New Jersey. But there wasn't a lack of star power with most of the sport's top names ready to tee off on Thursday afternoon, April 9. The favorites included Craig Wood (the event's defending champion), Ben Hogan (early money leader on the 1942 Tour and two-time Vardon Trophy holder) and Byron Nelson (winner of the 1937 Masters, the 1939 National Open, and the 1940 P.G.A. Championship). In a straw poll of pros conducted the previous week, Nelson was the most popular pick despite Hogan arriving in Georgia fresh off his third consecutive Land of the Sky Open triumph in Asheville, North Carolina. But Hogan, according to Associated Press writer Ronmey Wheeler, was the 5-to-1 betting favorite followed by Nelson, Wood, and Sam Snead all at 6-to-1. Nelson did nothing to dissuade anyone from plunking down a friendly wager on the day before the tournament began, recording a score of 2-under 70 in his final practice round.

On the other side of the globe that Thursday morning, about 80,000 American and Filipino soldiers became prisoners of the Japanese army when the peninsula of Bataan fell to the emperor's forces. The commander of the ill-equipped Allied unit was Lieutenant General Jonathan Wainwright, left in charge when President Franklin Roosevelt evacuated General Douglas MacArthur to Australia (during which he made his famous "I shall return" speech). During the following six days, Wainwright and his fellow prisoners suffered through the Bataan Death March – a trek of between fifty-five and ninety miles depending on the account. Along the way, some prisoners were executed. Some were forced to dig their own graves and then buried alive. Estimates are 1,000 Americans and 10,000 Filipinos died that week.

Nine of the forty-two Masters competitors conquered par during the opening round, paced by the 5-under 67s shot by Paul Runyan and two-time Masters champion Horton Smith. Nelson trailed the leaders by only one stroke along with Sam Byrd. Hogan was amid a trio at 1-over 73. The biggest cheers of the day went to Bobby Jones for the even-par 72 round that equaled his best score in Masters play. Day two saw Nelson add a 5-under 67 to reach the midpoint of the tournament in first place at 9-under 135, equaling the event's 36-hole record set by Henry Picard in 1936. After recording his sixth birdie of the day on no. 16, thanks to a 10-foot putt, Nelson blurted, "When I get back to the clubhouse, I think I'll break all my clubs – out of sheer excitement." Still, he stood only one shot ahead of Byrd. Runyan and Smith recorded 1-over 73s and were joined in a three-way tie for third at 140 with Jimmy Demaret, the 1940 tournament winner. Hogan shaved three shots off his Thursday total for a 1-under 143, eight strokes behind Nelson. On Augusta's par-5 second hole, Hogan reached the green in two, needing to sink a 15-foot putt for an eagle. His putt didn't fall, forcing him to "settle" for a birdie.

After Friday's round, Nelson confided to reporters gathered around him as he ambled toward the clubhouse: "I've got a secret about playing this course. I could tell you fellows, except there are three or four boys in this field it might help. And I want to win this tournament. But if I do win, I'll tell you Sunday night." The ebullient Nelson didn't stop there in entertaining the Fourth Estate: "It was the easiest round of golf I ever shot with the possible exception of a 66 in 1937 [winning the Masters], when I had thirty-two putts. Everything clicked perfectly. I didn't miss a green, though my approach did kick off a bit on the first hole. And I have had only one bogey in thirty-six holes. That was one on the fifth Friday, where I took three putts, missing the second from no more than four feet."

Saturday's blustery third round belonged to Hogan, and he, like Nelson a day earlier, reveled in his performance shortly after it was over – without considering smashing his clubs. Hogan fired a 67, equaling the best round of the tournament. With Nelson recording a par 72, Hogan headed into Sunday's finale having pulled within three shots of the lead and soared into second place. "It was the best managing I ever did," Hogan said. "I mean manipulating the ball, allowing for wind and roll. You had to do it in that wind." He took only twenty-eight putts, just thirteen on the back nine. Conversely for Nelson, the flat stick was his enemy on Saturday. "I just can't seem to get the ball in the hole unless it's three feet from the cup." And his third-round struggles weren't confined to the putting surface. His round began with overshooting the green on no. 1, leading to a bogey 5. On the last four par 4s, Nelson bogeyed three of them. But that momentum swing wasn't enough to sway defending champion Wood (out of contention at 13-over 229) when asked on Saturday night by NBC sportscaster Bill Stern on nationwide radio to predict who would win: "Three shots separate Nelson and Hogan going into the final round, and I don't think Hogan can pick up those three strokes Sunday."

On Sunday at Augusta, the twenty twosomes began marching off at 1 p.m. Hogan and Demaret started at 2 p.m. in the eleventh pairing. Twenty-five minutes later, Nelson and Runyan comprised the fifteenth group. Nelson's round again began inauspiciously with a bogey on the par-3 fourth hole, the culprit being a two-foot par putt that couldn't find the hole. Through eight holes, he was 3-over for the round and had lost all of the eight-shot cushion that separated Hogan and him after thirty-six holes. With the world all but falling in on him, Nelson responded with a birdie on the 430-yard ninth hole to restore his one-shot advantage. With a pitch that sailed twenty-two feet past the hole, Nelson managed to send the downhill putt straight into the cup. The lead was back up to two after Nelson birdied the par-4 eleventh hole with another long-distance putt, from forty feet.

Hogan required little time to respond. On the 480-yard, par-5 dogleg thirteenth, he placed his second shot on the green and two-putted for a birdie to halve Nelson's margin. When Nelson reached no. 13, he nearly added another stroke by getting on in regulation only twelve feet from the flag. But his putt missed, and he settled for a par 5. Then Nelson counterpunched with a birdie on the par-5, 485-yard fifteenth. He reached the green in two, twelve feet separating him from an eagle and a three-shot lead. Nelson two-putted but again enjoyed a two-shot lead with three holes between him and the clubhouse.

On no. 18, with thousands of fans being held back with the aid of uniformed servicemen, Hogan's second shot on the par 4 came to rest only six feet from the hole. He sank his first putt for a birdie and a fourth-round score of 2-under 70. All Hogan could do then was wait to see what happened to Nelson, still with no. 17 and 18 to complete. He told reporters that he'd pretty much given up: "I don't see how Nelson can miss now." Nelson's second effort on the par-4 seventeenth, using an 8-iron, plunked into a sand trap only a foot short of the green. It appeared he might save par with a blast that landed twelve feet from the cup, but his putt went awry. With one hole to play, Nelson was again tied with Hogan. He lost his footing slightly on his downswing in the soft tee box on no. 18 and sliced his drive into the pines, prompting a collective moan from the gallery. He was glad to simply have an opening in the trees of about twenty feet for his second shot and again managed with a 5-iron to reach the green in regulation, some fifteen feet from the pin. But the putter again was his undoing, a soft stroke for a birdie and a Masters championship medallion traveling six inches wide and a foot beyond the hole. After sinking his putt coming back, Nelson recorded a fourth-round 1-over 73 that left him tied with Hogan at 8-under 280.

The Masters was headed to a playoff for the first time since Gene Sarazen defeated Wood in 1935, following a '42 fourth round that *Atlanta Journal* golf writer O.B. Keeler proclaimed "on the finest day for dramatic golf, or any other kind, that yet has smiled on the Big Show." Keeler humbly noted he'd stated no golfer could rally from a 36-hole deficit of more than seven strokes to claim a major championship. A tradition, he said, that Hogan had conquered. "Whatever may be the result of that playoff tomorrow afternoon, or possibly another playoff Tuesday, Ben Hogan has collared it with an iron grasp, not to mention a useful putting stroke and some tremendous wallops from tee to fairway." None other than Grantland Rice also heralded this ninth Masters as the best to date. He hailed Hogan – "the lean, grim battler, the human rattlesnake on a golf course" – and, like Keeler, wrote that Hogan's Sunday heroics would stand on their own no matter the result of the playoff: "This is one of the all-time tops in competitive sport. Hogan to me is one of the miracle men, and you can pick your game."

When the playoff combatants returned to Augusta National on Monday, Nelson was far from feeling his best. He was so worked up, his stomach battled him throughout Sunday night and he couldn't keep down his Monday breakfast. Hogan saw him at the hotel, said he'd learned of his overnight illness, and offered to postpone the playoff. Nelson declined and appreciated the offer. Later in the clubhouse, Nelson felt somewhat better after having half of a chicken sandwich and a cup of hot tea. They went ahead and played for a gallery that included most of the pros who had competed in the tournament.

Nelson couldn't have felt any good after playing No. 1. His drive wandered far to the right, into the woods and snuggled up to a pine cone. With that kind of a lie, Nelson's second shot was another adventure, a left-handed chip that found more trees. It took four strokes to simply reach the par-4 green. Nelson's opening double bogey 6 gave Hogan, who parred the hole, an instant two-stroke lead. On no. 3, a long par 4, Nelson's long-iron shot off the tee fell short of the green and into a bunker. He bogeyed again and trailed by three only three holes into the playoff.

Events began to greatly turn in Nelson's favor on the par-3, 185-yard sixth. His tee shot landed seven feet from the pin, and he putted in from there for a birdie. Hogan bogeyed, his chip for par missing by four feet, and Nelson was back within one shot. Two holes later, he was back in front. On the 510-yard, uphill par-5 eighth that victimized Nelson on Sunday, Nelson this time reached the green in two, his approach with a 4-wood sliding off the mound of the putting surface toward the flag and stopping six feet past the hole. His putt provided an eagle 3, a three-shot swing from his performance there a day earlier.

From a stroke down to a stroke ahead, Nelson led at the turn 35 to 36 and never trailed again. He built a three-shot lead through thirteen holes, though Hogan still had fight left in him. On the par-4, 425-yard fourteenth hole, Hogan sank an 18-foot birdie putt. On no. 15, Nelson settled for a par 5 when he three-putted while Hogan snagged another birdie to pull within one with three holes to play. But Hogan bogeyed the par-3 no. 16 after his tee shot found a bunker. The gap was still two shots heading to the home hole, enabling

Nelson to play the par 4 somewhat safe. Each golfer put his second shot in the trap to the left of the green. Hogan's blast out of the sand allowed him to one-putt for par. Nelson's escape from the trap wasn't as accurate, but his two-putt was good enough for a final score of 3-under-par 69 to Hogan's 70.

In the clubhouse afterward, Nelson noted all the breaks went against him on the first four holes. "When I got to the sixth, I could feel I was in the groove again. I was hitting the ball true every time." He identified the key to the playoff being the tenth hole, where Hogan had a bad chip. Hogan cited his missed short putts on nos. 6 and 8. And it was time for Nelson to make good on the promise that he made to the press on Friday evening, to reveal his secret strategy for mastering Augusta National. He said he simply concentrated on getting on the green instead of seeking to land as close to the pin as possible. (But his explanation for the Sunday afternoon bogey at no. 17 contradicted his statement: "I was shooting at the pin, of course, and should have used a 7-iron.") And, he added, "Except for the first hole, I think that was the finest round of golf I ever shot." For Nelson, he finished in the money for the thirty-fifth consecutive tournament. The winner's share of $1,500 raised his season's bankroll to $5,822, third on Tour behind Hogan's $9,598 and Snead's $6,078.

Nelson would technically reign as the Masters champion for four years. Soon after the '42 renewal, Augusta National devoted its greenery to the war effort and became a pasture for cows and turkeys. The Masters wouldn't be contested again until 1946, when the P.G.A. Tour resumed a full schedule of events for the first time following the war. That year, Hogan trailed after two rounds by only seven shots instead of eight. Yet he needed merely a down-hill par putt of about two-and-a-half feet on the seventy-second hole to complete another incredible comeback and claim his first major title by one shot over little-known Herman Keiser. Hogan coaxed his putt with little more than a nudge. The ball slowly rolled downhill, scraped the side of the cup and continued on another four feet. The subsequent uphill putt needed for Hogan to join Keiser in a playoff also lipped out. Possibly the most unlikely three-putt of Hogan's career banished him to second place.

"Pop" Boone of the *Fort Worth Press* mused a few days after the 1942 Masters about the curious geographical phenomenon that existed in P.G.A. Tour play: "Of all the cities and towns in the country which are adorned or defaced by several golf courses, it seems strange that the two top hands should have grown up together. Ben and Byron are as opposite a type as it is possible to be. Ben, small and dark, is so full of business he does not make friends easily. He hasn't time to cultivate casual friends. Byron, on the other hand, is bulky and on the blond side. He's amiable as a rule, although not garrulous or exuberant like Jimmy Demaret of Houston. It's pretty nice for Ben and Byron right now, but it was a tough haul for a long time. Maybe it's the memory of that period of their golfing lives that made the two guys realize the truth of that old saw: "Hero today, bum tomorrow."

Nelson's final P.G.A. Tour event of the year was late-July's Tam O'Shanter Open, which became his third victory in seventeen Tour outings. He later won a couple of non-Tour competitions played in his neck of the woods, the Ohio Open and Toledo Open. And in August 1942, Nelson played his first competitive baseball game – sort of – since his days as a proud member of the Poly Parrot nine. He agreed to play for Toledo's minor league baseball club, the Mud Hens of the American Association, in a Friday night exhibition game against their major league affiliate. That was the American League's St. Louis Browns, who had yet to claim a pennant in forty-one years of play. The Mud Hens were about as futile competing in the minors' Class AAA, having finished first only once in thirty-eight seasons. The club's unique nickname was linked to the fowl that occupied property adjacent to one of the team's two home ballparks in 1896. Fans of the famed sitcom *M*A*S*H* might recall

Corporal Max Klinger would often wear a Mud Hens cap or jersey in honor of his hometown – when he wasn't decked out in a strapless evening gown – because actor Jamie Farr is a Toledo native.

Nelson would start in right field for the Mud Hens on "Golf Night" at Swayne Field. Related events included a pitching contest – as in pitching wedge – with various local golf pros taking aim at a "pin" placed behind home plate from a spot in center field. George Wakely of Chippewa Country Club put his effort one foot, eight inches from the cup to win. Nelson hit sixth in Toledo's batting order and hit once, failing to solve the breaking pitches of St. Louis' Stan Ferens and striking out. During Nelson's time in the field (four or five innings, depending on which local newspaper account you believe), he didn't have to catch any fly balls and only handled one chance. After the Browns' Glenn "Red" McQuillen singled to right, Nelson returned the ball to the infield cleanly. Unfortunately for the 5,000 local fans in attendance, McQuillen also homered in the top of the eighth inning to provide the margin of victory in the 3-2 St. Louis triumph. Fortunately for those same fans, the Mud Hens that afternoon on the same field won a game that counted – 12-3 over the St. Paul Saints.

13

MANHATTAN MERRIMENT

THE **1943 P.G.A.** Tour season became a mere shell of its former self in deference to the world war that took precedence over virtually every aspect of American life. The schedule amounted to only a handful of events with a field of competitors that didn't resemble the usual array of top pros. But that didn't mean golfers who were not part of the country's fighting force, like Byron Nelson and "Jug" McSpaden, weren't busy on the links. Nelson and McSpaden in particular committed to playing in multiple exhibitions from coast to coast to benefit American soldiers at home. And there were still their jobs as club professionals, in Nelson's case the duties at Inverness in Toledo, Ohio.

Ben Hogan was fully aware that he would be drafted for military service. In order to choose his branch of service rather than be assigned, he enlisted so that he could join the Army Air Corps. When he reported for duty, the officer who dealt with him was about to stamp his papers for the Navy. Hogan brought the discrepancy to the officer's attention before he was unwittingly sent off to sea. The night before his induction date, Hogan presented Valerie with a star sapphire ring and said he couldn't be sure that he'd ever be able to give her another present; she wore it for the rest of her life. When it came time for Hogan to board the bus at the county courthouse in downtown Fort Worth, he asked Valerie to leave before. As she told Dave Anderson, she protested, wanting to see him off right to the time the bus pulled away. Hogan ended up spending his first days in the military right there in Fort Worth before heading off to officer candidate school in Florida.

North of Fort Worth, the Nelson family was struggling to produce a crop on its farm because of severe drought. John Byron Nelson had no choice but to sell his cow to buy more seeds. Up in northeast Ohio, Byron offered an idea that could help the family through the tenuous financial times. He invited brother Charles, seventeen years old, to come to Toledo for the summer and earn money working in a stamping factory. Byron, as the pro at Inverness Country Club, was rubbing elbows with many of the elite in the industrial town located about sixty miles south of Detroit. And many factories were running at nearly full capacity as part of the war effort.

Charles worked six days a week, ten hours a day for eighty-five cents an hour, a wage that many then would have coveted. His job was to stamp out rocker arms for tractor engines. It was a monotonous task, and it included an added indignity for the musically inclined Nelson who considered his hearing a valuable tool. The factory was a cacophony of noise. To simply speak with anyone on the production line required yelling. But Charles accepted the role he was playing in helping bolster the family's financial situation back home. He took up residence in an extra bedroom in the home of Byron and Louise. He also accompanied them on dinner trips around town at homes of Inverness members, including the owner of the factory. Charles says he recalls interaction between the Nelsons and the Hogans, mostly by phone. "I would hear Byron and Louise mention that Ben had called or Valerie had called. Or Byron called Ben." One of the exhibitions that Nelson played in took place right there in Toledo. He invited Craig Wood, the Masters and U.S. Open champ of 1941, to come up and play a 36-hole match to benefit the Red Cross. To increase attention and the ability to generate contributions, Nelson arranged for Walter Hagen, who lived in Detroit, to come down to officiate the competition. The match for charity proved to be little fun for Wood, as was the case in their 1939 U.S. Open "double" playoff. Nelson won 19-and-17 though they played out the full thirty-six holes. One Inverness member suggested to Nelson that he should have taken it easier on Wood to better entertain the large gallery. As Ben Hogan once said he never played "friendly golf," Nelson was miffed by the recommendation that he shouldn't have played his best.

As Charles' time in Ohio was drawing to a close, Byron suggested that his brother quit the factory job a week early to enable the three of them to travel by train to Philadelphia. Byron was scheduled to play in an event, and they would all bunk down at the home of McSpaden. Then, with whatever money Byron earned, the trio would head up to New York for an Indian summer holiday. In New York, Byron arranged for the three travelers to attend a live performance of Fred Waring and the Pennsylvanians' weekly musical radio show, "The Chesterfield Hour." The show was broadcast five nights a week, 6:00–6:15 p.m., but went on for another forty-five minutes for the benefit of the studio audience. Byron had met Waring somewhere along his golfing travels and took Louise and Charles backstage following the performance to meet the famed music maker. This was, of course, a particular treat for Charles, who was seeking a career in music. Waring said to Charles, "You look like Bennie Goodman!" Charles, having only listened to Goodman on the radio and never having seen the man, wasn't sure what to think. Byron informed Goodman that his brother was a singer, and Charles added, "Not high enough for a baritone;

not low enough for bass." Waring then told Charles that he would arrange for him to audition there the following morning, which Charles balked at. "Young man, you'll need all the auditions you can get in your career," Waring advised. "See you at nine." And he told Charles to report to a gentleman named Bob upon arriving the next morning. Bob happened to be Robert Shaw; Charles Nelson would eventually sing thirteen solos for Shaw all across the country in the years to come. Charles reported the following morning right on time and sang "Without a Song" for Shaw and was fairly crestfallen to learn it was Shaw and not Waring himself who handled thousands of auditions that resulted in the selections for the Pennsylvanians.

Waring also provided the three Nelsons with tickets to "Oklahoma!" which was a huge hit on Broadway since its opening the previous March. The trio also attended a rodeo at Madison Square Garden and ate at Toots Shor's Restaurant that often served the sporting elite. They all went out clubbing one night with golf pro Herman Barron – the first Jewish golfer to win a P.G.A. Tour event – serving as their unofficial guide. When the four of them arrived at a club, Barron could whisk them to the front of the line once the staff realized their party included Byron Nelson. The group walked by the Waldorf Astoria and sauntered in to take a look around to see how the other half lived – or at least temporarily stayed. Byron was the only one of the three facing the main entrance when he discreetly told the others, "Turn around and look." Walking in the door was film star Lana Turner, her husband, and their entourage. The Nelsons followed Turner through the hotel as far as they could before reaching a point that required special approval for admittance. The travelers the next day took a train back to Toledo, where a letter from Waring was waiting for Charles. Waring told him that he had a fine voice but didn't read the music well enough to gain entry to the Pennsylvanians. "I knew that before I sang," Charles says.

14

DOMINATION IN DALLAS

THREE YEARS AFTER Colonial's successful staging of the U.S. Open, P.G.A. Tour golf returned to the area for the first time when Dallas' Lakewood Country Club hosted the $13,333 Texas Victory Open during the second weekend of September 1944. Lakewood, located east of downtown Dallas, opened in 1912 as the city's second 18-hole course. The club, noted for its three-story clubhouse, warded off the financial challenges of the 1920s and '30s thanks in part to slot machines installed in the men's clubhouse. That made possible the improvements to the course that brought the Tour event in 1944. Proceeds from the tournament, expected to reach $20,000 going in, would go into the P.G.A.'s national program for the rehabilitation of wounded war veterans. Specifically, the money was earmarked to build a nine-hole golf course on the grounds of Ashburn General Hospital for veterans located about forty-five miles northeast of Dallas in the Collin County town of McKinney. Tournament officials asked golf fans to buy extra tickets that could be donated to servicemen and servicewomen through Dallas' USO office.

The return of Tour competition to north Texas meant a homecoming of sorts for Byron Nelson amid his extraordinary 1944 campaign. He dominated play at a time when some pros were still off at war; Nelson was classified as 4-F because of a blood condition called "free bleeding." While not hemophilia, his blood didn't coagulate within an amount of time that met the military's standards. Speaking of the military, the most pressing question going into the event was whether Lt. Ben Hogan, stationed only a few miles west of Dallas at Tarrant Field, would be given leave to play. Even if granted liberty, there were whispers Hogan wouldn't play because of poor health. Such fears were dispelled on the Sunday before the tournament, when he came over and played a practice round while most of the touring pros were competing in the Nashville Invitational, which would end on Labor Day. Hogan started with a relatively irregular 2-over-par 37 on the front nine but finished with a 4-under 32 to record a 2-under 69. He played with Harry Todd, who planned to turn pro at the Lakewood event and shot a 1-under 70. Lakewood's pro, Larry Nabholtz, predicted the victor would shoot 276 and that no more than two pros would score 280 or better.

Nelson left Music City with yet another victory, his sixth official Tour triumph of the year (including one team event), his second consecutive win, (following the Tam O'Shanter in Chicago), the thirty-fourth of his career, and nearly a piece of golfing history to boot. His first two trips around Nashville's Richland Club layout resulted in an 11-under-par 131. If he'd equaled that pace over the last thirty-six holes, a final score of 262 would break the Tour's 72-hole scoring mark of 264.

In Monday morning's third round at Richland, Nelson shot a 3-under 68. That required him to finish with a 7-under 64 to break the record. Nelson instead "ballooned" to a 1-under 70 to finish at 15-under 269. He defeated "Jug" McSpaden by only one shot and actually had to scramble to avoid a playoff – which would have complicated matters for the two of them in Dallas. Nelson needed to par the par-3 eighteenth to maintain his one-stroke lead but sent his tee shot into a sand trap. He blasted out to eight feet of the cup and sank his putt to win $2,400 in war bonds. That brought Nelson's earnings for the year to $34,267. The third-place finisher was Bob Hamilton, who only a few weeks earlier had nipped Nelson 1-up in the final of the P.G.A. Championship at Manito Golf and Country Club in Spokane, Washington. On the final day in Nashville, Hamilton might have deserved the biggest cheers. He was stricken with appendicitis the previous night and played Monday's final two rounds wearing ice packs. (Hamilton later became the youngest known golfer to shoot his age with a round of 59 shot in 1975 at a course that he opened in his hometown of Evansville, Indiana a year earlier.)

Hogan got in another nine holes of practice that Monday and afterward identified for local reporters four holes that he believed would greatly determine the tournament winner – par 4s and par 3s all located on the front nine. There was the 368-yard, par-4 fourth ("An east-west hole that you have to play north-south," Hogan assessed. "You have to hit a distinct slice off the tee, and I don't mean a mere fade, in order to have a shot at the green with your second."); the 329-yard, par-4 fifth (a narrow fairway bordered by trees on both sides); the 208-yard, par-3 sixth (a lake located two-thirds of the way from tee to green and traps guarding the front of the green); and the 239-yard, par-3 ninth (a ditch running down the right side and traps again guarding the green had pros calling this one of the toughest par 3s in the country).

Hogan then dismissed Nabholtz's prediction of a winning 276, saying Nelson would shoot 269 or better. Why? Well, Nelson just shot 269 in Nashville. And, Hogan added, someone would shoot a round of 65. Fred Corcoran, the P.G.A. tournament manager, only threw fuel on Hogan's fiery prognostication for Nelson, noting Nelson's Nashville play included seven missed putts of two feet or shorter during the final day's thirty-six holes. "The greens were very rough and bad," Corcoran said. "If you tried to roll the ball up slowly to the cup, it would spin away. If you tried to slap it in soundly, it bounced over." (Richland was a first-time P.G.A. Tour host and would lose the event after hosting it a second time in 1946.)

On Tuesday, Nelson was en route from central Tennessee by car with wife Louise. She dutifully informed him that he had never played well in Texas and it was high time that changed. While that conversation was taking place, Hogan promptly bolstered his contention that a 65 would be scored. He shot a practice round of 5-under 66 despite missing short par putts on Nos. 6 and 9 (two of the holes he'd identified as toughies). For better or worse, he played right after a brief downpour. One of Hogan's playing partners was McSpaden, who flew in from Nashville on Monday night, landed in Fort Worth at 3 a.m. Tuesday and drove to Dallas before getting any semblance of sleep. McSpaden still shot even par and then tossed in his prediction for the winning score: "It will take four rounds of 69 or a total of 276." Rain pelted Lakewood again that Wednesday, cutting short some practice rounds. Hogan got his in and shot a 2-under 69, finishing with a bogey on no. 18. Nelson didn't arrive in time to get in any holes. He did join in the speculation, saying a 12-under 272 would be needed to win. That from someone who shot 11-under days earlier.

Nelson's inability to get in at least one practice round was of concern to one person at Lakewood, even if it wasn't Nelson himself. Bernard Smith was a fourteen-year-old who had just finished his freshman year at Jesuit High School, Dallas' all-male Catholic high school, and was a top caddie at Lakewood. Bernard lived over in Highland Park – ironically right across the street from Dallas Country Club – and landed the caddying position at Lakewood through one of his Jesuit classmates, Jack Nabholtz, son of the club pro. He usually earned $1.25 for carrying a bag, the standard fee plus a quarter tip. In a family with eight children, Bernard's caddie job helped pay Jesuit's annual

Byron Nelson selects a club from his golf bag, held by fourteen-year-old caddie Bernard Smith, during the 1944 Texas Victory Open at Dallas' Lakewood Country Club. (Courtesy of Bernard Smith; Associated Press)

tuition of $100. (The annual tuition at Jesuit College Preparatory School of Dallas for the 2011-12 academic year was $13,600.) Bernard was assigned to Nelson by Larry Nabholtz as a special favor considering the family's travails at the time. Bernard's mother, Julia Smith, had recently been hospitalized for gallbladder surgery, was given the wrong type of blood during a transfusion, and was suddenly fighting to stay alive.

During the first round of the Texas Victory Open, the Nelson-McSpaden act continued to command center stage. They each shot 2-under 69s – Nelson in the morning, McSpaden in the afternoon – and were the only golfers to break par that Thursday. Hogan struggled through a round of 5-over 76. McSpaden got off to a poor start in Friday's second round and skied to a 4-over 75. Nelson's second consecutive 2-under 69 gave him a two-round score of 4-under 238 and a six-shot lead over runner-up McSpaden. Hogan had a much better day, equaling par, but that left him nine strokes off Nelson's pace. The day's head-turning result was recorded by an amateur who, like Hogan, was on holiday from military duties. Seaman First Class Al Smith – from Virginia but stationed just up the road from Dallas at the naval air base in Clinton, Oklahoma – singed Lakewood with a 3-under 68. That was eleven shots better than his Thursday effort, the combination leaving him tied with Hogan. After Friday's second round, the field was reduced to sixty low scores and ties.

Nelson came back to the pack slightly during Saturday's eighteen holes, watching the six-shot lead skimmed to four following his 1-under-par 70 in part because he missed two short birdie putts. Naturally, it was McSpaden nipping closer at his heels with a 3-under 68 that included what he called the best shot of his career. On the 349-yard, par-4 eighth hole, McSpaden jerked his tee shot into high rough only inches from the boundary fence guarding the left side of play. He could think of no other option than simply getting the ball back into a playable situation by hitting off the fence, and he asked the fans behind him to back up and provide him more room. As McSpaden began to address his ball, he thought otherwise. He asked some men in the crowd to boost him over the fence to hit from there with a 6-iron. "Well, if I make it, it'll be a good shot," he offered. And it *was* a good shot, clearing a tree and traveling about 135 yards to the green and within four feet of the pin. Heroics behind him, McSpaden's putt for birdie missed (that Bermuda grass!). Hogan's third round equaled Nelson's 1-under 70, their nine-shot gap unchanged with only eighteen holes to play.

Nelson did no more backing up. He finished that Sunday with a 3-under 68 to run away with his third consecutive win. His final score was 8-under 276 – not the 269 that Hogan predicted, not the 272 that Nelson said would win, but precisely the score that McSpaden said would win. McSpaden was runner-up to Nelson for the second consecutive event, this time by ten shots instead of one. Hogan and Ray Mangrum tied for third, twelve behind. Maybe it was a team event in a way; in accepting his trophy, Nelson cited his wife's coaching role as a source of inspiration.

Bernard Smith was paid $65 for his four days' work with Nelson. He recalls Nelson asking what clubs the members played on certain holes, only to have Nelson always choose a club other than the one that he identified. One fan offered Nelson a beer, Smith says, but the pro declined. Smith's mother fought off the near-fatal effects of the botched transfusion but was hospitalized for months. Because of that, the older daughter in the family – thirteen-year-old Kathleen – didn't return to St. Elizabeth's Academy in Dallas for her sophomore year that fall, instead staying at home to take care of the family. Young Elizabeth had long done chores at home so the shift to "full-time" duties wasn't a drastic transformation. And her burden was eased somewhat with the Smiths' two youngest children sent away temporarily to live with friends and relatives. Their mother came home in the fall and was bedridden for another couple of months, a makeshift bedroom set up in the first-floor dining room since the master bedroom was located upstairs. But Elizabeth received little outside help. An aunt who was a nurse back east helped somewhat early on, but there was no home health service as is available today.

Bernard added another job, as a bagger at the local A&P grocery store, and graduated from Jesuit in 1947. Elizabeth returned to school in the fall of 1945, transferred to Jesuit's sister school, the all-female Ursuline Academy, and graduated in 1948. All eight of the Smith children attended college. Bernard graduated from Notre Dame and Elizabeth from St. Mary's College, the all-female university affiliated with Notre Dame. Julia Smith lived to the age of sixty-five, dying of cancer in 1969.

Nelson was voted the Associated Press' male athlete of the year, named on sixteen of seventy-nine ballots to edge out St. Louis Cardinals shortstop Marty Marion, the National League's Most Valuable Player as the Cardinals won the World Series over the crosstown Browns (they finally made it, but only in a year in which many major leaguers were drafted into the service). Nelson was the second golfer to claim the award, the other being Gene Sarazen in 1932.

15

FAMILIAR FINISH LINE

ON FEBRUARY 13, 1945, Byron Nelson shot a 7-under-par 65 to defeat "Jug" McSpaden by five strokes in a playoff to win the New Orleans Open. It was the sixth event of the calendar year; Nelson had already claimed three victories and placed second or tied for second in the other three starts. Going back to late August 1944, he'd notched seven wins in a dozen tournaments. The previous day, Glen Garden secretary-treasurer Harry Gantt spoke by telephone with Fred Corcoran of the U.S.G.A. about the prospect of the club landing a date on the pro schedule for the 1945-46 winter tour and followed up the conversation with a letter.

"As stated to you today we would prefer to have our dates immediately following San Antonio, Corpus Christi then to Ft. Worth, via New Orleans," Gantt wrote. "It is our idea now to offer $10,000 in war bonds and we would prefer to have it listed as 'Glen Garden Golf and Country Club Open,' Ft. Worth Texas. Since Ft. Worth is the home of both Byron Nelson and Ben Hogan, and since both of these boys grew up as Caddies at this Club, and further since Byron's name appears several times as the winner of The Glen Garden Annual Tournament, we feel that Ft. Worth could in a small way repay them for the National Publicity which they have brought to both our city and Club."

Glen Garden indeed was granted a tournament, but to be played in mid-December 1945 in what turned out to be the final Tour date of the calendar year. Nelson was consulted in the process, asked by Tour officials if the weather in December would be prohibitive. He told them it would be fine. It would be the first pro event played in Fort Worth since the U.S. Open's visit to Colonial in 1941. With Dallas hosting an event for the second consecutive year (the Dallas Open, played in early September at Dallas Country Club), north Texas would enjoy the rare privilege of multiple stops from the pros.

Gantt's letter didn't mention an atypical "hazard" on the course – an electrical tower located smack dab in the no. 12 fairway, with accompanying wires that were also a hazard on the no. 13 hole that doubles back adjacent to no. 12. (The tower can be a hazard on no. 13 as well if a player's tee shot flailed badly to the right.) Wendell Waddle recalls the tower being there when he first became acquainted with Glen Garden in the late 1930s. The twelfth hole is currently 533 yards long, and the tower is about 340 yards from the tee box. Waddle explains there's a special club rule dealing with the metal monster. A red stake was planted into the ground, 150 yards from the tee area. The stake is called the "Peter Post," and Waddle says he doesn't know the origin of the name. If a tee shot goes farther than the "Peter Post" and leaves a second shot that's obstructed by the tower, the golfer is allowed to move the ball as far to the right as desired to render the tower no problem without a penalty. Waddle says the tower usually isn't much of a factor. He does recall an episode in 2007 when he drove no. 12 into the rough on the left side of the fairway. The tower was an impediment for his second shot, but the placement of his tee shot didn't qualify him for relief. Waddle's second shot smacked the tower, which made a ringing sound heard across much of the course. That meant he had to hit again from the same spot. But he hit the tower a second time. And a third. And a fourth.

By the time the Tour hit Dallas, Nelson was the sporting sensation of the country. He and McSpaden teamed to win the Miami Four-Ball in early March for his first victory since New Orleans, and thus began Nelson's jaw-dropping streak of eleven consecutive victories that extended into early August at the Canadian Open. Along the way, he broke the record for the lowest score in a 72-hole tournament by shooting a 263 at the Atlanta Open (which filled the first week of April on the P.G.A. Tour schedule during the war-prompted suspension of the Masters). Nelson's winning finally came to a halt at the Memphis Invitational, where he finished in a tie for fourth place at an event won by amateur Freddie Haas. Of the eleven straight, nine came in stroke play events. In the thirty-six collective rounds of those nine tournaments, Nelson played thirty rounds under par, two rounds even and four rounds over; his worst 18-hole performance was 2-over. He shot a cumulative 109-under par with an average round of 67.86. As the streak progressed, Nelson often skipped playing practice rounds. That served multiple purposes. It limited his exposure to the increasing interest that fans and reporters had in him. It also prevented him from over thinking play. As opposed to the detailed notes that Sam Parks Jr. used to conquer Oakmont during the 1935 U.S. Open, Nelson sometimes benefitted from not even seeing a course until competition began.

The week after Memphis, the Tour continued its three-week stay in Tennessee that featured the return of Ben Hogan to regular play following his discharge from the Army Air Corps. Nelson's "losing streak" came to abrupt halt at one; he captured the Knoxville Invitational while Hogan showed no rust in finishing third. (The event intended to pay the top twenty finishers, and only eighteen pros entered. "Lefty" Stackhouse suffered a sleepless night before the final round and completed only nine holes the following day – even after being allowed to return to the clubhouse for a nap – so he failed to collect a check that required him to simply finish play.) Then at the Nashville Invitational, Hogan recorded his first victory since August 1942 before the pros headed for the Dallas event worth $10,000 in war bonds under the first-year sponsorship of the city's Salesmanship Club.

On the day before competition began at Dallas Country Club, Hogan and Nelson both elected not to play a practice round. Hogan hit town with a slight case of the flu and decided it would be better to simply spend the day resting, also skipping Wednesday night's big celebrity dinner. Nelson also rested, taking the opportunity to bed down at his ranch near Denton. Hogan didn't appear sick during Thursday's opening round, shooting a 4-under 68 (birdieing the final two holes) to share the lead with McSpaden. But following play, Hogan hurried back to his hotel room for continued rest. Nelson's first effort of the tournament was a par-72 leaving him four strokes back; three three-putt greens prevented him from finishing the day in red numbers. Hogan returned to the course on Friday stating he felt much better, but he began his second round pushing tee shots and struggling on the greens. Hogan went out in 6-over 42, rallied for a 4-under 32 on the back nine and finished with a 2-over 74 for a two-day total of 2-under 142. That left him five shots behind McSpaden, whose 3-under 69 provided an overall score of 5-under 137. Nelson's 2-under 70 allowed him to join Hogan at 142.

Hogan and Nelson drew closer to McSpaden during Saturday's third round, but it was Sam Snead who turned a two-shot deficit into a one-stroke lead – 8-under 208 to McSpaden's 209. Hogan's 3-under 69 thanks to consistently reaching greens in regulation put him in third place, three behind at 5-under 211. Nelson, still baffled by his flat stick, stood fifth at 3-under 213 following his 1-under 71. That morning, Nelson, Snead, McSpaden, and Vic Gheezi traveled north to McKinney to put on a pitching and driving exhibition for the servicemen quartered at Ashburn General. Nelson was asked before his round back at Dallas Country Club if he and Hogan were about to overtake McSpaden, Nelson answered, "There is a chance, but Ben is more likely to deliver than I am. I can feel myself going awfully stale. I've played too much golf over too long a stretch. Now I catch myself trying shots that are ridiculous when you give them a second thought." The Saturday charge came from Snead, and that's who won the tournament on Sunday. He recorded a 4-under 68 for a finishing total of 12-under 276 to defeat McSpaden by four shots. Nelson played his best round of the tournament, a 68 that vaulted him to third place at 7-under 281 good for a $1,000 check. Hogan shot 6-over 42 on the front nine for the second time in three days and finished fourth at 3-under 285 because of a 2-over 74, collecting $800.

Before the pros returned to north Texas three months later to finish the 1945 schedule at Glen Garden, Hogan, and Nelson exchanged an incredible one-two punch of heavyweight golf. It began in late September at the second annual Portland Open, where *Oregonian* golf editor Bruce Hamby identified Hogan as the favorite going in: "Many believe Hogan is ready to regain his prewar standing as the nation's top golfer and this may be the spot."

Hogan wasted no time living up to that billing on the par-72 Raleigh Hills layout in Thursday's opening round, playing in a group that included his old Glen Garden mentor, Ted Longworth, the pro at nearby Waverley Country Club. Parring the first three holes, Hogan started his domination of the course with birdies on nos. 4 through 7. His first tour of the course ended in 7-under-par 65 and a four-stroke lead over McSpaden and Ralph Mangrum. Nelson, who struggled off the tee much of the day, was among a group at 1-under 71 along with Longworth. Reporters flocked to Hogan in the clubhouse and practically awarded him the championship, to which he argued, "Let's wait for Sunday before we do any celebrating." On Friday, he opened by bogeying the 397-yard, par-4 first hole and came back to the field slightly with a 3-under 69 and a two-day total of 10-under 134. McSpaden

Charles Nelson [right] visits brother Byron during the 1945 Portland Open, during which Ben Hogan set the 72-hole record with a score of 261. Two weeks later at the Seattle Open, Nelson broke that record with a 259. (Photo by Hugh Ackroyd for *The Oregonian*)

was four shots off the pace. Nelson – visited that day by brother Charles, who hitchhiked down from his post at Fort Lewis, Washington – was eight behind. In the clubhouse afterward, they indicated to reporters they were weary of the Tour schedule. "Three more tournaments, and then we're going hunting," McSpaden said. "Some place deep in the woods of Montana."

Deep in the woods well behind Hogan, the field didn't receive a break from the Hawk during Saturday's third round. His 9-under 63 not only swelled his lead to ten shots over McSpaden (19-under 197 to 9-under 207) but placed him within striking distance of Nelson's record-low score for a 72-hole tournament. Hogan would need another 7-under 65 and responded with an 8-under 64 to finish at an incredible 27-under 261. Afterward, he acknowledged he went into Sunday's final round – played an hour later on the day the nation returned to Standard Time – aiming to set the record: "I figured up Saturday night that a 65 would break Nelson's mark, and that's what I was shooting for." Nelson finished with his best round of the tournament, a 6-under 66, and claimed second place – fourteen strokes behind. "From the looks of the score," he said of Hogan afterward, "I think he still has nine holes to play." Asked how long he thought Hogan's freshly minted scoring standard would last, Nelson answered, "Well, you don't know in this game. It could be forever or it could be broken next week."

That same weekend, sports fans celebrated on the north side of Chicago. The hometown Cubs, playing in Pittsburgh, clinched their first National League pennant in ten years when right-handed pitcher Hank Borowy shut out the Pirates. Borowy was the key to the Cubs' success. The twenty-nine-year-old who'd helped the New York Yankees reach the World Series in 1942 and 1943 compiled a win-loss record of 10-5 record in late July after making the American League All-Star team. But the Bronx Bombers looked to make room for star pitcher "Red" Ruffing returning from the service, and there was con-cern among the club's brass that Borowy had a sore arm and wouldn't match his first-half success. For the Cubs the rest of that season, Borowy went 11-2 as Chicago finished three games ahead of the defending N.L. Champion St. Louis Cardinals. The Cubs would soon try to win their first World Series since 1908 in a rematch of the '35 Fall Classic against the Detroit Tigers.

The Tour moved from Portland up to Tacoma, Washington the next week, and Hogan's record indeed was safe; Jimmy Hines' victorious score at the Tacoma Open was 275. But the *following* week, Hogan's mark not only fell, it was reclaimed by its previous owner at the second Seattle Open. Nelson raced from the gate over the par-70 Broadmoor Golf Club with an 8-under-par 62; his front nine featured two eagles, one on the 500-yard, par-5 ninth hole com-ing courtesy of a 30-foot one-putt. His closest pursuer was a local amateur named Harry Givan, the "Broadmoor Bomber" who also happened to serve as the tournament's general chairman. Hogan shot 2-over 38 on the front and finished at 1-over 71. When Nelson shot "only" a 2-under 68 before a throng of 2,000 fans on Friday for a two-round 10-under 130, Givan stubbornly stood only one shot behind thanks to a second-round 5-under 65. Hogan, with another 71, trailed by a dozen shots.

Nelson's 7-under 63 during Saturday's third round increased his lead over the second-place Givan to nine strokes. *Seattle Times* writer William F. Steed-man advised tournament organizers to save time and affix Nelson's name to the trophy on Sunday morning. At 17-under 193, Nelson needed a 3-under 67 in the final round to take back the scoring record. A 4-under 66 sealed the deal. He realized while making the turn he was within reach of the record and took literal aim. Years later, Nelson admitted being motivated by the fourteen-shot gap between his second-place total at Portland and Hogan's winning score. "I was so embarrassed," he wrote. "I might not have played as well at Seattle if

I'd only been two or three shots back at Portland." Hogan's Sunday score was 1-under 69; his overall 1-under 279 placed him in ninth place.

The Nelson mark lasted until February 1955, broken at the Texas Open by Mike Souchak. Another lasting sports legacy was shaped at the same time during the 1945 World Series between the Tigers and Cubs. Though the war essentially ended with the Japanese surrender that summer, the wartime series scheduling format for minimizing travel continued with the first three games scheduled for one city (Detroit in 1945) and the balance of play to be played in the other city. At the Tigers' Briggs Stadium, Borowy shut out Detroit 9-0. The Tigers evened the Series in Game 2 with a 4-1 victory, but the Cubs headed home with a Series lead of two games to one after blanking Detroit 3-0 in Game 3.

As the Cubs prepared to host Game 4, a popular local restaurateur named William "Billy Goat" Sianis eagerly anticipated attending the ballgame. He arrived at Wrigley Field with something a little unusual – his pet goat named Murphy. The ballpark ushers didn't allow "Billy Goat" to enter with the goat, and Sianis appealed to the highest level – club owner P.K. Wrigley. Denied, Sianis responded by declaring in anger that the Cubs would never win a World Series while his goat was prohibited from taking his rightful place among other loyal Cubs fans. In Game 4, the Tigers won 4-1. Borowy made his second start in Game 5 and was knocked out in the fifth inning, Detroit going on to win 8-4 and take the Series lead three games to two. Game 6, with the Cubs clinging to life, went into extra innings. Borowy was called upon in relief in the ninth inning after the Tigers had scored four times in the eighth to tie the score at 7-7. He pitched four scoreless innings and became the winning pitcher when Chicago scored in the bottom of the twelfth inning to win and force a seventh game. With one day off before Game 7, Borowy was brought back for his third start of the series – having pitched four relief innings two days earlier. He allowed the first three Tigers to reach base in the top of the first inning before being pulled, but the damage was already done. Detroit scored five runs in the first and cruised to a 9-3 victory to win the Series.

What has followed in the Cubs' star-crossed history is widely known: the black cat crossing in front of the visitors' dugout at New York's Shea Stadium in 1969; Leon Durham's error in San Diego in 1984; Steve Bartman's notorious reach over the railing in 2003. The club still hasn't won a World Series since 1908 or even played in one since 1945.

As Glen Garden was about to host a P.G.A. Tour event for the first time in mid-December, the city of Fort Worth dressed up in its Sunday best for a two-day visit from General Jonathan Wainwright. The festivities wouldn't rival the ticker tape parade that the Bataan hero received in New York in September, but he made it clear he was quite pleased to be coming to Cowtown. For one, he contained a soft spot for Texas from his tours of duty in the Lone Star State in 1909 (straight out of West Point) and 1938. He also was eager to help the Tarrant County Victory Bond Campaign in whatever way he could. (And he planned to follow his stay in Fort Worth with a trip to south Texas, Del Rio to be specific, to go quail hunting.) He was honored with a banquet at the Hotel Texas and was made an honorary member of the Sons of the Confederate Veterans.

A Fort Worth resident named David R. Pittman wasn't having such a grand time despite his upcoming wedding to one Marguerite O. Wallace. Days before the big event, Pittman was arrested in Oklahoma, charged with theft and didn't offer much if any defense. Miss Wallace pleaded with the judge to allow the couple to be married before Pittman was relocated to the county jail. Call it multi-tasking – the judge brought together bride and groom on a Friday afternoon (even provided Miss Wallace with a free cab ride to the courthouse) before breaking them apart at least temporarily. A kiss for luck, and he was on his way; Pittman promised the judge that "he would go straight."

Nelson arrived at Glen Garden having sat out the seven events sandwiched between Seattle and Fort Worth. He had won a record seventeen times during the year playing in twenty-seven tournaments. Even with the modest schedule, the pile of victories allowed Nelson to set the record for winnings in a calendar year at $64,528 – topping his 1944 bankroll of $46,600. Hogan came to Glen Garden having played only seventeen tournaments that year yet stood third in victories with five and third on the money list at $26,209. He was in contention at the preceding Miami Open through three rounds before stumbling on the final day with a 74.

Also arriving in Fort Worth was an unusual cold snap, the chilliest of the season to date. The high temperature on the Sunday before the tournament was forty-five degrees, but by 9:30 that night the mercury reached only thirty-two on the way to an overnight low of twenty-eight accompanied by a 28-mph wind. On Monday, it warmed to thirty-two degrees with a hint of snow. Nelson was among those who braved the elements to practice, working his irons on the no. 1 fairway for an hour before playing nine holes with a group that included included Glen Garden's "Smiley" Rowland (who recently became the club's new head professional), and Rockwood's "Skeet" Fincher – he of the marathon golf record in the 1920s. Some observers believed Nelson had put on a few pounds during his golfing sabbatical. Hogan traveled in from south Florida that day and put his military skills to good use; he co-piloted a former Army transport plane flown by pro Johnny Bulla, who flew for Eastern Airlines during World War II when many commercial pilots were drafted. On Tuesday, another pro guided his own aircraft in – right onto the course. McSpaden got in a day later, weather forcing him to spend the previous night in Shreveport, Louisiana. But he set his craft down on the no. 1 fairway, where Wendell Waddle – working part-time in the pro shop – considered tying up the plane like a horse from the old West next to the golf shop. The weather on Wednesday improved – sort of. Temperatures crept into the low forties with a chilly mist, leading one pro to quip, "Fort Worth is much closer to the South Pole than I thought." A slippery road caused Nelson, who was driving in from Denton with Louise on Wednesday to practice, to crash his car on the Denton Creek Bridge about twelve miles from his home. He'd glanced over his shoulder at a car that had skidded into the bridge. Then his car swerved and flipped. Neither of the Nelsons was hurt, though Byron was suddenly wearing parts of ten dozen eggs that were stored in the car. A wrecker that arrived minutes later to haul off the first bashed-up vehicle took Louise back home.

Ben Hogan [left] and Byron Nelson pose during the 1945 Glen Garden Invitational, which Nelson won by eight strokes. (Courtesy of Martin Davis)

Byron followed along later when his car was towed away. Hogan didn't practice on Wednesday, either, but did participate in a "bull session" in the clubhouse.

Frosty or not, Glen Garden was spruced up for the visit from golfing royalty – though nothing could be done about the electrical tower out on no. 12 – with the assistance of a $7,500 deposit in the tournament till directly from the pocket of club president Tom Brown. A total of 135 yards were added, giving the course a total length of 6,296 yards. Seventeen new sand traps were installed, including three each on the 315-yard, par-4 no. 6 and 414-yard, par-4 no. 16. At the previous length earlier in the year, Nelson had fired a course record 63 playing in an exhibition along with McSpaden, Dallas' Raymond Gafford and Rowland. On Thursday, Nelson finally played eighteen holes for the first time since the 66 that capped his record-breaking effort in Seattle. He shot a 1-over-par 72 and said afterward he was lucky to do so given Mother Nature's fickle mood. Friday morning arrived with more flurries, and the temperatures that afternoon poked only into the mid-30s. The day's largest galleries stuck with Nelson, but the day's co-leaders at 2-under 69 were "Dutch" Harrison (a former staff sergeant who was discharged in September) and Joe Zarhardt. Hogan was one of nine golfers at 1-under 70, dipping below par by nailing a 50-foot birdie putt on no. 18. Nelson shot 72 again, leaving him tied for nineteenth place.

But Nelson's game suddenly came alive during Saturday's second round. He set a course record on the front nine with a 6-under 31 that featured six birdies and three pars and played even-par on the back nine. The 5-under 137 pushed him into the lead, one shot ahead of Jimmy Demaret (making his first tournament appearance since being discharged from the Navy). Nelson's most spectacular shot of the round came on the 437-yard, par-4 eighth hole. Eight feet off the green and thirty feet from the flag stick, he chipped in, the ball circling the cup for dramatic effect. He also provided some counsel along the way to amateur playing partner and protégé Frank Stranahan, whose family owned a membership at Inverness. After Stranahan missed what Nelson considered a makeable putt on no. 6, Nelson bluntly admonished him: "You didn't line that one up, Frank. That's half of putting." In the warmth of Glen Garden's clubhouse following the round, Nelson was asked if he'd ever played in colder Fort Worth weather. "I remember once on this same course," he recalled. "I fouled a drive. It hit on the ice-covered lake, bounced up on the other side. The ice was so thick, I walked straight across the lake to retrieve the ball." (This from the man who endorsed playing a tournament in Fort Worth in mid-December.) Hogan stood three shots behind at 2-under 140 and tied for fourth place following a second consecutive round of 70; he lamented his flawed chipping that day.

Sunday's thirty-six hole schedule was delayed for an hour to allow the frozen greens to become something closer to thawed out. The day remained cold but sunny, with a crowd of about 5,000 eager to see if Nelson could hang on and finish 1945 with an eighteenth victory. He didn't disappoint, compiling rounds of 5-under 66 and 1-under 70. He cruised to an eight-shot victory at 11-under 273 to pocket $2,000 (in war bonds). Demaret fought off McSpaden for second place. Hogan tied for seventh at 3-over 287, good for $425. Nelson later called his performance at Glen Garden his worst winning golf of the year. But "Pop" Boone of the *Fort Worth Press* was enamored with Nelson's play on the final seven holes of the morning round, played in 4-under par to provide a nine-stroke cushion going into the fourth round. "Over a stretch of a great many years," Boone wrote, "I have seen all of 'em play from Bobby Jones through Walter Hagen, Gene Sarazen, Byron himself, and Ben Hogan. But I've never seen anybody play seven as tough holes as those which finish the back nine of Glen Garden as Nelson played them yesterday morning – 4-4-3, 3-3-2, 3. Remember it, will you? You'll never see it again."

Nelson repeated as the Associated Press' male athlete of the year, to which the winner reacted by saying: "I didn't know I was in the running." Thirty-six of the eighty-two sportswriters polled chose Nelson first. He was followed by "Doc" Blanchard (Heisman Trophy winner on Army's national championship team), Hal Newhouser (winner of the "triple crown" for major league pitchers in leading the Tigers to baseball's world championship), Glenn Davis (also on Army's football team, who would win the Heisman in 1946) and Phil Cavaretta (catcher for the Cubs). Since the award was started in 1930, Nelson joined tennis star Don Budge as the only two-time recipients to that point.

16

KING OF COLONIAL

DINERS AT THE Milam Cafeteria in downtown Fort Worth on Saturday morning, February 10, 1946 displayed their loyalty to the popular Houston Street eatery as well as something of an appetite for anything cooked well done. For thirty minutes early that morning, a fire raged in the kitchen after starting in an oven that had accumulated an excessive amount of grease. Yet some fifty customers went about their business as the fire reached two-alarm status and three ambulances were dispatched. The fire marshal estimated the damages at $1,250; the cafeteria's manager assured service would continue apace, apparently looking ahead to the day's lunch crowd.

Byron Nelson was one of the few pros entered in the 1946 San Antonio Texas Open who traveled due south to reach the tournament. Most of the field came east by car or train from the Tucson Open, where Jimmy Demaret scored his first victory in six Tour starts since his discharge from the Navy in December 1945. Ben Hogan headed into the Arizona event as the favorite but was out of contention by Sunday's finale, finishing seven strokes behind Demaret in a tie for eleventh place.

When Nelson teed up at Brackenridge Park for a practice round on the sunny Wednesday, it marked the first time that he had touched his clubs in weeks. He opened the winter tour playing in Los Angeles and San Francisco – winning both events, to bring his total of titles since the beginning of the 1945 season to a staggering twenty – then headed home for north Texas instead of crisscrossing the continent to play in the Tour stops at Richmond, Phoenix, and Tucson. Maybe the prescient among golf scribes of the day suspected Nelson's hunger for playing week after week was waning, which would result in 1946 being his final year as a Tour regular. Likewise, Nelson by that point in his career wasn't apt to spend hours practicing. Fred Corcoran, the P.G.A. tournament manager, offered that Nelson and Walter Hagen benefitted from cutting their practice time after joining the elite of the tournament hierarchy. Corcoran indicated Hagen and Nelson were convinced they were better off working out the kinks of their games in actual competition rather than in simulated conditions. There was another effect of those weeks away from play – and, apparently the availability of that good farm food – Nelson arrived in San Antonio eight pounds heavier than his playing weight in San Francisco.

Hogan's finish at Tucson was atypical of his play during the early season: second at L.A., third at San Francisco, tied for third at Richmond and the victor at Phoenix. Hogan came to San Antonio as the young season's earnings leader with $6,200 (in war bonds). Nelson was second, despite playing only twice, with $4,600. When Hogan arrived at the course on Wednesday intending to play a practice round, he was sorely disappointed to discover Brackenridge otherwise occupied by a qualifying round. His conclusion: "I'll sit this one out and go on to New Orleans." He tossed his clubs in his car and left the course. Hogan was convinced to play, rejoining the pros' schedule of events that night at a tournament dinner hosted by the junior chamber of commerce. That day, he joined "Jug" McSpaden in a spin over San Antonio in McSpaden's small plane. Hogan peered down at the course and later declared, "Looks simple that high up."

The Friday and Saturday rounds at the tight, wooded par-71 Brackenridge layout saw Nelson paired with "Dutch" Harrison, the 1939 Texas Open champion, and amateur Mario Gonzalez while Hogan was teamed with Bob Hamilton, the defending P.G.A. Championship winner, and Lawson Little. Nelson showed no signs of rust, his first tour of the course completed with eleven pars and seven birdies for a 7-under-par 64. That gave him a share of the lead with Art Doering, a 29-year-old from Denver who turned pro the previous summer. Next on the leaderboard at 4-under 67 were Hogan, Little, Demaret, and amateur Frank Stranahan. In all, twenty-seven golfers bettered par. Maybe that's why Harrison, after shooting an even-par 71, considered dropping out after only eighteen holes.

No one shot 64 during Saturday's second round at Brackenridge, but Hogan came the closest. He fired a 6-under 65 for a two-day total of 10-under 132 that was equaled only by Nelson. Hogan's round was highlighted by a pair of eagles on par-5s. The first took place on the dogleg no. 3 hole, where Hogan holed out from a sand trap. On no. 13, with a creek standing guard in front of the green, he reached the putting surface in two shots thanks to a fairway wood and needed only one putt. Hogan put his exclamation point on the round with a birdie on no. 18. Nelson again recorded seven birdies, but bogeyed four holes.

For Sunday, Nelson, Demaret and Doering made up the seventh of eleven threesomes sent off no. 1. Hogan, Jim Ferrier and Vic Gheezi comprised the final group at no. 1. As Clarence Weikel wrote in the *San Antonio Express*, "Bantam Ben Hogan showed no respect whatsoever to the supposed mastery of the fairways by Lord Byron – known as 'Mr. Big Golf,' to Sammy Byrd's tournament record or to par figures yesterday at Brackenridge Park." Hogan closed with his second 6-under 65 of the tournament to break the event record with a 20-under 264. Nelson's 2-under 69 might have looked good on most days; instead it dropped him to nine shots behind the winner and into third place. The runner-up was Byrd, the former Texas Open record-holder, whose own 65 put him at 14-under 270.

Hogan met Valerie on the edge of the eighteenth green at the conclusion of the tournament. The victor was certainly expecting some expression of congratulations from his bride. Instead, she first put out her arms to reveal four golf balls that some young ladies had asked to have autographed. Hogan exclaimed, "Good lord. You, too?" Nelson termed his performance "ragged." "I three-putted six times, had that five on no. 8 when I missed the green and didn't hit the ball hard enough through a bunker," he moaned. "That accounts for eight strokes on my last two rounds. You can always look back and see where you lost out." Someone did point out the handicap of having to play in a group that included the sartorially daring Demaret, clad in a bright green cap, loud yellow sweater, green-and-white striped trousers and two-toned shoes. Nelson declined to accept the excuse.

Colonial Country Club made its return to P.G.A. Tour activity three months later, five years after hosting the National Open, with the establishment of the Colonial National Invitational Tournament. (Today, no other Tour event has been played at the same venue longer.) What set the tournament apart from most Tour stops was a small, exclusive field of only a couple dozen pros and a handful of amateurs instead of the typical 100-plus players cut following two rounds. Marvin Leonard and the Cowtown golfing establishment had actually lobbied to receive an annual Tour date earlier than 1946 but were forced to wait because of the volatile scheduling that took place during World War II. The Colonial offered a purse of $15,000, the third largest on Tour at the time.

Both Hogan brothers were entered – Royal as one of the select amateurs – as was Nelson, with Nelson edging Ben by two shots to claim the Houston Open championship before traveling up to Fort Worth. Neither Nelson nor Hogan played a practice round on Tuesday; Hogan worked on his clubs in the shop and afterward never left the practice range while Nelson spent the day up in Denton. Wednesday's work on the course had to wait for an inch of rain that fell in the morning. (Could have been worse; about three hours west of Fort Worth in the town of Ballinger, 10-inch-wide hail was reported.) An unknown from Utah by the name of George Schneiter attracted most of the attention during Thursday's opening day of competition. At least he was unknown to the fans if not the players since Schneiter was also the chairman of the P.G.A. tournament committee. He fired a 3-under-67 to not only claim the first-round lead but also break Ben's competitive course record by a stroke. Neither of the hometown stars managed par that first day despite excellent scoring conditions following early morning rain and a sunny afternoon, Nelson finishing at 2-over 72 and Hogan at 3-over 73. The undoing of Nelson, who was sick early in the week and didn't get in a practice round, was putting his tee shot on no. 8 into the river. Hogan was haunted by hooks and also regularly overshot greens on the front nine. Royal Hogan struggled to 9-over 79. Friday wasn't much different for Nelson and Ben Hogan. In fact, Nelson copied his Thursday result with a 38 on the front nine and a finish of 72 that left him four strokes behind new leader Sam Snead's even-par 140. Hogan also shot a 72, still hooking many drives, and trailed Snead by five at 5-over 145. Royal was 2-over for the round headed to the par-5 eighteenth but found the lake for a double-bogey 7, a round of 4-over 74 and two-day total of 13-over 153.

The golfer who charged to the front following Saturday's third round was a north Texan who wasn't named Hogan or Nelson or even Lloyd Mangrum. It was Harry Todd from Dallas. His third-round par-70 put him at 1-over 211 for the tournament, good for a one-shot lead over Snead, two over Schneiter, and three over Hogan and Mangrum. Hogan played his best golf of the tournament to date with a 1-under 69. "I needed a 67 today," Hogan said. "My woods and second shots are all that I could ever want for." That would leave putting, which he proceeded to practice for two hours that evening. Nelson also played his best so far, his 1-over 71 placing him at 5-over 215 after the same pattern of struggling early and rallying late. "If I played the back like I do the front," he fumed afterward, "I'd have been dead long ago."

Yet a hometown hero emerged in the nick of time to capture the first Colonial National Invitational Tournament championship. Hogan pieced together a round that was both consistent and spectacular – 33-32-65 – to reclaim the course record (which would last until 1970) and win the tournament by one shot over the game Todd (1-under 279 to even-par 280). Maybe the rest of the field was worn down; no other golfer broke par on Sunday. Hogan birdied the first two holes and then missed birdie putts on the next three. Such a start coaxed the majority of 7,000 fans to follow Colonial's favorite son for the balance of the day. Nelson continued to improve his scoring – an even-par 70 – but it wasn't enough to contend with Hogan. His final score was 5-over 285, six strokes off the pace.

During the tournament, a reporter in New York called Nelson with a curious question. The reporter had gone through the entries for the upcoming National Open at Canterbury Golf Club in Cleveland – the first official Open staged since 1941 – and didn't see an entry for Nelson. Oops; he had not sent his in yet. Quick thinking by the intrepid scribe made possible one of the most thrilling finishes in a major championship as Nelson, Gheezi, and Lloyd Mangrum competed in a three-way playoff. Nelson would have claimed his second Open championship and sixth career major title were it not for a gaffe committed by his caddie in the third round. On the par-5 thirteenth hole, Nelson's caddie lost sight of his second shot and accidentally kicked the ball to incur a one-stroke penalty. Eighteen holes of "overtime" golf settled nothing since all three shot 72. After a second extra round, Mangrum shot 72 to edge his two competitors by one shot each.

If Hogan and Herman Barron had not three-putted no. 18, there would have been a five-way logjam of the playoff at Canterbury – that following Hogan's putting collapse on the final hole of the Masters two months earlier.

17

MAJOR BREAKTHROUGH

BEN HOGAN HAD one final chance to cap his stellar 1946 season with his first major championship. The P.G.A. Championship would be played in late August at Oregon's Portland Golf Club, the course Hogan had personally annexed during the 1945 Portland Open with the record-sheering 27-under-par 261. Yet Byron Nelson came into the tournament considered at least the co-favorite, despite a sore back, on the basis of being the event's defending champion along with the fact that he'd won three of his last five starts. As Hogan and Nelson reached the quarterfinals, Nelson had little to worry about other than his sacroiliac. He eliminated Frank Rodia 8-and-7 (playing twenty-seven holes in 10-under-par), host pro Larry Lamberger (3-and-2) and his 1943 New York City tour guide, Herman Barron, (3-and-2). Hogan's victories to reach the three 18-hole rounds began somewhat tight but became progressively easier. He downed Charles Weisner (2-and-1), Bill Heinlein (4-and-3) and Arthur Bell (5-and-4).

In the quarterfinals that started 36-hole play, Nelson was pitted against "Porky" Oliver while Hogan's foe was Frank Moore. Nelson owned a two-hole lead with five holes to play but couldn't put Oliver away. The match was square going to the thirty-sixth hole, when Nelson yanked his second shot into the woods. That left him needing to convert a 25-foot putt to save par and extend the match beyond regulation; the putt didn't fall, and the defending champion was shockingly out in the quarterfinals. There had been talk earlier in the tournament that Nelson was hampered by a bad back, but after being eliminated he denied that. "My back never bothered me at all," Nelson said, sipping a Coke and chewing on some ice. "I lost to a man who shot better golf. Ed's a great guy and a fine competitor."

Meanwhile, the Hogan express continued to pick up steam. He defeated Moore 5-and-4, then routed his pal, Jimmy Demaret, 10-and-9. "Sunny Jim" actually built a lead of 2-up through the match's first three holes, but that only seemed to inject life into Hogan's game. He birdied three of the next four holes to swipe the lead as he completed the morning round 6-up. Afternoon competition wasn't much different. The match was over at twenty-seven holes. The drastic margin of victory prompted reporters to see if the normally jovial Demaret was provoked by Hogan's killer instinct. It was after this round that Demaret contributed to the legion of quotes pertaining to how little Hogan would say while playing. Asked if Hogan talked to him during the one-sided day, Demaret said, "Yes. 'You're away.' "

The final provided a contrast in silhouettes, Hogan at 137 and the somewhat slimmed-down Oliver at about 220. Hogan fell behind by three holes during the morning round because of – naturally – putting predicaments. But he immediately made amends with a 30 on the front nine of his afternoon play, taking a two-hole lead into the back nine. Hogan played the final fourteen holes in 8-under-par and defeated Oliver 6-and-4 to win the Wanamaker Trophy. Henny Bogan had won a major championship. "The only time I was sure of winning was when 'Porky' walked over and shook my hand," Hogan said. "No one gets as many birdies as I did without being lucky, and, boy, was

I tickled when those long putts started to drop. It's impossible to explain how much this means to me, so I'll just say, 'Thank you,' to the P.G.A. and my wife, Valerie." The path to a first major championship was so much more of an odyssey, a test of will and skill and guile for Hogan, than it appeared to be for Nelson. Whereas Nelson won the 1937 Masters in only his third season of week-in, week-out Tour competition, Hogan's path covered the better part of eight seasons – which followed the fits and starts that began eight years before that, when he first teed it up as a professional at Brackenridge in San Antonio at the 1930 Texas Open.

A month before P.G.A. Tour pros would come through Dallas and Fort Worth that fall, the chairman of the Glen Garden-based event renamed the Fort Worth Invitational had a curious interaction with Hogan, according to a story in the *Fort Worth Press* written by Bill Wood. Willard White was not only the tournament chairman but also Glen Garden's unofficial game warden. When adventurous water moccasins would venture up into the trees surrounding the course's central lake to sun themselves, White would dissuade them from bothering golfers with his shotgun. White ran across Hogan in front of the Blackstone Hotel. As Hogan was leaving, White said, "Well, be seeing you at the tournament beginning of next month." Hogan turned and half shrugged, and his reply was almost inaudible. That left White to wonder whether Hogan had said yes or no. This exchange was repeated twice more with White still unsure of what Hogan said. Finally, with White nearly apoplectic that one of the biggest stars in golf and a hometown hero wasn't planning to play at Glen Garden, Hogan offered, "Of course I'm going to play in the Glen Garden Open. Couldn't you see me laughing when I said, 'No.'?"

In 1946, the young Dallas Open moved yet again, from Dallas Country Club to Brook Hollow Golf Club. The course, a Tillinghast design that opened in 1920, is located just west of downtown Dallas. Defending champion Sam Snead looked quite at home despite the change of venue, shooting an

8-under-par 62 during a Tuesday practice round followed by a 4-under 66 the following day. Hogan wouldn't reveal his Wednesday practice score when asked by newsmen. (Demaret was happy to spill some beans and said Hogan shot either 5-under or 6-under.) Hogan was willing to speculate that a score of 4-over-par 284 would win the tournament.

Even with Nelson extending his hiatus from competition to six weeks since his quarterfinal loss in Portland, *The Dallas Morning News* proudly proclaimed "Greatest Field in History Tees Off in Dallas Open Tourney Today." But the opening round provided a jolt for the galleries when Snead followed a front-nine 1-over 36 with a disastrous 7-over 42 for a first-day score of 8-over 78 that virtually eliminated him from championship contention. Afterward in the locker room, he dropped his watch, which smashed into pieces. "I guess this isn't my lucky day," he mused. The first-day leader was Vic Gheezi at 1-under 69 with Hogan amid a group one stroke behind. Hogan added a 69 on Friday to share the midpoint lead with Dallas' own Harry Todd.

Hogan backtracked on Saturday with a 2-over 72, but that was still good enough to grab the lead solo by one shot over Buck White, the Mississippian who'd won the previous week at Memphis. Hogan followed with his worst round of the tournament on the windy Sunday, a 3-over 73, yet extended his lead and won by two shots over Paul Runyan and Herman Keiser to claim the $2,000 winner's check. He never shot the low score of the day, and his winning score was 4-over 284 – precisely the number that he'd cited before play began. Which impressed *Dallas News* sports editor Bill Rives: "On the assumption that eventually his game will desert him, Ben Hogan can always make a living; all he need do is buy a crystal ball at a 10 cent store, pick up an Army surplus tent and set himself up in business as a prognosticator."

18

CHANGE OF PLANS

THE P.G.A. TOUR returned to Glen Garden in 1946 amid more favorable meteorological circumstances – thanks simply to a change in scheduling. The tournament was moved from mid-December to early October. And, not coincidentally, it immediately followed the Dallas event. And there was no mystery as to who was primarily responsible for the Tour's return to southeast Fort Worth. Glen Garden president Tom Brown donated another $3,000 in July 1946 to ensure the tournament would take place. The club sent him an official letter of thanks a few weeks later written by club secretary Liston Jackson: "This is only one of the many things that you have so unselfishly done for Glen Garden over a period of years and the officers, directors, and entire membership want you to know that they appreciate what you have done."

While Ben Hogan was finishing up his twelfth individual or team victory of the year over in Dallas, Byron Nelson was getting in a tidy practice round of 1-under-par 70 back at his former home course. He and Cecil Nottingham teamed to defeat Glen Garden pro "Smiley" Rowland and tournament chairman

Willard White 3-and-2. Nelson's most recent P.G.A. Tour appearance came six weeks earlier, in the P.G.A. Championship played at Portland Golf Club. On Monday, Hogan made his first appearance at the course. That night, the club held a dinner for Brown. Hogan and Nelson were presented with Glen Garden life memberships dated the following Sunday, October 6.

Byron Nelson sinks a par putt on the ninth green at Glen Garden Country Club during a practice round before the Fort Worth Invitational played in October 1946. (Courtesy, *Fort Worth Star-Telegram* Collection, Special Collections, The University of Texas at Arlington Library, Arlington, Texas)

Wednesday's final day of practice saw Hogan spend only ninety minutes on the course, working strictly on his iron play, before exiting early and saying he had walking flu. The prospect of losing Hogan's presence in the tournament was compounded that same day when Sam Snead withdrew following a difference of opinion with tournament officials regarding an appearance fee. Snead requested $250 to help with his lodging expenses. Tour traveling secretary Gerry Moore released a statement that attributed Snead's hasty exit to other reasons: "Snead has not been feeling well, and he needs a lot of dental work. Too, he hasn't been playing well." The *Fort Worth Star-Telegram* reported Hogan and Lloyd Mangrum had also requested appearance fees of $250 and agreed to play though their requests were also denied. White addressed the impasse with Snead and didn't mention poor play or aching gums: "When we made arrangements for the tournament with the P.G.A., no such items [like appearance fees] were mentioned. We feel that putting up $10,000 for the boys to play for, we have done all we should. We did not feel that the additional expenses of nearly $1,000 was justified. After reading our contract with the P.G.A., which makes no mention of the additional expenses, the committee stood pat." A contingent from Glen Garden took one last stab at convincing Snead to stay and play. If he didn't earn $250 with his tournament finish, the tournament would make up the difference. Snead declined.

Hogan was listed in Thursday's starting field, though many observers had their doubts whether he'd be well enough to compete. Indeed, White received a phone call just before noon from Hogan. Bed ridden with a temperature of 103 degrees, Hogan informed the chairman that he was under doctor's orders not to play in the event. With Snead and then Hogan missing from play, it probably was difficult to determine who felt worse, Hogan or White. At least the tournament began with a measure of curiosity when Ellsworth Vines, the 1932 Wimbledon gentlemen's singles champion who switched over to golf in 1940, shot a 6-under 65 on Thursday to grab the first-round lead. It was a day in which almost two dozen players broke par. George Fazio and Frank Stranahan, the amateur from Toledo, trailed by only one shot. Nelson's 1-under 70 left him tied for seventeenth place. And there was a Hogan on the scoreboard; amateur Royal Hogan finished at 2-over 73.

With Friday play hampered by occasional thunderstorms, Stranahan kept his hot hand with another round of 66 – despite twice hooking shots out of bounds – for a 36-hole total of 10-under 132 good for a four-shot advantage. Nelson shot par and trailed by nine. Royal Hogan's tournament ended with a 4-over 75 that prevented him from making the cut. Saturday's third round belonged to Fazio. He shot a 6-under 65 to make up five shots on Stranahan and pull ahead by one over Stranahan and Jim Ferrier. If the tournament organizers had hoped Nelson would begin a charge and drum up more local interest, it didn't happen. His scores continued to improve – this time, a 3-under 68 – but the Denton farmer went into Sunday's round trailing by eight strokes.

Stranahan bolted from the gate strong on Sunday, firing a 6-under 31 on the front nine. A round of 3-under 68 gave him a two-shot victory over Ferrier. It was the amateur's third P.G.A. Tour victory, all three taking place within twelve months. Nelson finished with another 3-under 68 and a final total of 7-under 277, seven strokes behind the winner. Stranahan was somewhat unpopular with most Tour pros who resented what they considered a silver-spoon upbringing – not only did his parents own a membership to the ritzy Inverness club, but the family wintered in fashionable Palm Beach, Florida – and his willingness to speak his mind to reporters. He'd enrolled at the University of Miami with the intent of playing football but was deemed too small for the gridiron. After he turned his athletic attention to golf, he continued to lift weights, hardly the practice among the golfers of the day. Stranahan was the top-ranked power lifter in his weight class from the mid-1940s through the mid-1950s and later on ran in more than 200 marathons and some 50-mile events. Nelson and he first crossed paths in

1940 at Inverness, and Nelson continued to provide unofficial instruction and encouragement during Stranahan's forays against the pros. "The 'Lord' is the only golfer on the P.G.A. circuit who will give a guy a helping hand," Stranahan said of Nelson after winning. "Most of them just haven't the time. Maybe they don't notice that you need it. But the 'Lord' does, and he takes time then and there to point out your mistakes and make little suggestions which sharpen your game."

But the day's action was hardly over; two announcements of varying significance to the golfing world were made as Glen Garden emptied out. Club officials stated Glen Garden's run as home to a P.G.A. Tour event had ended with this second annual event. Revenue from ticket sales, program sales and concessions barely reached $5,000. That was less than half of the amount needed to simply pay the players' purse. Whereas the 1945 event struggled to attract paying patrons by being played in frigid mid-December, playing in early October relegated the '46 tournament to afterthought status in an area whose sporting attention was riveted to college football. During the four days of tournament play, the *Star-Telegram* didn't feature a bylined story from Glen Garden. The newspaper was much more interested in the weekend's football games involving Fort Worth's two most popular Southwest Conference elevens, the hometown TCU Horned Frogs and the Longhorns of the University of Texas. The Horns, behind quarterback Bobby Layne, thumped Oklahoma A&M (now Oklahoma State) 54-6 before a crowd of 45,000 in Austin to run their early-season record to 3-0 while outscoring their overmatched opponents 172-6. A few miles below Colonial Country Club in southwest Fort Worth, the Frogs fell to Arkansas 34-14 before a gathering of 13,000 that surely featured a fair representation of visiting Razorback fans. (In one of the greater national upsets of the season a month later, a TCU team that would win only twice tripped up sixth-ranked Texas 14-0 to end the Longhorns' chances of winning the conference.)

And news was also made that Sunday afternoon at Glen Garden by Nelson. Already in semiretirement, he told Bill Wood of the *Fort Worth Press* that he would play no more tournament golf except for rare appearances such as an annual visit to Augusta. Wood included no direct quotes from Nelson, writing:

"Byron said that the second annual $10,000 Fort Worth Invitational, which ended yesterday, would be his last tournament appearance except one meet a year – the Masters. Both Nelson and Glen Garden have taken a beating from the game. Byron's has been physical because of the pressures of long circuit tours, increasingly sharp competition and outside business demands. Byron told us that he would continue in close association with the game – making exhibition match appearances, completing a golf book he is writing and representing McGregor [sic] Sporting Goods by personal appearances at the biggest meets of the year."

Nelson and wife Louise had discussed the topic of his retirement from full-time competition since the previous December. It wasn't as simple as walking away from the game since he had a contract with MacGregor. Oddly, it was after he won the season's first two tournaments (the Los Angeles Open and the San Francisco Open) that he withdrew from the next event, across the country in Richmond, to meet with Louise in Phoenix. They traveled together back to Texas to talk about the next chapter of their lives, a chapter brought into clearer focus when Nelson identified a three-bedroom ranch house on a 630-acre piece of property between Dallas and Denton in the town of Roanoke. They bought it for $55,000 cash.

The October Glen Garden event was indeed Nelson's final Tour competition of 1946, his twenty-first Tour event. In 1945, the first full tournament slate following World War II, Nelson played in every Tour event from the initial Los Angeles Open right after New Year's through the P.G.A. Championship in mid-July. He skipped the St. Paul Open, then made the next eleven consecutive through the Seattle Open in mid-October, when he shot the unbelievable

259. Of course, Nelson didn't confine his future big-time play to Augusta. He frequented the Crosby Clambake, the Colonial N.I.T. and occasionally other stops for various reasons. He also played regularly in Texas P.G.A. tournaments. But he no longer would be a Tour regular, a competitor for player of the year honors that had previously come his way.

Charles Nelson says Byron talked to him during the 1946 golf season about the prospect of stepping back from being a regular player on the P.G.A. Tour. "He wasn't distraught," Charles says. "But it was taking a toll, a physical strain. He said, 'I'm thirty-four, and men are just beginning to succeed in their profession. I'm a has-been.' He felt like he was a novice at everything else."

Nelson sat out the Tour season's final seven events, with the Fort Worth Invitational followed the subsequent week by the tournament in Alabama's capital city of Montgomery. Technically, the first victor of the post-Nelson era was the irrepressible Ky Laffoon, claiming the last of his ten career titles. The Oklahoma native appeared to many to be an American Indian, with high cheekbones, a deep tan and slick, black hair. Maybe the name sounded some-what exotic, too, though his first name actually was George. He wasn't an Indian. But early in his career when was asked by a sportswriter if he was, he said yes. That was all "Porky" Oliver needed to start calling him "Chief." Laffoon's golf shots often strayed from their intended paths, but his ability to spit chewing tobacco at a specific target was uncanny. Snead said Laffoon could spit into a golf hole from twenty feet and never missed from eight feet in.

But because Laffoon's golf shots weren't as reliable, he often reacted by launching into curse-filled tirades and busting one or more of his golf clubs. After three-putting no. 18 at one event, he marched directly to his car, opened the trunk, pulled out a pistol and shot the offending flat stick three times. And yelled expletives during the execution as well. It reached the point that his wife threatened to leave him if he couldn't be more civil during play. But Laffoon could also employ his talents in more constructive ways. He once ground down his wedge while driving to the next tournament, leaning out the door and barely being able to see over the dashboard as the club scraped along the pavement. Witness to this was Hogan, who was snoozing in the backseat before being rousted by the noise and smell of Laffoon's inventive undertaking.

In May 1947, Charles Nelson and Betty Brown tied the knot. They'd met in her hometown of Gainesville, Texas, right on the state line with Oklahoma, when he was in the Army in 1945 and stationed at nearby Camp Howze. Charles went into town on Easter to attend church and was one of the soldiers invited to the Browns' for a home-cooked meal prepared by Betty's mother. Before the ceremony, Charles reminded his brother that the best man is supposed to see to the needs of the groom on his wedding day. And in this case, the groom decided the two of them should play a round of golf at the nine-hole course located at North Texas State Teachers College at 1 p.m., in plenty of time to get to the church late that afternoon. Charles wasn't a regular golfer. As a young teenager, he first played a round at a nine-hole municipal course near Fort Worth in the town of Arlington and shot about 50. He was thirteen when Byron won the U.S. Open and was often asked if he wanted to be a golfer. He didn't but tried to be as polite as possible in responding to the question: "Whatever I do, I want to do it well." Charles eventually played regularly just for fun, often with a saxophone player named Don McIver. Charles invited McIver to join in the pre-wedding golf date. While McIver probably wouldn't have dropped what he was doing to play with Charles, the circumstances were quite different when Charles phoned to ask, "Would you like to play a round of golf this afternoon with Byron Nelson?"

McIver rushed to the course and spent the rest of that morning hitting practice balls. Unfortunately for him, playing in a threesome with the two-time Associated Press male athlete of the year adversely affected his game when play began. The most notable aspect of the activity probably took place on North

Texas' short par-4 no. 3 hole that required a drive over a small lake that was closer to the tee box than the green. Byron's shot was even with the green but landed a couple of yards to the right of the putting surface. Charles' effort wasn't nearly as good, a topped shot that barely cleared the water. His second shot wasn't much cleaner, a bladed 4-iron, but the ball rolled onto the green to within thirty feet of the flag stick. Byron's short chip wasn't close enough to the cup for a one-putt, and he parred the hole. Charles struck a healthy putt that covered the thirty yards with ease and dropped into the cup. Charles Nelson had "won the hole" from his famous golfing brother. Byron seemed to take his medicine in stride; it was all McIver could do not to lose his lunch right there on the no. 3 green.

In the autumn of 1947, Hogan made his Ryder Cup debuts as both player and captain – having previously been chosen as a player in 1942 for matches that were cancelled because of World War II. At one of Hogan's favorite layouts, the Portland Golf Club, he and Jimmy Demaret played first-day four-somes and downed the British pairing of Jimmy Adams and Max Faulkner 2-up as the Americans rolled up a rout of 11 to 1.

19

DIFFERENCE OF OPINION

O N THE MONDAY before the 1948 Texas Open, Ben Hogan was on the road before the sun heading out of Tucson, Arizona. He tied for ninth place in the $10,000 Tucson Open, his 9-under-par 271 leaving him seven strokes behind winner Stewart "Skip" Alexander. The $2,000 first-place check was definitely earned by Alexander, a 29-year-old product of Duke University, on the seventy-second hole. He trailed John Palmer by one shot but reached the par-5, 513-yard finishing hole in two shots – a mere twelve feet from the flag stick. Needing to two-putt for a birdie to force a playoff, Alexander sank his initial putt for an eagle and outright victory, which would be the first of three in his P.G.A. Tour career. Placing twentieth – the final position to collect a check, for all of $55 – was Sam Snead. He was prepared to cut short his participation on the winter tour right there in Arizona. But Jimmy Demaret convinced him to travel on to Brackenridge, where he had not played since 1941.

Hogan nearly made it all 868 miles to San Antonio but stopped along U.S. Highway 90 about ninety miles short of San Antonio and spent the night in the small town of Uvalde. He said he would have come all the way if he'd previously arranged for lodging in San Antonio. And it turned out Hogan didn't need to cover all those miles on Monday. He thought he needed to get at least close to San Antonio by Monday night in order to get in a Tuesday practice round before playing in the pro-am on Wednesday. But the schedule actually called for the pro-am to be played on Thursday. Told by local sportswriters that Brackenridge's greens were the portion of the course most affected by recent rains, Hogan said his biggest concern regarding putting was his own play and not the condition of the putting surface: "I've been missing so many two-foot putts, it's discouraging. My putting has been miserable."

Hogan was considered at least among the tournament favorites if not the top pick. The $10,000 Texas Open was assured a new champion before the first group began play at 8:30 a.m. on Friday. "Porky" Oliver, who had won at Brackenridge in 1947 and finished the year fourth in the money standings, didn't travel to San Antonio after leaving the Tucson event before it ended. It turned out he was busy finalizing a deal to become the new pro at Inglewood Country Club in Seattle. The field of 129 pros and sixteen amateurs was called the best in the event's history by *San Antonio Light* sports editor Dick Peebles. It included four previous Texas Open champions and the victors in all five of the Tour events played to date on the 1948 winter tour. Glen Garden's "Ivey" Martin, a veteran of the *San Antonio Light*'s junior tournament, would make his Texas Open debut. But also present was more bad weather, a steady drizzle that dogged the golfers all day Friday. The weather kept down the size of the gallery, but among the fans was a certain farmer from Roanoke, Texas who turned a few heads. Byron Nelson took a holiday from his sixty-six head of Hereford cattle and plunked down the $2 admission fee. Nelson assured journalists that he wasn't planning a comeback to regular Tour competition: "I was thirty-six years old Wednesday and have had fourteen years of tournament golf without a break. That's enough for any man, and it's enough for me. I don't intend to give up the game entirely and will play this year in the Masters in Augusta, Georgia and the Texas P.G.A. at El Paso. But no more, except for exhibitions." The exhibitions, Nelson announced, would include a barnstorming series beginning in April in Hobbs, New Mexico and heading east to New York – featuring the likes of Hogan and Demaret.

Hogan's threesome was the thirty-third group to tee off on Friday, called to the no. 1 tee box at 12:35 p.m. and including Jimmy Thomson of New York and amateur O'Hara Watts of Dallas. Hogan finished his round and turned in his card with a 1-under-par 70, five shots behind the leading group that consisted of Jim Ferrier, Ky Laffoon, Eric Monti, and Norman von Nida. But minutes after Hogan signed his card, two P.G.A. officials – F.A. Burttschell, chairman of the rules committee, and George Schneiter, tournament committee chairman – informed him that his scorecard was in error. Hogan's card gave him a 7 on the par-4 thirteenth hole. He'd put his second shot into a creek bed in front of the green. Hogan assumed the entire creek bed was to be played as a casual hazard, moved his ball out and assessed himself a one-stroke penalty. The officials told him his lie fell under the definition of "river water," according to local rules as printed on the back of the players' scorecards. It was unplayable, they told him, and should have been a two-shot penalty. His score for the hole should have been an 8, they said, giving him a 71 for the round instead of 70.

Burttschell and Schneiter told Hogan they considered it an honest error, to be simply resolved by officially recording a par 71 heading into Saturday's second round. But Hogan didn't consider that the resolution at all. He told the officials that, since he'd signed an incorrect scorecard, he was disqualified to continue play according to U.S.G.A. rules: "If I continued to play and won some money here, I would feel like I was cheating somebody else. I won't do it." Coincidence or not, Hogan never again played in the San Antonio event.

With Hogan gone, Snead followed his opening round 66 with a 65 during Saturday's muddy play to take a one-shot lead over Dick Metz. Sunday brought a brisk, cold wind to San Antonio. Snead's finishing thirty-six holes resulted in a third-round 65 and a fourth-round 68 that left him tied with Hogan's 1946 score as the event record. More important, he held the lead to finish two shots ahead of Demaret to collect the $2,000 winner's purse. Metz's 67-70 relegated him to third place with a 269. The finish marked Snead's first Tour individual victory since the Miami tournament that ended the 1946 season. He was photographed afterward sipping some hot chocolate and was asked if the cold hindered his play. Snead pointed to the scoreboard and said, "I was praying for a blizzard."

In June 1948, Charles and Betty Nelson arrived home in Denton after enjoying a dinner only a few miles to the west in the small town of Ponder with a couple of friends, Sidney Burke and Julia Mudd, to celebrate Betty's twenty-second birthday. Overnight, Charles became sick and vomited. But since he felt relatively fine the next morning, he headed off to classes as usual and later that day reported to his job at a brickyard as well. About two weeks later, he began to feel a sharp pain in the upper portion of his right hip. The discomfort not only didn't go away, it started to increase in severity. It reached the point that he didn't feel he could walk home, and his boss drove him instead. Walking at anytime became increasingly difficult by the end of July. But there was a night when the pain in his hip was so excruciating that he preferred the pain that came from walking to the pain that he endured while laying in bed.

That evening, after taking prescribed codeine aspirin to get some rest, Nelson couldn't relieve himself in the bathroom. His doctor's office was closed for the day, so he went to the college infirmary. The nurse on duty reported that Nelson wouldn't be able to see a doctor until the following morning. He stayed the night, left to simply endure the pain. When the infirmary doctor came to see him the next morning, Nelson tried to get out of bed only to discover that his legs wouldn't support him. The doctor catheterized his bladder, but it appeared Nelson was paralyzed from the waist down. The nurse telephoned Betty to say Charles was being transferred to Parkland Hospital near downtown Dallas. There, he was given a spinal tap and diagnosed with polio. Since he was a military veteran, he was sent on to Lisbon Veterans Hospital in southern Dallas.

Because polio was considered an infectious condition, Nelson was given a private room though not quarantined. He often felt too sick to sleep and finally began to see some improvement after about a week when he could urinate without the aid of the catheter. For a brief time, the paralysis spread to his right arm and also affected his breathing. He learned later that the medical staff was about ready to put him in an iron lung assisted breathing machine. His appetite eventually returned, starting with a breakfast of Rice Krispies. Two weeks into his stay at Lisbon, he was moved into a semiprivate room with a 75-year-old veteran of the Spanish-American War. Nelson would remain at Lisbon for six months, spending much of the remaining time working with a physical therapist who taught him what life was going to be like without the use of his legs.

That same month, only weeks after Hogan doubled his career total of major championships at St. Louis' Norwood Hills Country Club by winning his second P.G.A. Championship, Hogan again focused on the elusive prize of an official U.S. Open title. The site was Los Angeles' Riviera Country Club, a venue that was fast becoming his personal playground and his second golfing home behind Colonial Country Club. His L.A. Open career record included a tie for third place in 1941, a victory in 1942, a runner-up finish after the war in 1945 and two more triumphs in 1947 and 1948. How convenient for Hogan with the National Open coming to the Pacific Palisades course five months after he recorded his third "regular season" victory there. His best official Open finish to date was a tie for third place in 1941 when the Open came to him, at Colonial. There was also his victory at the 1942 Hale America Open, staged at Chicago's Ridgemoor Country Club as the substitute for the U.S. Open during the first year of the four-year span in which the major tournament was suspended because of World War II.

Hogan needed little time to reacquaint himself with the layout. His first-round score on Thursday of 4-under-par 67, bursting out of the gate with a 4-under 31 on the front nine, equaled the best score recorded in the first round of National Open competition. He might have shaved another stroke with the aid of rules that were adopted more than a decade later; he settled for a par 3 on the fourteenth hole when his mud-caked ball died short of a hole when putting for a birdie. The 67, though, only left him tied for the lead with Lew Worsham. Hogan followed with a 1-over 72 on Friday, bogeying the eighteenth by missing a 10-foot putt, putting him in second place one stroke off the lead. That belonged to Sam Snead, whose consecutive rounds of 2-under 69 provided him a 138 for an Open record through thirty-six holes.

Snead's record of snake bitten results at the U.S. Open continued when he faded during Saturday's closing thirty-six holes. Despite starting morning play with an eagle and a birdie, he shot a 2-over 73 followed by a 1-over 72. Meanwhile, Demaret – two shots behind Hogan when the day began – surged into the lead on the heels of a third-round 3-under 68. When he added a 69 in the afternoon, his four-round total of 6-under 278 broke the four-round U.S. Open record by three shots. But Hogan was still out on the course following his own morning 68. He again matched Demaret in the fourth round with a 69. For a course toughened to testy National Open standards, Hogan shot an 8-under 276 that nearly equaled the 275 that won the Los Angeles Open there in January. Before the ink was figuratively dry on Demaret's U.S. Open scoring mark, it was erased by Hogan by two strokes. "Sunny Jim" noted in awe that Riviera should be called "Hogan's Alley." And Bantam Ben was hardly about to let up. The U.S. Open title won at Riviera would be the first of six consecutive victories in events in which Hogan participated, a streak second only to Nelson's eleven of 1945. In the five tournaments that Hogan played in before the U.S. Open, he collected one win, two runner-ups finishes and two thirds. He finished the year with thirteen wins, again second to a Nelson record – the eighteen of 1945.

20

ULTIMATE TEST

AFTER LLOYD MANGRUM christened the 1949 P.G.A. Tour season with a victory at the Los Angeles Open, Ben Hogan and Jimmy Demaret did their best to turn the rest of the month's schedule into a match race. Hogan won the Bing Crosby Pro-Am. Then they finished in a tie at Long Beach with Hogan taking the playoff 67 to 69. On to Phoenix and another playoff between them, won this time by Demaret 67-70. There was no reason to believe things would be any different at the Tour's next stop, the Tucson Open, except that Hogan was headed back to Texas for a break before resuming play in San Antonio following a week's break.

If the Hogan-Demaret heroics weren't enough to gain the attention of golf fans across the country, Hogan was the cover story of the January 10, 1949 edition of *Time* magazine. The cover display offered the advice on which he based his career: "If you can't outplay them, outwork them." The extensive profile was written by Marshall Smith, who gave Hogan a taste of his own medicine while interviewing him. When Hogan was made aware of something that would be in the story that he wasn't enthusiastic about, he confronted Smith: "You're not going to say *that* in your story." To which the writer replied, "Look. Your game is golf. This story is my business. Let me handle it my way."

As January gave way to February, post-war tensions between the United States and the Soviet Union reached a new milepost. Soviet Premier Josef Stalin had offered President Harry S. Truman the opportunity to engage in disarmament talks – but only at a location behind the Iron Curtain because of his health. The administration recoiled; the new Secretary of State, Dean Acheson, replied in a news conference that the United States wasn't interested in such a summit. Stalin, Acheson said while referring to voluminous notes, had previously rejected invitations from the Americans to meet in Washington. Plus, Acheson added, such talks would involve many other countries and shouldn't be confined to simply the two well-armed superpowers.

Everything was going Hogan's way until the Greyhound bus coming at him in far west Texas knocked his Cadillac off the road, nearly killing him and his wife. Hogan skipped the Tucson tournament and left Phoenix on Tuesday, February 1 bound for Fort Worth, where that night "Jug" McSpaden was giving a golfing lecture at TCU's auditorium. The Hogans nearly covered half the distance in driving about seventy-five miles beyond El Paso. They reached the small town of Van Horn and called it a day, stopping at the El Capitan Motel. The following morning was frigidly cold across much of the Lone Star State, with snow covering parts of Waco and Austin. In Fort Worth, Oscar the Groundhog saw his shadow. Out in far west Texas, there was early morning fog and at least a slight glaze of ice on U.S. Highway 80, the main route between El Paso and Dallas-Fort Worth. The Hogans were back on the road at eight looking at almost another full day's drive before arriving home. They had not gone far when Hogan told his wife, "I think we've got a flat tire." He pulled off the two-lane road, determined there was nothing wrong with the tires, and continued driving. Having noticed ice on the road for the first time that morning, he told Valerie that he'd drive slightly slower.

Only a few minutes after the Hogans were rolling again, the glow of headlights – right in front of their Cadillac – came seeping through the fog. It was a bus in their lane, the driver in the midst of passing a truck. The driver, Alvin Logan, had spent about six miles behind the truck and decided this stretch of winding, dipping road was suitable for trying to make the pass. As the Cadillac and Greyhound bore down on each other, the Hogans were crossing over a culvert with a concrete barrier that prevented Hogan from swerving to the right. Valerie screamed, "Honey, he's going to hit us!" Hogan instinctively threw himself over his wife's lap to shield her from the impending collision. Had he remained in the driver's seat, the impact of the steering column being thrust back into him surely would have killed him. The car was knocked well off the road and into the ditch. Hogan was concerned the Cadillac would catch fire and yelled for Valerie to get out of the car. As they both managed to escape the vehicle, passersby began to come to their aid. With people frantically concerned for the Hogans' welfare, it somehow took about an hour for someone to summon an ambulance. Hogan tried to assure people that he was fine, though it was already obvious that he'd suffered at the very least a broken ankle and an injured left leg. While they were waiting to make the trip to the Hotel Dieu Hospital back in El Paso, Hogan kept asking about his golf clubs, which were in the trunk of the Cadillac. Valerie asked police on the scene to please get the clubs and send them along with them. It turned out Hogan had sustained a double fracture of the pelvis, a fractured collar bone and a chipped rib in addition to the leg and foot issues. As for Valerie, her injuries were limited to some bruises and a black eye thanks to her husband's quick thinking.

Hogan initially recovered at an encouraging pace in El Paso. Royal Hogan, who rushed there upon hearing the news, indicated to hometown reporters that his brother would be transferred home within a matter of days. But the timetable soon changed when Hogan suffered a significant setback; blood clots worked their way from his injured left leg into his lungs. For the first time since the initial aftermath of the crash, there was legitimate concern for Hogan's life. A specialist in vascular surgery was contacted in New Orleans, but he couldn't immediately get a seat on a commercial plane bound for El Paso because of the ongoing Mardi Gras celebration. Valerie then recalled one of the visitors in Hogan's first days in the hospital was a brigadier general stationed nearby. She contacted him at midnight and, with his help, a plane was sent to bring Dr. Alton Ochsner to Hotel Dieu. The operation was a success, but Hogan remained hospitalized in El Paso for two months and never fully recovered from the leg injuries. They would require daily attention – massages, baths and extensive leg wrappings – for years to come. The Hogans were overwhelmed with well-wishers and expressions of people's concern for Ben while in El Paso. Valerie told the *Fort Worth Star-Telegram* the episode had made her husband realize how much people cared for him.

By the time the Hogans rode a train to Fort Worth in early April, no one was possibly considering Hogan would play P.G.A. Tour golf again – except for Hogan himself. Maybe he doubted he could do it or maybe he was building his own target for motivation when he told reporters, "Don't waste your time writing about me. People are tired of hearing about Ben Hogan. They're interested in the guys who are playing now. It won't be long until they forget all about me." His return to golf came as captain of the United States' 1949 Ryder Cup team, which retained the trophy with a 7-to-5 victory at the Ganton Golf Club in Scarborough, England. By that autumn, he was prepared to take steps to return to the game. In early November, he was on the practice range at Colonial. About a month later, Hogan played his first round of golf, with the aid of a cart, since the playoff in Phoenix about eleven months earlier. News of the Saturday afternoon jaunt around Colonial on a chilly, cloudy day appeared in the next day's *Star-Telegram* without a writer's byline and beneath a headline that began with the word FLASH! "I didn't hit them very well," Hogan allowed. His playing partner, Ridglea pro Raymond Gafford, offered that Hogan hit them "well enough." That following day's *Press* noted Hogan played another eighteen holes at Colonial that Sunday, shot 71 and 72 for the weekend and complained of being "a little tired."

His next step – literally – was to complete a round while walking, which he did a week later. His goal was to enter the first event of the 1950 season,

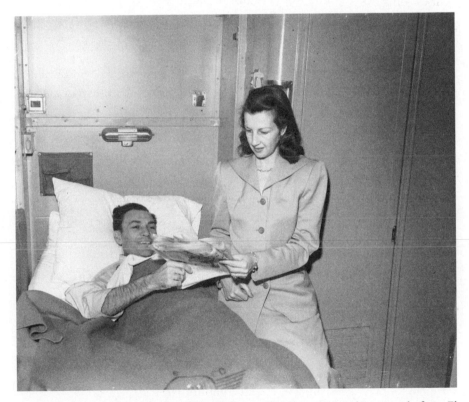

Ben and Valerie Hogan look through mail from well-wishers during the train ride from El Paso to Fort Worth almost two months after the horrific car-bus collision of February 2, 1949. (Courtesy, *Fort Worth Star-Telegram* Collection, Special Collections, The University of Texas at Arlington Library, Arlington, Texas)

the $15,000 Los Angeles Open scheduled for Friday through Monday, January 6–9. About the same time that Hogan was first playing eighteen holes without a cart, representatives of the L.A. event asked him if he could come out to the tournament and serve as the honorary starter. A few days later, the Hogans were on a train headed to California. He piqued the interest of reporters at the station in Fort Worth by indicating he was interested in actually playing at Riviera Country Club, where he won the 1948 National Open. At least one Hogan fan was certain he would return to tournament play – Alton Ochsner, the surgeon who saved his life. "Ben has the kind of determination that leaves no doubt as to the ultimate outcome," Ochsner was quoted in the *Star-Telegram* during the Los Angeles tournament. "Doctors not infrequently recognize this will in patients, but in few people has it ever been more evident than in Hogan."

Oh, Hogan indeed played; his performance at the 1950 Los Angeles Open would have been the story of the year on the Tour were it not for his later heroics on a grander stage. The four practice rounds that he played totaled three shots less than Mangrum's winning score a year earlier, though he brought along a chair for resting between holes. "It's all a question of my legs," he said after a practice round. "They've been tiring in the latter parts of rounds." Among those who played practice rounds with Hogan was Cary Middlecoff, the defending U.S. Open champion. "He pinned our ears back," reported Middlecoff, the former dentist who gave up his practice to play professional golf. At one point, Hogan told his playing partners that his legs hurt like hell and then deposited his next shot twenty feet from the pin.

Hogan opened with a 2-over-par 73 that left him five shots behind leader Ed Furgol. As per his fears, his play withered along with his legs on the back nine. Hogan also appeared unusually distracted by things that previously didn't affect him, like noises from a construction crew working on a home site above the seventh green. But he then incredibly fired off three consecutive rounds of

69 on Saturday, Monday, and Tuesday (with Sunday's play rained out) and no longer seemed impacted by potential agitations such as an amateur photographer facing down his putting line. Hogan tied for first place at 4-under 280 with Sam Snead, who required a 15-foot birdie putt on his seventy-second hole to force the playoff. An exhausted Hogan obviously didn't welcome the prospect of another grueling eighteen holes. "I'm awfully tired," he told reporters. "I wish I didn't have to play tomorrow."

Hogan didn't have to play tomorrow. More rain washed out the Wednesday playoff and, with the popular Bing Crosby Pro-Am scheduled to start up the coast on Friday, the decision was made to re-schedule the L.A. playoff until *after* the Crosby event. Hogan played at the three-round Pebble Beach tournament, where he was the defending champion. He didn't experience the same success that he enjoyed at Riviera. His best round there was "only" a par-72 – still remarkable given what had happened to him in the previous year – and finished in a tie for nineteenth place. Byron Nelson, playing in a Tour event for the first time since the previous May, shot 4-over 148 for two rounds and withdrew.

Snead was among four players who tied for first at the Crosby – missing an eight-foot putt that would have claimed the championship – and tournament officials didn't bother with a playoff; all four were declared winners. Hogan was glad to be leaving chilly northern California, but the forecast on Monday called for showers in Los Angeles on Wednesday. The rain held off, but the combatants were greeted at Riviera by low fog. The proceedings began with a dismal omen for Hogan when his initial tee shot went hooking out of bounds. Snead led by two shots after two holes and maintained that edge through the front nine. He did the same coming home, holding even par while Hogan shot 2-over to win 72 to 76. "I was lousy," Hogan growled afterward. Snead countered: "He was terrific. He's the same old Hogan. He scares you to death."

There was an awkward episode on no. 13 when Snead became impatient with the amount of time that Hogan was taking on putts and walked off the green while Hogan was putting. Years later, Snead told the *Los Angeles Times* that he thought Hogan purposely took that much time, trying to drain his opponent's momentum. For those in Dallas-Fort Worth who wished to watch a delayed telecast of the playoff, WBAP-TV provided that opportunity the following Sunday night – sponsored by Royal Hogan's office supply store.

Hogan skipped the Long Beach tournament but played in Phoenix, where organizers renamed the 1950 event the Ben Hogan Open; following a first-round 65, he faded and finished in a tie for twentieth place. Hogan didn't make another start for almost two months, appearing in the non-Tour Seminole Pro-Am in Palm Beach, Florida in mid-March. He was working out of a hole opening with a 79 and could manage only a tie for twenty-fourth place. Then it was on to a triumphant return to Augusta. Incredibly, Hogan stood only two shots out of the lead heading to the final round. But he closed with a 4-over 76 leaving him in fourth place, five shots behind three-time Masters winner Demaret.

If there was any animosity between Hogan and Snead given the events of the Los Angeles Open, it didn't prevent Hogan from showing up for Snead's Greenbriar Open a few weeks later. The event featured only twenty-five players, and Hogan shot a 21-under 259 to beat the host pro by ten shots. Hogan's plan had been to follow the West Virginia stop with a trip to the Western Open, but he decided against that. Next up would be another emotional experience – as if any appearance at this stage wouldn't be – returning to Marvin Leonard's course. It appeared the Colonial National Invitational Tournament couldn't be played without Bantam Ben; the 1949 event that was scheduled while Hogan was convalescing was cancelled because of flooding. At Hogan's homecoming in May 1950, Snead gained a measure of revenge by winning on Hogan's home layout. Hogan was hardly a disappointment, though, placing third. The following day, he caught a train for Philadelphia to play in two weeks in the U.S. Open at Merion Golf Club, where he would be required to play thirty-six holes in a single day for the first time in his return.

In the days leading up to the National Open, Snead acknowledged to the *Richmond News Leader* that Hogan was on his mind – either that or he was writing another chapter of gamesmanship. "The man who wins it will have to beat me," Snead said. "I'm not playing sensationally, but I'm playing well. I actually think Hogan is the man who might make some trouble. He's the man I've got to beat." During Hogan's practice rounds at Merion, he made the decision to replace his usual 7-iron with a 1-iron after determining there were no 7-iron shots on the historic East Course. Like it was at Riviera, the issue of Hogan's durability seemed to be the most popular topic of pre-tournament repartee. Gene Sarazen, the 1934 Open winner, was forthright if not polite in his assessment: "If they were going to play it without walking – just hitting the shots – I would pick Ben without hesitation. But, unfortunately, he will have to walk."

For at least a day, events pushed the story of the historic Hogan comeback to the back pages. Lee Mackey Jr., a 26-year-old from Birmingham, Alabama with no professional wins, broke both the course record and the National Open one-round mark in Thursday's first round by one-putting ten holes and firing a 6-under-par 64. Hogan opened with a 2-over-par 72, recovering from a rickety start shooting 39 on the front nine. When reporters sought an explanation from Mackey for his implausible taming of Merion, he replied, "I guess I just got lucky." Alas, he failed to pack luck into his bag the next day; he stumbled through an 11-over 81 that took him out of contention. Hogan's second-day score of 1-under 69 was shot with a mid-morning tee time that enabled him to miss the most scorching portion of a Philadelphia day that reached a humid 95 degrees, though he did experience some cramping at the no. 12 hole. His overall 1-over 141 placed him only two shots behind leader "Dutch" Harrison in fifth place.

For Saturday's 36-hole finale viewed by a National Open record 12,500 spectators, Hogan was paired with Middlecoff going off at 9:30 a.m. and 2 p.m. As would be the case for the rest of Hogan's career, early starting times were problematic because the hours of preparation required for getting his legs ready for competition. He completed the morning round in 2-over 72, putting him two behind Mangrum and one behind Harrison. On the twelfth hole of the afternoon round, owning a three-stroke advantage, Hogan suffered through more than cramping this time around; he grimaced after striking his tee shot and began to stagger, grabbing onto a friend to prevent himself from falling and went on to bogey the hole. Years later, Hogan told the *Star-Telegram* that his legs had turned to stone and he wasn't certain he could finish. For the balance of the round, Hogan's putts were extracted from the cups by either his caddie or Middlecoff's. And then after playing the thirteenth, according to separate interviews that Hogan gave years later, the pain was so great he was resigned to the fact that he couldn't finish – only to have his caddie insist on meeting him at the no. 14 tee box.

Suffering bogeys on nos. 15 and 17 because of putting issues, Hogan trudged to the par-4, 458-yard eighteenth having lost a three-shot lead over six holes. He needed a par to force a three-way playoff with Mangrum and George Fazio, the latter a hometown boy whose two Tour triumphs consisted of the 1946 Canadian Open and the '47 Crosby. After a tee shot that nestled in the middle of the fairway more than 200 yards from the pin, he called upon the 1-iron that he'd subbed into his bag just before play began. His approach, captured in the renowned photograph shot by Hy Peskin for *Life*, carried the treacherous rough lurking right of the fairway and in front of the green and landed just short of the green but carried up onto the putting surface about forty feet from the flag stick. His first putt rolled four feet past the hole; he quickly struck the return putt to earn his par for the hole – a 4-over 74 for the round – and another day's play. (Hogan told long-time golf writer Charles Price that he struck the putt hastily because his legs hurt so much he was eager to end the round and get off his feet. On the way back to his hotel afterward, Hogan became sick to his stomach.) In the chaos of excitement in the aftermath of the drama, the club that Hogan used to reach the eighteenth green – years later, debate raged over whether it was his 1-iron or 2-iron – was absconded from his golf bag. If it *wasn't* the 1-iron, the granite marker placed in the fairway to honor the achievement is in error.

Valerie Hogan feared her husband couldn't endure another eighteen holes that Sunday. Wasn't she pleasantly surprised, as she recalled for Dave Anderson, when Ben awoke that morning and exclaimed, "Isn't it a nice day?" In the lobby of the Barclay Hotel, reporters diligently checked on Hogan's condition – and some all but rooted him on as he and Valerie left for the 30-minute drive to Merion. Hogan's day would ordinarily have started much earlier with a morning tee time for the playoff, but state blue laws prohibited starting before 1 p.m. In the three-way battle, Hogan took his first lead on the par-4 seventh when his approach landed only four feet from the pin and he converted the birdie putt. He gave back the stroke with a bogey on the eighth hole, and Hogan and Mangrum stood even following nine holes. Hogan was back on top through twelve holes, his even-par round providing him a one-shot lead over both of his competitors. When Fazio and Mangrum each bogeyed the par-4 fourteenth, Hogan enjoyed a two-stroke cushion with four holes to play. Mangrum managed to birdie no. 15 to get back within one.

Then came the infamous turn of events at no. 16. With Mangrum preparing to putt, he unwittingly committed a rules violation when he addressed his ball, then picked it up to blow a bug off it. He was assessed a two-stroke penalty; prior to 1960, U.S.G.A. rules allowed players to mark and pick up their ball on the green only when the ball interfered with another player.

Mangrum later stated he was initially unaware of the ruling, thinking he'd putted for a par. It was only in the tee area on no. 17 that U.S.G.A. official Ike Grainger explained to him what happened. Hogan was ahead by three shots with two holes to play but played like a man needing to shoot a birdie. Which he did on no. 17, thanks to a 50-foot uphill putt. On no. 18, missing the club that he used for his second shot on Saturday afternoon, Hogan played a 5-iron – and sent the ball over the green. His chip back came to rest seven feet from the cup, and a one-putt gave him a 1-under 69 to Mangrum's 73 and Fazio's 75. The crowd around the green was prepared to hoist the victorious Hogan on their shoulders but was halted by the local constabulary. Hogan admitted to reporters that winning the 1950 Open topped even his first Open victory in Los Angeles two years earlier: "This was my biggest thrill. And I'm awfully glad that those two strokes Lloyd lost on the sixteenth green penalty didn't make the difference." One of the wags later mentioned something about retirement. "Retire?" Hogan replied with a laugh. "I love golf, and I'll never quit it competitively."

And it was something of a big weekend as well back at Glen Garden. The 22nd annual match play Men's West Texas Golf Tournament was held there, with Royal Hogan in the field. Defending champion Bob French of Odessa, Texas reached the 36-hole final with a victory over Glen Garden regular Doug Higgins in the semifinals to meet another Glen Garden golfer, Claude Blackwell. French eased past Blackwell 7-and-5 to become only the fourth golfer to win multiple titles in the event.

21

UNPARALLELED ENCORE

THE 400 GUESTS who crowded into the Crystal Ballroom on the eighteenth and top floor of Dallas' Baker Hotel on June 9, 1952, rose in unison as baseball immortal Tris Speaker (who made the game-winning hit for the Red Sox in Fenway Park's inaugural game the year Hogan and Nelson were born) greeted the center of the evening's attention. The 63-year-old Speaker said, "Ben, the competition is great. There are many sports figures in Texas who belong in the Hall of Fame, but you are a fighter. You've won this one as you have won many others you richly deserve." Ben Hogan accepted his inclusion into the Texas Sports Hall of Fame's second induction class – and the accompanying adulation of the ballroom throng – only three days before he would head a few miles to north Dallas' Northwood Country Club and attempt to repeat as U.S. Open champion and claim his fourth title in the prestigious event. Hogan and the late Joe Routt (a two-time All-American lineman for Texas A&M in the 1930s who was killed in the Battle of the Bulge during World War II) were the '52 entrants to join the one-man class that established the Texas Sports Hall of Fame the previous year – none other than Speaker, a native of the central Texas town of Hubbard. (Byron Nelson's induction came in 1955, nine years after his voluntary withdrawal.) Hogan's résumé to that point included six official major championships plus participation in Ryder Cup winning teams in 1947, 1949, and 1951.) "This is something I never dreamed of happening," Hogan told the audience. He thanked wife Valerie and repeated the story from his lean years, when she innocently advised him to hit his second shots closer to the holes. Hogan called his induction the "greatest achievement or honor I've ever received."

Byron Nelson [seated far left] and Ben Hogan [seated far right] were among the Glen Garden figures who honored club president Tom J. "Coke" Brown at a dinner in the clubhouse on May 30, 1949. (Courtesy, *Fort Worth Star-Telegram* Collection, Special Collections, The University of Texas at Arlington Library, Arlington, Texas)

Hogan had actually already been out at the 6,764-yard, par-70 layout that would play host to the fifty-second National Open. At the course over the weekend, he complained of a crick in his neck caused by the air-conditioning in the club's dining room. He assured he'd be ready for Thursday's opening eighteen holes, which would be followed by another eighteen on Friday and the final thirty-six on Saturday. Nelson had not played in a U.S. Open since his Tour departure in 1946 – he played annually at the Masters through his final year of competition, 1966, and spent the week at Northwood dictating columns to the *Dallas Times Herald*. Nelson didn't hazard a predicted winner but narrowed his choices to Hogan and Lloyd Mangrum. He played North-wood the previous weekend "and I can vouch for the fact that this course will be a fine test of golf," he said. Later in the week, Nelson waved toward the tree-lined layout and told *Fort Worth Star-Telegram* golf writer Gene Gregston, "Here, a bad shot can bring more trouble than it would at Colonial." During Tuesday's practice round, the U.S.G.A. appeased pros who complained that the 435-yard, par-4 sixth hole was unfair with a tree perched directly in the path of any good tee shot; the tree was cut down. Nelson wrote the greens would be made firmer than usual. "If they were soft, a big field such as the Open provides [162 players] would trample the soft greens to the point that they would be uneven and a disadvantage to the late starters the first day."

Northwood was only in its sixth year, the first country club course built in Dallas since the 1920s. Postwar Dallas contained more young men interested in playing golf than could be accommodated by the city's existing clubs. One of those clubs was Brook Hollow, home to the Dallas Open in September 1946. A regular Brook Hollow tennis foursome of Estill Heyser, Billy Moore, John Pace, and Hugh Prather decided to do more than simply rant. They put together a group of businessmen who formed Northwood Club in August '46 and eventually bought 160 acres of land in north Dallas (then a remote area, now just north of the bustling LBJ Freeway). To finance the acquisition, the club's founders followed the lead of clubs like Lakewood and installed slot machines. And they also endorsed the sale of lifetime club memberships. One of those life memberships was sold to the father of Jack Munger. Jack was a skilled player, had played in several national events and once reached the quarterfinals of the U.S. Amateur. He also served on some U.S.G.A. committees and was acquainted with people who made decisions like where the U.S. Open would be held annually. Munger proved to be the one-man lobbying group that convinced the U.S.G.A. to stage the 1952 Open at Northwood – by guaranteeing a minimum payment of $25,000, an increase of $10,000 over Colonial's offer that landed the '41 Open – to the national body.

Northwood's par-70 layout for the National Open covered 6,764 yards. Its most striking hole was the 210-yard, par-3 sixteenth that featured a fairway basically tunneling through trees and lined on the left by White Rock Creek. The course was designed by noted Indiana golf course architect Bill Diddel, who lettered at Wabash College in baseball, football, basketball, and track (the school had no golf program) and went on to win multiple Indiana Amateur titles. Diddel designed more than 300 courses, Northwood being his only project in Texas.

Hogan came to Dallas for what would be his final Tour appearance of the year. In 1951, he cut back his schedule drastically to play only the Masters (he won), Colonial (tied for fourth), the U.S. Open at Oakland Hills near Detroit (won again), and the World Championship of Golf (won yet again). For 1952, he would play only the Masters (tied for seventh), Colonial (won for the third time in six appearances) and at Northwood. He arrived with the Open practically on a string, his personal property, having scored back-to-back victories beginning with the emotional triumph at Merion in 1950 in his comeback season followed by his taming of "The Monster" at Oakland Hills. Since he won the 1948 Open at Riviera and missed the '49 event at Medinah following the terrible car crash that February, he came to Dallas having won in each of his previous three appearances at the National Open. He was officially seeking a fourth title that would make him the third man to do so, joining Willie Anderson and Bobby Jones. For those who count the 1942 Hale America as that year's surrogate Open, Hogan was seeking to become the first golfer to win the tournament five times.

"It's not as tough a course as Oakland Hills last year, but it is far from easy," Hogan told reporters on the Monday before play. "I think 283 or 284 will win. I figure I am playing as well as at the same stage a year ago, but for some reason I'm not getting near the hole with my approaches. I can't explain it." He played Northwood four times the previous week, reporting his best result to be a 1-over-par 71. Sam Snead, longtime bridesmaid at the National Open, stole some thunder during Tuesday's practice by scorching Northwood with a 6-under 64. That day, Hogan said he "just fooled around" and revealed no score. He didn't play another round on Wednesday, instead beginning his day playing at Dallas' Brook Hollow Country Club and returning to Northwood for only four holes and some time on the putting green.

On the opening Thursday, Hogan began play at 9:36 a.m. teamed with Lew Worsham and Charles Gocsis. For all of his U.S. Open heroics to date, Hogan had never finished the first or second rounds of a National Open in the lead. That appeared to change when he rallied from two bogeys on the first six holes to card a 1-under 69 in temperatures that reached into the mid-90s with winds whipping at 20-25 miles per hour when he headed for the clubhouse in the early afternoon. He was stopped by an ever-vigilant clubhouse guard who forced Hogan to present his player pass before being allowed entry; and to avoid what he considered the dining room's unreasonable air-conditioning, Hogan took his lunch into the locker room and ate while straddling a bench.

But the first-round leader came in later in the day. It was Al Brosch, a 40-year-old whose claim to fame was being the first player on Tour to shoot a round of 60 (at the 1951 Texas Open). Brosch fired a 2-under 68 for a one-stroke advantage and joined Hogan as the only players to break par.

Hogan recorded another 69 on a sweltering Friday following a mid-afternoon tee time, bolstered by birdies on two of the first three holes, to claim his first midpoint Open advantage, a 2-under 138. (At Oakland Hills in 1951, Hogan trailed by five after two rounds.) Second place belonged to George Fazio at even-par 140, Brosch having plummeted to a 7-over 147 with a second-round 79. Hogan, one of three golfers to break par on Friday, was on pace to equal the Open scoring record of 276 that he set at Riviera. He professed little appreciation for his lead, his pace or the fact that his 36-hole score also equaled the Open record set by Snead in 1948: "They don't give any prizes for that." He expressed appreciation that his putting was better than he'd expected and admitted to being "tired as I can be."

The *Star-Telegram*'s Gregston stated Hogan wouldn't be caught Saturday, "which is nothing new." Bill Rives of *The Dallas Morning News* pretty much equated the two-shot cushion to ten: "He dominates the field like a colossus and appears to be a cinch to win." That same opinion apparently was shared by a woman who asked Hogan to autograph a cap for her son back in West Virginia shortly after his round. "I'm leaving tonight," she said, "and I know you'll win and he'll want to have your autograph." Hogan complied and replied, "Let's just leave it as it is." Veteran golf writer Oscar Fraley of United Press International left no plaudit unturned: "Little Ben Hogan is already regarded as one of golf's immortals, but he'll stake a solid claim to the title of all-time greatest if he manages to win the U.S. Open a fourth consecutive time. Even those who hold out for Bobby Jones admit that a win for Hogan would surpass Jones' more spectacular grand slam because competition is far tougher today."

Local "scribe" Byron Nelson stated he felt sorry for Hogan, that he was in the roughest place a golfer can be – leading the U.S. Open going into the 36-hole final day. But he also tempered that warning: "Hogan will be affected by the terrific pressure . . . but not as much as any other golfer in the world would be." Fifty-three players advanced to Saturday's play with a cutline of 11-over 151; that's right where Dallas' Raymond Gafford, Northwood's pro, found himself following rounds of 77 and 74. "Normally, Ray can play his home course in about even par," Nelson wrote in the *Times Herald*. "Ray was the first-day leader at the Masters this year, and he led the field in the Colonial Invitational in Fort Worth for three rounds. So he isn't exactly what you would call a novice."

Hogan drew the fifteenth pairing among the twenty-four for Saturday's play, starting the third round at 9:30 a.m. and the fourth at 2:06 p.m., joined by "Porky" Oliver (tied for fifth place at 3-over 143). As temperatures headed toward the upper 90s, his game suddenly abandoned him during Saturday's morning round. He struggled through to a 4-over 74 while Julius Boros, who began the day four shots off the pace in fourth place, surged to the lead on the strength of a 2-under 68. Hogan, trailing by two at 2-over 212, couldn't regain his touch during afternoon play. His greens play went sour, three-putting three times on the first eleven holes, and another 74 left him at 6-over 286 in third place behind Boros (281) and Oliver (285). Northwood allowed only seven total sub-par rounds over the four rounds, and Hogan was the only player to break par twice. The tournament essentially got away from him on the 408-yard, par-4 fifteenth hole on Saturday afternoon, trailing Boros by four shots with four holes remaining. Hogan bogeyed no. 15; behind him, Boros birdied the 485-yard, par-5 fourteenth.

After Hogan closed his seventy-second hole with a par-4, he received a standing ovation. Pleased with his putting through two rounds, he identified the greens as an object of his scorn in the locker room: "This is like trying to play around an ice rink. You just hit and hope." But Hogan also offered praise to the victor, equating Boros to the Sunday funnies character Mandrake the Magician: "Any man that can play around here in 281 must be a magician. It's not with pleasure that I relinquish the Open championship to Julius Boros, but I will have to say that it couldn't have happened to a nicer follow." He later thanked Northwood's host committee: "They made the golf course too tough for me but made it up by many acts of kindness." The *Star-Telegram's* Lorin McMullen sought a silver lining in Hogan's Saturday travails: "The 'loss' may prove a good thing for Hogan in one way. He may live longer. So long as he was on top, Ben, knowing no other way, kept himself at fiddle-string tightness in an effort to stay there. Now that the string is broken, perhaps he'll relax."

What laid just ahead for Hogan, who turned forty in August 1952, was golf's greatest season in 1953. He won his second Masters with a 14-under-par 274 that erased the tournament's previous 72-hole mark by five strokes. A 5-under-par 139 at the midpoint provided only a one-shot lead over Bob Hamilton. Hogan's game then went into overdrive with a 6-under 66 that gave him a four-stroke cushion over Oliver going into Sunday. Oliver gamely supplied a modicum of competition for Hogan during the final round by shooting a 2-under 70. Hogan, though, wasn't to be caught, wasn't to suffer any seventy-second hole calamities. He responded with a 3-under 69. The first person to congratulate him after his final putt was his final-round playing partner, Nelson. Hogan soon after won his fourth official U.S. Open, at Oakmont near Pittsburgh. Just to get to the four-round tournament proper, players that year had to endure two qualifying rounds at Oakmont and Pittsburgh Field Club. Hogan was fighting pain in his back and beat the qualifying score of 156 by only six shots. Once medal play began, he was immediately in command by grabbing the lead in the opening round with a 5-under 67 and never letting go.

With a total of 5-under 283, Hogan became the first golfer since 1921 to lead all four rounds of the National Open.

And that was all topped by his magical victory at Carnoustie in his only venture to the British Open. He climbed out of a three-shot deficit following the first round and improved each day. The sequence was 73-71-70-68 for a 6-under 282 and a four-shot winning margin for the small, laconic Yank whom the Scots immediately adored and affectionately labeled "the wee ice mon." "I do not play to break records," Hogan later told Gregston of the *Star-Telegram*. "I play to win, and I think the Lord has let me win for a purpose. I hope that purpose is to give courage to those people who are sick or injured and broken in body." Hogan's glorious achievement nearly fell into the crosshairs of what would have been one of the most bizarre incidents in big-time golf. On the tenth hole of the final round, he struck his driver as a large dog pranced across the fairway about ten feet in front of the tee box. The ball sailed over the dog by only a few inches.

Playing for the year's grand slam was impossible because the P.G.A. Championship overlapped with the British Open's total time period of play and round-trip travel. The Hogans traveled to France before the voyage back across the Atlantic when Ben was reached by the *Dallas Times Herald*'s Jim Lawson by phone at the Paris Ritz. Hogan answered a few minutes before retiring for the evening, reporting a touch of the flu but reviewing the momentous event. "I felt more pressure in the British Open than any other tournament I have ever entered," Hogan said. "This was because everyone was interested to see if I could win." (One would think there was equally intense interest and curiosity when he teed it up at Riviera in January 1950 in his first appearance following the crash eleven months earlier. All he did then was force a playoff in the Los Angeles Open with Sam Snead and finish second.) "I made the trip to Scotland because many people urged me to do so. Naturally, I got a great deal of satisfaction out of winning, but it was not my biggest golfing thrill. Winning the National Open in 1950 was the big one for me." When Lawson asked what gave him the most trouble, Hogan routinely replied, "I didn't have any trouble." Flu or no flu while in France, Hogan played through a rainstorm a few days later for the benefit of more than 1,000 American and Allied servicemen in an exhibition appearance. He shot a 69 on a course that he'd never seen before. "This is great – except I don't know where I'm going," he confessed. "I just keep shooting."

A few days before Hogan completed his conquest of Carnoustie, Nelson went to sudden death to win the Arkansas Open over amateur Paul Collum at Texarkana Country Club (pocketing $300). Next on his schedule was a pro-junior event in San Antonio in a few days when a reporter for the *Star-Telegram* phoned to get reaction to Hogan's achievement. He was cutting away weeds at his ranch in Roanoke when his father called him to the phone. "I knew what it was when Dad called me to the phone," Nelson said. "No, I don't think it's surprising. In fact, I think it would have been surprising if he hadn't won. ... He's winning everything he tries and breaking all the records while doing it."

The Hogans' return to America began in the New York harbor, and Ben was honored with a ticker tape parade through Manhattan. Ben was saluted by an assemblage of celebrities at Toots Shor's Restaurant, the likes of baseball star Stan Musial, boxing champion Gene Tunney, actor Don Ameche, and golf's own Gene Sarazen and Jimmy Demaret. Back in Texas a few days later, the City of Fort Worth paid tribute to its hero and his wife with Ben and Valerie Hogan Day on Monday, July 27. A testimonial luncheon was held before more than 600 people in the Crystal Ballroom of the hotel that hosted the celebration for General Jonathan Wainwright in 1945, the Hotel Texas. (Another Crystal Ballroom? No coincidence. T.B. Baker built Fort Worth's Hotel Texas, Dallas' Baker Hotel and similar accommodations, primarily across Texas. On the night of November 21, 1963, the Hotel Texas' guest list included President and Mrs. John F. Kennedy.) Among the speakers that day in Fort Worth was the Reverend Granville Walker, pastor of University Christian Church, where the Hogans worshiped. "Ben Hogan has had every reason for quitting more than once," Rev. Walker said. "He has known what it means to fight the dread specter of poverty – to be hungry and still not cease to dream. He has known what it means to enter the lists and lose and then make of the loss an opportunity to re-examine his game, discipline himself once more and try again. He has known what it means to see the things he gave his life to broken … and stoop and build them up with worn tools. Behind the record stands a man who has never known what it means to throw in the sponge."

Another family friend, Colonial member Lacy Boggess, told a story that he cited from 1929 in which Clara Hogan asked Ben why he spent so much time playing golf rather than getting a more formal job like Royal. As Boggess told it, young Ben told his mother, "I intend to become the greatest golfer in the world." (Years later, Hogan denied saying that.) Hogan looked over the ballroom crowd: "I see here men I have caddied with, men I have caddied for, men I've played golf with. Even the barber who cuts my hair is here." He noted he and his wife had enjoyed good times and endured bad times through the years. "But lately it seems that every week or so, something good happens to us," he said. "After this week, I just don't see how anything better could happen." More was about to happen, though, and soon. Hogan started his own business late in 1953, a company that manufactured golf clubs. The Hogan Company became a giant in the industry and was bought by AMF in 1960, though Hogan stayed on as chairman of the board for some time.

The same day that Hogan was honored in Fort Worth following his performance at Carnoustie, Glen Garden pro "Smiley" Rowland reported the largest advance registration in the history of the club's invitational with 110 players. The club remained an attractive local golf destination. In the late 1940s and early '50s, people would come from across Fort Worth to Cobb Park, located just north of Glen Garden, to ride horses, hold family reunions and go bird-watching. The tournament was played a few weeks later, won by city champion Richard Patton, "pushed to the precipice and perspiring" in the words of the *Star-Telegram*'s Gregston. Patton hung onto first place by one stroke by sinking a 25-foot putt to bogey the final hole.

Hogan remained competitive when playing in major championships despite his infrequent appearances in tournament play. Playing the 1954 U.S. Open at Baltusrol as only his second event of the year, he was four shots off the lead going into the final round and finished in a tie for sixth place, seven shots behind winner Ed Furgol. At the 1955 Masters, Hogan placed second to Cary Middlecoff. And the 1955 U.S. Open at Olympic Club's Lake Course found Hogan as the unwitting foil in the Cinderella tale of unknown Jack Fleck rallying from a two-stroke deficit with four holes to play in the fourth round and winning in a playoff.

A few weeks later back home, Hogan came upon the July 8 copy of the *Dublin Progress* weekly. In the paper's tribute to town history, there was a photo of Chester Hogan at work at the bottling plant circa 1905. Hogan crafted a polite letter to the newspaper and requested a glossy reproduction of the photo that was printed in the paper. Albert Jackson of the *Progress* replied that the photo was the property of Dr Pepper Bottling. (Dr. Pepper became Dr Pepper – no period after the abbreviation for Doctor – during the 1950s when a change in the company's advertising typography inadvertently resulted in "Dr." looking like "Di:" and the punctuation was removed.) Jackson was forwarding Hogan's request on to the plant manager, Grace Lyon. About a month later, Lyon mailed a copy of the photo and a letter:

. . . Please find enclosed the glossy print, per your request. We are most happy for you to have this picture. Perhaps you have a vague memory of my father, S.H. Prim, and the bottling plant in Dublin. It is doubtful that you would remember me as Grace Prim, but since my fathers [sic] death, I have carried on the business.

It is with great pride that I can point to the old records, and say how closely we were associated with the now famous Ben Hogan.

Thanking you and hoping the picture is all that you expected, we are
Sincerely,
Dr Pepper Bottling Company
(Mrs) Grace Lyon, Mgr.

To which Hogan replied:

. . . I would like to express my appreciation to you for your time and effort in getting this for me. Incidentally, you failed to advise the expense incurred. Please let me know so I might reimburse you promptly.

I must admit my memory of those days is very vague, but it is always nice to renew old acquaintances!

Thank you again . . . and with all good wishes and kindest personal regards, I am

Sincerely
Ben Hogan

By the 1956 season, the truncated playing schedules of Nelson and Hogan often only intersected in Fort Worth, Augusta and a handful of other Tour stops. But they were together in northern California in March 1956 when they were cajoled by a mutual friend from the area, Eddie Lowery, into playing a four-ball match against promising amateurs Ken Venturi and Harvie Ward at Pebble Beach's Cypress Point. In an extraordinary display of golf skills, the Hogan-Nelson tandem nipped the kids 1-up as both teams sprinted to the finish with birdies on the final four holes. Their individual cards read: Hogan 9-under-par 63, Venturi 65, Nelson and Ward 67 each. It's considered the greatest match play event ever.

When the pros arrived at Augusta National for the twenty-second Masters in April 1958, there was important business to tend to before play began. Club co-founders Bobby Jones and Clifford Roberts escorted Nelson and Hogan back to Amen Corner. There, they introduced the bridge leading to the twelfth green as the Ben Hogan Bridge and the bridge leading from the thirteenth tee area to the fairway as the Byron Nelson Bridge. In particular, Hogan was honored for shooting the course-record 274 in winning the 1953 Masters, Nelson for playing the twelfth and thirteenth holes in five total strokes during the final round of the 1937 tournament to gain six shots on Ralph Guldahl en route to the first of his two Masters triumphs.

In 1958, Hogan took up a new golfing home address – though still with a direct connection with Marvin Leonard. Leonard had sold Colonial Country Club to its membership in 1942 and by the early 1950s was itching to recreate his handiwork with a course and facilities that would even trump what he'd built in southwest Fort Worth. Shady Oaks Country Club was built in the up-scale community of Westover Hills, within Fort Worth only a few miles north-west of downtown with top-notch amenities, and the course wasn't designed for championship competition. The intent was a layout that would present an intriguing challenge without being overwhelming to the weekend player. The quote from Hogan that appears on Shady Oaks' web site states: "Anyone who is building a golf course anywhere in the world and doesn't come down here to see what has been done at Shady Oaks will be making a big mistake."

While Hogan shifted his base of operations away from Colonial, he wrote one more chapter of his personal golfing history there in 1959. At age forty-six, he captured his fifth Colonial National Invitational Tournament championship – his first since the fabled 1953 season – and what would be the final Tour win of his career. Who could have been shocked at him winning after he preceded the tournament by shooting a course-record 63 in a practice round? Hogan continued his hot play with Thursday-Friday rounds of 1-under-par 69 and 3-under 67 that put him in second place among the field of forty-eight entries at 4-under 136, two shots behind Lionel Hebert. The 67 included birdie putts that were long, longer, longest: fifteen feet, twenty feet and twenty-five feet. As he left the scorer's table, he chirped, "I'd sure hate to have to make a living doing this." Nelson, designated as Colonial's ceremonial leadoff hitter starting in 1953 and making his third and final Tour appearance of the season, followed an opening-round 6-over 76 with a 1-under 69 that featured a 31 on the back nine Friday to equal the course record.

Hogan stumbled in the third round with a 7-over 77, his worst round in Colonial National Invitational play, that contained something that had become common in Hogan's later playing years – putting woes that sometimes were extreme. A Sunday 2-over 72 was good enough to tie with Fred Hawkins to force a Monday playoff after Hogan missed a three-foot putt for the win by an inch. "I was completely confident I could sink that putt," he said. "I guess I didn't hit enough club." Here was a playoff matchup between Hogan, three-time owner of the Vardon Trophy, and Hawkins, whose sole Tour victory was the 1956 Oklahoma City Open. But they both played Hogan clubs – and Hawkins got his from the company's owner. Monday brought winds to north Texas that gusted to forty miles per hour. Hogan kept the ball low for the most part, out of the elements. Soon after Hawkins put his tee shot on no. 5 into the river, he was staring up at a three-shot deficit from which he wouldn't escape.

Hogan shot 1-under-par 69 to Hawkins' 3-over 73. "It's been quite a dry spell," Hogan said. "I've had five years of poor putting. But I've gone back to my own stroke instead of fooling around with everyone else's." When it came time for the trophy presentation, a familiar scene was played out as Leonard presented Colonial's championship cup to Hogan for the fifth time. And he got to keep it. "He promised me I could keep it if I won a fifth time. The trophy is mine now. He'll have to buy a new one." As Dan Jenkins wrote in the *Fort Worth Press*, "The calendar was being ridiculed before your very eyes."

22

FINAL BOW

ONE DAY IN 1959, Glen Garden member Talmadge Tubb finished his round of play and continued to satisfy his thirst for friendly competition in the clubhouse by settling in at the poker table. One of Tubb's adversaries pushed two $20 bills to the center of the table and crowed, "I think I'll just waltz out there with about $40." Another couldn't resist contributing to the pot and added, "Then I think I'm fixin' to waltz across Texas," and flashed all four aces. Tubb found the phrase appealing and jotted it down. Back at his home on the south side of Fort Worth, he began to use the phrase as the foundation for writing a country and western song – which he often did for his uncle, singer Ernest Tubb. But the song lay dormant for years before Ernest finally recorded "Waltz Across Texas" in autumn 1965.

Despite the proliferation of well-appointed country clubs across Fort Worth, Glen Garden's membership in the early 1960s reached a high of approximately 525 members. "Smiley" Rowland was a popular head pro, holding the position for twenty-two years before stepping aside in 1967 for Bill Bradford. One of the new members was Clarence Dowdy, the owner of American Tile in Fort

Worth. Tile was the Dowdy family business; his father was a tile setter during the Depression and he got into contracting in 1939. Clarence and other neighborhood kids were eager to pick up odd jobs with the elder Dowdy, and he estimates about half the kids in the neighborhood grew up to be involved in the tile business in some way. The early 1960s at Glen Garden also saw the formation of a group called the Dirty Dozen that exists to this day (though now expanded to about forty members, who have a separate golf game each day Tuesdays through Sundays). The Dozen was initiated by Charles Stanley, its first "commissioner," whose name now graces the clubhouse room where men are apt to spend hours playing cards or dominoes. Like a secret fraternity, the Dirty Dozen employed a set of hand signals for conveying a par, birdie or bogey while out on the course. Since alerting fellow members to a birdie must have been a priority that couldn't always be trusted to the hand signals, Dirty Dozen players also were heard to yell following a birdie, "Wak-a-wak-a-woo!"

Ben Hogan's few appearances during the decade often produced better than anticipated results beginning with the near fairy tale that was Denver's Cherry Hills in 1960. At age forty-seven with legs that might have felt sixty-seven, he incredibly put himself in position to win his fifth official U.S. Open title playing the final thirty-six holes on Saturday with a 19-year-old who was also in the hunt, an Ohio State University junior named Jack Nicklaus. Hogan was tied for the lead with Arnold Palmer through seventy holes, heading to the par-5 no. 17. His third shot barely cleared the water in front of the green only to spin back and drop into the drink. Were the bogey there not enough to snuff out his chance for unlikely glory, Hogan double-bogeyed no. 18.

He placed in the top ten in all four events that he entered in 1964, including the Masters and P.G.A. Championship. But he couldn't keep that up much longer, especially dealing with the injuries to his legs incurred decades earlier, and took leave from Tournament participation after the 1967 U.S. Open.

Early in 1968, his doctor cancelled plans to operate on Hogan's bothersome left knee because of his fears the procedure could leave him crippled. The result was an alteration of Hogan's famed swing, hitting the ball off his right side before shifting his weight to the left.

Hogan ended a hiatus of almost three years in May 1970 with a return to the Houston Champions International, the $115,000 event co-hosted by longtime friend Jimmy Demaret. From 1961 through '67, his schedule was confined primarily to Colonial's National Invitational Tournament and the majors. Of Hogan's two weeks of practice in Houston prior to the tournament, Demaret trumpeted: "Nobody can hit it like Ben has been hitting it the past week. He's placing the ball exactly where he wants it. If he gets the touch of the greens, he is going to be mighty tough to beat."

Hogan wowed the galleries – and his fellow pros – with a par-71 in the windswept opening round, which would have been even lower had he not missed a gaggle of short putts. His 33 on the back nine tied the best of the day, and he trailed leader Deane Beman by three strokes. As Hogan prepared to tee off on no. 4, a reporter heard a fan say, "As far as I'm concerned, there is only one man on this golf course and he is on the tee right now. I'd follow that man every day to hell and back." One person apparently wasn't wowed by Hogan's play – Hogan. "I'm never satisfied," he blurted afterward. "I hope to get better. I must admit, I was nervous out there, and I was a little tired at the end." More putting problems on Friday resulted in a 4-over 75, four shots within the cut line. One of his playing partners during the first two rounds was Bob Goalby. "He drove the ball so beautifully," Goalby recalls from his home in Iowa. "Our mouths were just watering when we finished those thirty-six holes. I'd played with him in practice rounds at the Open in Baltusrol in 1967, the last time he'd played. Beautiful shot. I told him, 'Who do you think you are, Ben Hogan?' We said that all the time when you hit a great ball. He kind of wheeled around and looked at me with those steely eyes. 'Oh, shit, what did I say?' And then he busted out laughing."

Hogan stubbornly rebounded in the third round with another 71, giving him a 4-over 217, eight strokes behind leader Bruce Crampton. In the club-house following Saturday's play, Demaret couldn't resist ribbing his old friend about the metal brace that Hogan wore on his left knee. "If it starts raining and lightning out there, you had better head for cover. You're a walking lightning rod." Demaret wasn't through, turning to tournament trainer Bobby Brown and adding, "Ben had a hard time getting a caddie. He has to be a mechanic and carry screwdrivers, pliers and bolts just in case his brace breaks up."

On Sunday, Hogan played the first seven holes at 4-under to climb back in contention. *Houston Chronicle* sports editor Dick Peebles noted, "The other players in the field behaved like kids when the preacher comes to call. They seemed to walk in awe of Bantam Ben, old enough to be the father of most of them." Hogan couldn't keep up that pace because of continued difficulties on the greens, yet finished with his best round of the tournament (1-under 70) to finish five shots out of the lead with a 3-over 287 good for a tie for ninth place and $2,600. In the locker room afterward, Hogan was quoted as saying the following week's National Invitational Tournament, at his beloved Colonial, would be his final event, then amended that to specify he wouldn't compete anymore at the Masters or in the U.S. Open. Three days later in Fort Worth, pain in the left knee forced Hogan to end his practice round after only nine holes and skip the Wednesday pro-am. He was ready to go for Thursday's first round, and the *Fort Worth Press* listed him as a 50-to-1 pick to win.

Hogan opened with a more than respectable 1-under-par 69, putting him three strokes behind leaders Gary Player and Lee Trevino. Afterward, he faced further interrogation from the press regarding whether Colonial would mark his farewell from tournament competition: "I simply told that guy I had no other plans after Colonial. I didn't say I was quitting. If I get a yen to play in a tournament, I'll play. But I'm looking for a flat course. I don't think I can go those hilly ones anymore." One scribe observed Hogan had stopped and shook hands with a fan while walking the first fairway and therefore asked if he'd mellowed. The reply, following a long pause, was, "I don't think I'll answer that." Friday wasn't as kind to the Hawk, a 77 battling stubborn winds tying his worst Colonial round and dropping him ten shots off the pace at 6-over 146. "Everything I hit today, I did something wrong," he said.

Weekend rounds of 3-over 73 and 2-over 72 gave Hogan an 11-over 291 to finish in a tie for fifty-sixth place and a pay day of $192. The only previous time he'd finished outside the top twenty at Marvin Leonard's golfing jewel was when he had to withdraw from the 1954 event after two rounds because of a cold. And, during Saturday's play, Dale Douglass wrested from Hogan the Colonial 18-hole record (that Hogan had set with a 5-under 65 at the first National Invitational Tournament (N.I.T.) in 1946) by firing a 7-under 63. When his left knee wasn't a problem from the tee boxes and fairways, his fading eyesight – and maybe some rust – haunted him on the greens. "I hit the ball pretty good; I was pleased with that," he said. "You've got to play in competition to score well, and I have not been. It really hurts you around the greens." Again non-committal regarding his next appearance, Hogan said it was unlikely he'd play in consecutive weeks again.

Hogan made one more appearance that season, in Westchester County, New York, his temporary stomping grounds of the late 1930s and early 1940s when he was employed at Century Country Club. He entered the Westchester Classic with the hopes of a later tee time that would accommodate his pre-play physical preparation. But the tournament staff played no favorites and, needing to start particularly early overall with a field of 171, slated Hogan to start on the no. 10 tee at 7:24 a.m. "The only spectator will be the official scorer," Hogan groused to the Tour's Fred Corcoran, who tried to make the best of things with a reply of, "You may be pleasantly surprised." Hogan considered withdrawing right then and there, but Corcoran reminded him that tournament proceeds would be shared among six local hospitals and Hogan would indeed be a big draw.

The club chef, Haelmut Kischowski, had Hogan's breakfast order of fresh orange juice, plenty of coffee, eggs over easy, and bacon delivered promptly at 5 a.m., and Hogan was ready and waiting. Likewise, Kischowski was ready amid the gallery at the tenth hole when Hogan began play about two-and-a-half hours later. Hogan shot a 78, 39 on each side, which left him eleven shots off the first-day lead. He decided he was finished for the tournament, for the year and possibly for his career. Three weeks later, Hogan suffered a different and more profound loss with the passing of John Marvin Leonard. Finally giving in to persistent liver and stomach ailments, Hogan's surrogate father was seventy-five years old.

When the pros returned to the Champions Club in Houston in mid-May 1971, Hogan was ready to greet them once again. With the Colonial N.I.T. coming up the following week, he ignored his personal prohibition of playing in consecutive weeks. Hogan practiced the previous week while the Byron Nelson Golf Classic was being contested at Dallas' Preston Trail Country Club (where Mickey Mantle would often hold court in his adopted hometown). Jack Nicklaus won there for the second consecutive year, coming from behind with birdie putts on nos. 15, 16, and 17 to give him three victories within eleven weeks – and reason to skip Houston and spend a few weeks at home in south Florida. (Nelson not only hosted the tournament but served again as a "golf consultant" in the *Dallas Times Herald*.)

But Hogan's encore effort in Houston didn't make it through twelve holes. His heart was betrayed by his legs, particularly the balky left knee. Hogan nearly fell while hiking down a slope in pursuit of an AWOL tee shot using a 3-iron on the 228-yard, par-3 fourth hole. Eschewing the opportunity to continue from the drop area, Hogan returned to the tee box, pulled out the 3-iron again and sent another errant drive into the ravine. And a third time. A fan sighed, "I've never caught Hogan before, and I guess I've waited too late." His fourth attempt reached the green, and his score for the hole was a 6-over 9. He almost lost his footing again teeing off on no. 12. Before attempting another shot, he conceded to his playing partners that he couldn't continue and begrudgingly accepted a cart ride back to the locker room. As he climbed into the cart, he told a friend, "Don't ever grow old." But Hogan was composed when dissecting the day's efforts afterward. Explaining why he didn't take advantage of the drop zone on no. 4, he stated, "I thought it was an easier shot from the tee."

The pros returned to north Texas the following week, to Fort Worth, and Hogan was determined to take his place back on Colonial's center stage if at all possible twelve years after recording his sixty-fourth and most recent P.G.A. Tour win, which was his fifth victory in southwest Fort Worth. Hogan practiced on Monday with the youngest player in the field, fellow Texan John Mahaffey (making his P.G.A. Tour debut). On Wednesday, he invited old friend Mike Souchak, five years removed from regular Tour competition himself, to pair up for a practice round beginning at noon. Hogan's bad knee began acting up on the seventh hole and, as in Houston the previous week, Hogan nearly fell while striking his approach to the green. Souchak asked if he wanted to stop there, and Hogan – in visible pain – declined. Hogan almost sliced his tee shot on the par-3 eighth hole into a stream, and he told Souchak that he'd had enough – but not enough for him to immediately return to the clubhouse. Hogan stayed with his friend as Souchak played the ninth hole and, only afterward, was sure he wouldn't go back out for the back nine. That afternoon, he informed N.I.T. officials that he wouldn't be playing in the tournament.

The Dr Pepper bottling plant in Dublin grew into the town's landmark and took on an even greater profile in the 1970s, when the soaring price of sugar led to many soft drink manufacturers settling for artificial sweeteners. The Dr Pepper plant in Dublin was still under the management of Sam Prim's daughter, Grace Prim Lyon. Her right-hand man was Billie Kloster, who began working there even before he graduated from Dublin High in 1937. They were determined to continue making Dr Pepper with real sugar – Imperial Pure Cane Sugar, to be specific. While Dr Pepper took on a greater national profile thanks to increased national advertising in the late '70s – "Wouldn't you like to be a Pepper, too?" – the drink that was produced in Dublin began to take on a near cult following since many soda drinkers considered its sugar-based taste superior to the Dr Pepper that was made everywhere else and it became commonly known as Dublin Dr Pepper. The little plant on Highway 377/67 and only a block from Highway 6 was a convenient stop for folks traveling across Texas. In the area of the building where Chester Hogan was photographed near the beginning of the twentieth century, a retail area was built in 1995 called "Old Doc's Soda Shop." Visitors could stock up on Dublin Dr Pepper, stop at the lunch counter and even buy all sorts of Dublin Dr Pepper souvenirs and memorabilia.

23

HAIL AND FAREWELL

BYRON NELSON'S LONG goodbye to the Tour lasted twenty years, from 1947 to his withdrawal following the first round of the 1966 Colonial. He was still representing himself well as a fifty-year-old in his infrequent appearances on the 1962 schedule: tied for fifteenth at the Crosby, tied for seventeenth at Colonial, and tied for thirty-third at the Masters (an event that he had not missed since being passed over for the inaugural staging in 1934). But there were more misses than hits over the next few years, and one of the greatest careers in American golf came to a quiet conclusion early in 1966. After lasting only two rounds at the Masters, Nelson withdrew from the Colonial after Thursday's opening play. He hit the tournament's first shot for the fourteenth consecutive year – Colonial's Olympic torch bearer, as one local writer put it. After shooting a 5-over 75, he told tournament officials that he wasn't feeling well and wouldn't be back for Friday's second round.

With that nearly unnoticed departure, the pro career that began with a $5 entry fee at the 1932 Texarkana Open fell silent. Most notably after Nelson's regular Tour participation ended, he played on the United States' 1949 Ryder

Cup team that won 11½ points to 1 at Portland Golf Club. Nelson never won the Colonial National Invitational, which began awarding plaid jackets to its champions in 1952, but tournament officials awarded him one in the 1990s. He started doing analysis on televised events beginning with the 1957 Masters on CBS alongside Chris Schenkel and moved over a few years later to ABC (reunited in 1964 with Schenkel, who became one of Nelson's closest friends). Nelson captained America's victorious Ryder Cup squad in 1965, making him a participant in three Ryder Cup wins in three tries. The Yanks team led by Arnold Palmer, Dave Marr, and Tony Lema dominated play 19½ to 12½ at Royal Birkdale.

Nelson also dabbled in golf course designing and combined with Ralph Plummer (who was a caddie at Glen Garden before Nelson and Ben Hogan arrived) to give birth to Preston Trail Country Club in Far North Dallas in 1965. Dallas had joined Fort Worth as home to an annual Tour event beginning in 1956 with the tournament bouncing among various clubs. After the 1967 installment was played at Oak Cliff Country Club on the city's south side, the event found a new home at youthful Preston Trail. And, for the first time, a Tour stop was named for one of its former competitors. The Greater Dallas Open became the Byron Nelson Golf Classic.

The tournament was (and still is) operated by Dallas' Salesmanship Club, which was started in 1920 with the mission of contributing to local children's charities. The Dallas Open wasn't one of the more successful events on the Tour schedule. A longtime, respected Texas journalist and former sportswriter named Felix McKnight was co-publisher of the *Dallas Times Herald* and approached Nelson with an idea. The tournament could earn much more money for the Salesmanship Club's many affiliated charities if it established a direct connection with a high-profile name in the golf community. While Nelson stopped making even his handful of Tour appearances in 1966, he became known to an entire new portion of golf fandom with his TV work. A huge kickoff party for the first Byron Nelson Golf Classic in April 1968 was held in downtown Dallas at the Southland Center Hotel. The emcee was Schenkel from ABC, the network that would televise the tournament, and the guest list of more than a thousand well-wishers included Hogan. While Nelson couldn't play favorites, he was pleased that the inaugural Byron Nelson Golf Classic was won by fellow Texarkana Country Club alumnus Miller Barber.

Hogan told *Golf Digest*'s Nick Seitz in a 1970 interview that he was invited to lend his name to a Tour event but declined, concerned that he wouldn't enjoy control over the quality of the tournament. Seitz also wrote that Hogan was pondering building his own course, which would be the perfect home of a Ben Hogan Classic. One possible home for a Hogan course, maybe the Hogan Classic, was near Shreveport in the northwest corner of Louisiana, about four hours from Fort Worth. He inspected the site near Lake Wallace and loved the property. He was prepared to rent an apartment nearby and provide hands-on supervision of the project. But the real estate deal fell through.

Hogan turned his attention to a similar project on land located northeast of Fort Worth near where northern Tarrant County meets southern Denton County. It was in the town of Westlake, coincidentally next door to the Nelsons' adopted hometown of Roanoke. Working with two developers from Houston, Hogan would design two courses meant to be the collective centerpiece of an upscale residential and retail community with its own schools. The first course was Trophy Club Country Club, opening in 1975; the name identified another purpose for the undertaking – to establish a home for Hogan's vast collection of championship trophies and other golfing keepsakes. But as the parties prepared to embark on the second course, they couldn't come to an agreement on a timetable for continuation of the project and other financial roadblocks proved too troublesome. Trophy Club went on to become an incorporated municipality, but Hogan's involvement came to an abrupt halt. Trophy Club Country Club's Hogan Course would be the only golf course that he designed.

The Hogan name expanded some years later when the Hogan Company's new parent company, Cosmo Sports of Japan, announced late in 1989 that it would subsidize a new arm of the P.G.A. Tour that would resemble big-league baseball's minor leagues. The Hogan Tour began a five-year commitment in 1990 to stage thirty tournaments annually for lesser pros, primarily young ones starting out, to hone their games in hopes of joining the major league of American golf. As it turned out, the investment by Cosmo Sports was a crippling blow to the Hogan Company and led to the shuttering of Hogan's once proud facility in Fort Worth. And within three years, sports manufacturing giant Nike bought the Tour's naming rights, which today belong to Web.com.

On April 1, 1983, Louise Nelson suffered a stroke while driving home from a trip to the post office. The Nelsons' family physician, James D. Murphy, immediately consulted a neurosurgeon, who estimated she would live no longer than a few weeks. Louise lived well beyond a few weeks. The following spring, on the Monday night between the 1984 Nelson Classic and the Colonial National Invitational Tournament, local dignitaries and a sizable representation of Tour players gathered at the Loews Anatole hotel on Stemmons Freeway just west of downtown Dallas. Officially, the night's banquet was a fund-raiser to kick off the Byron and Louise Nelson Golf Endowment Fund at Abilene Christian University. There were many connections between the Nelson family and Abilene Christian, located about three hours west of Dallas-Fort Worth. A cousin of Byron's, Don Morris, served as school president from 1940 to 1969. Ellen Nelson started her college career there in 1938. Charles Nelson's music career brought him to Abilene Christian as a professor in 1984, and he was named artist-in-residence two years later.

Byron and Louise Nelson pose during the early 1980s amid much of Byron's championship hardware. (Byron Nelson estate)

With a gathering of about 1,200 at the Anatole, the evening raised more than $350,000 for Abilene Christian's golf program. The day was declared Nelson Day by both Fort Worth mayor Bob Bolen and Dallas mayor Starke Taylor. The dinner's festivities were emceed by Verne Lundquist, at the time a familiar TV sports anchor in Dallas who had just ended a fifteen-year run in the Dallas Cowboys' radio booth and was about to embark on a new career as a network announcer. Also on the program was Schenkel, Nelson's longtime partner in the ABC golf booth. "In all the time I spent with him, we never had an argument," Schenkel told the audience. "We always headed to the clubhouse, not the bar, after working a tournament. And the biggest thing we argued about was what kind of ice cream to buy." Schenkel said Nelson once took him back out in the rain after a round they played together to make him work on his bunker play. "Today," Schenkel proudly added, "I'm probably the only golfer in my handicap bracket who can hit a good sand shot."

The celebrities in attendance included the only head coach the Dallas Cowboys had known to that point. Tom Landry didn't wear his signature fedora indoors, and the "plastic man" exhibited the dry sense of humor that most of the nation only discovered two years later in an American Express commercial when, decked out in cowhand garb, he found himself "surrounded . . . by Redskins." "One of the first stories I ever heard about Byron was how straight he hit the ball," Landry said. "He couldn't play thirty-six holes in one day over the same course because the second time around, he'd be hitting out of the same divot." Another of the speakers was Tour superstar Tom Watson, one of Nelson's most devoted golf disciples. He noted Nelson's feats from 1945 would surely never be broken and marveled that Nelson's third-place finish in his first pro event earned him $75 while Watson's third-place check for finishing behind Craig Stadler and David Edwards the previous day in the Nelson Classic was good for $34,000. "I recall our first meeting, after I shot 79 in the last round of the U.S. Open in 1974. He came up to me and offered me tips and said I could call him anytime and come down to Texas and he'd help me with my game. It took me two years to take him up on it. When I finally did, it was the best professional help I could ever find. And after he straightened me out, I had one of my best years ever in 1977." Namely five victories, including the Masters and U.S. Open.

Charles Nelson was present, though not feeling terribly chipper following a root canal procedure that day. He still managed to sing two songs and read the following poem that he wrote:

Poor is the child who has no brother to sooth his hurts, to dry his tears.

Poor is the boy who, through the awkward years, has no brother to treat him with respect.

Poor is the man who has no brother whose life is a model of honor and integrity, which inspires him to reach and stretch and strain to become the best he can possibly become.

I was not and am not poor.

But the true star that night from the Nelson family was Louise. She made her first public appearance since suffering the stroke thirteen months earlier that left her unable to speak. Her husband of almost fifty years told some stories, like her response years earlier at Oakmont when he complained about not being able to identify a good driver, while speaking on her behalf. "I wouldn't be standing here tonight if it weren't for Louise," Nelson said. "She encouraged me and helped me. There is no way a man can be friendly without a friendly wife. All I wanted to do was play golf, and that's all I cared about. But she taught me different, how to care about others. We have been a team for fifty years, and we've had so many wonderful things happen to us. I don't know what else you could possibly do. People have treated us so well. We are extremely blessed to have the best friends in the whole world." Louise suffered another massive stroke in September 1985 at the couple's home. Deemed brain dead soon after, she lived only a few more weeks and passed away on October 4, 1985. Louise and Byron, who was holding her hand when she died, were married for fifty years and four months.

Nelson's grief was so consuming that he began losing considerable weight, and Dr. Murphy feared Nelson would himself be dead soon. Nelson managed to take a rare trip in March 1986 to a friend's golf outing in Ohio and renewed an acquaintance with a woman whom he'd met there five years earlier. Nelson and Peggy Simmons, an advertising writer, kept in touch, and their communication soon bloomed into romance. She moved to Texas that September, and they were married on November 15, 1986. Nelson wrote in his autobiography of his new wife, almost thirty-three years younger than he: "I truly feel that if it hadn't been for Peggy, I wouldn't be alive today."

In the fall of 1987, Nelson and Hogan were among the nine inaugural inductees in the Fort Worth Sports Hall of Honor at the Amon G. Carter Jr. Exhibits Hall. (They also entered the World Golf Hall of Fame together as part of the 11-member charter class at Pinehurst in 1974.) Three of those honored that night in Fort Worth were in attendance, the golf legends joined by auto racing star Johnny Rutherford. The others were former TCU football coach "Dutch" Meyer, former Horned Frogs football stars Sam Baugh and Davey O'Brien, and two respected figures in the history of Fort Worth Cats minor league baseball, Jake Atz and Paul LaGrave. Hogan was the last of the three to address the audience and displayed some Hogan wit in noting the amount of time that his follow honorees took to speak: "I was told not to exceed three minutes. Everyone was told that. Well, I've been asleep twice already." After the guffawing abated, he cited the evening as being the second time that his adopted hometown had feted him – the other being his homecoming from the 1953 British Open. "I came here to live as an eight-year-old and am seventy-five now and have enjoyed every minute I've lived in Fort Worth. I have traveled and traveled and traveled all over the world, and these are the best people collectively I've ever been around. I will live here the rest of my life peacefully, quietly and pleasantly."

Ben Hogan [left] and Byron Nelson chat before they were among the inaugural members of the Fort Worth Sports Hall of Honor inducted on October 22, 1987. (Courtesy, *Fort Worth Star-Telegram* Collection, Special Collections, The University of Texas at Arlington Library, Arlington, Texas)

Nelson maintained a relationship with Glen Garden long after he initially left Fort Worth for Texarkana. Hogan didn't, most likely because he established other local golfing ties as Marvin Leonard built Colonial and later Shady Oaks. Some have speculated Glen Garden represented too close of an emotional connection to Hogan's young days of desperation, when he and his brother entered the working world as boys to help support a family that had lost its breadwinner through such ghastly circumstances. One occasion when Nelson frequented his old club took place in spring 1989, when he accepted an invitation to come play. Afterward, he sent a letter to the membership and expressed his appreciation for the receptions that he had received there then and years earlier.

Dear Members:

The junior membership and later life membership that you gave me was a great source of encouragement. I don't think it would have been possible for me to develop such a good game of golf. I shall always be grateful to you good people for the friendship and good wishes from all your fine members.

Playing golf again there on May 29th certainly brought back many pleasant memories. Even back to my caddy days.

Many, many thanks,

all my best wishes.

Sincerely,

Byron Nelson

Three years after *The Dallas Morning News* captured the milestones of north Texas' two golfing legends turning eighty in 1992, Hogan underwent colon surgery and also suffered through an episode of bronchitis. Such physical pains were compounded by the emotional trauma of brother Royal's death in December 1996. The following July, Hogan was rushed to Fort Worth's All Saints Hospital after he'd fallen at home. The next morning, he died on the eve of wife Valerie's eighty-fifth birthday. As reporters in Dallas-Fort Worth began feverishly collecting plaudits and remembrances, Nelson was naturally one of the first sought out. By the time he was called by the media, Nelson had already been informed of Hogan's passing by the physician that the two of them shared, Dr. Murphy.

"He was probably the most feared competitor out there, ever," Nelson told *Fort Worth Star-Telegram* golf writer Jimmy Burch. "They feared Palmer, Tiger, Watson, Nicklaus. But I think there was something about Ben's personality. He wasn't mean, but he was such a fierce competitor. No holds were barred." In an interview with another *Star-Telegram* writer, Gene Menez, Nelson said, "The players were afraid of Ben. It's just something about his personality that I never felt that way because I guess I knew him so well." In reference to the live radio interview that they gave in San Antonio before the playoff of the 1940 Texas Open, he added, "He didn't think I practiced enough. I thought he practiced too much. We both played all right." Talking to Brad Townsend of *The Dallas Morning News*, Nelson said, "He was very private, and I respected that. I think one reason Ben and I got along well is I respected his privacy. I never was in his home. I had his private number, but I never used it." He elaborated on not knowing the source of Hogan's desire for such privacy: "The only thing I could say about it is, in his childhood, I don't think he had many friends. In later years he liked being around other golfers, but strangers seemed to bother him."

Hogan was laid to rest at Greenwood Memorial Park on July 29, 1997 following a funeral ceremony at University Christian Church. The list of twenty-five honorary pallbearers was comprised mainly of longtime personal and business friends from Fort Worth. There were a few from the sports community – Sam Snead, Herman Keiser, Ken Venturi, and Pulitzer Prize winning sportswriter Jim Murray. Nelson attended the funeral with wife Peggy, quietly entering the back of the church. About three weeks after Hogan's death, the P.G.A. Championship was played at Winged Foot in Mamaroneck, New York. Golf author Martin Davis was working with Nelson on a book and hosted a pretournament party whose guest list included Nelson and *Golfweek*'s Jeff Rude. Nelson spotted Rude and told him abruptly, "Jeff, I need to talk to you." After pulling Rude aside, Nelson proceeded to explain how hurt he was that he wasn't one of the pallbearers at Hogan's funeral.

Longtime members of Glen Garden reached the point where they almost weren't comfortable without some sort of crisis. When the club decided to try bentgrass greens, the conversion didn't work well and some members left. When it was decided that going semi-private and allowing outside play was financially necessary, more members left. And they were bitterly split early in 2000 when a decision was looming on the future of the beloved but decaying clubhouse.

The ballroom floor that had hosted so many parties through the years was dull and creaky. The white ceiling tiles were sullied with brown water stains. The air-conditioning was, at best, finicky. The deal breaker might have occurred when set-up for a party that spring had to be halted when part of the ceiling collapsed and two raccoons fell to the floor. Wendell Waddle was among those who couldn't envision Glen Garden without the original clubhouse. Others cited it would be more expensive to repair the aging structure than to replace it. And part of their argument proved especially painful. There wasn't enough money to fix the old clubhouse because of the steady decline in Glen Garden's membership. The total often fluctuated through the years. From the peak of more than 500 in the early 1960s, the number dipped to about 200 in the late 1970s. The years in between saw the surrounding neighborhood steadily become home to more racial minorities. Many of the members who didn't give up their memberships did move from the neighborhood and were then willing to drive thirty miles or more to go to the club. Bill Bradford served as head pro from 1967 until 1989, equaling "Smiley" Rowland's twenty-two years; when the club faced serious financial hardship, Bradford and other staffers offered to work for free. There was another spike in membership in the 1980s when Glen Garden proved convenient for golfers in nearby cities whose courses were closed. Doug Higgins Jr. followed Bradford but stayed for only three years. He was replaced in 1993 by Alan Courtney, a native of southeast Texas whose college golfing career included a year at Mississippi State.

For many at the club, common sense dictated the 30,000-square-foot clubhouse with a ballroom that now often swallowed up its occupants should be replaced by a one-story, 10,000-square-foot version that better suited the club's evolved profile. That contingent included Clarence Dowdy. "I told Wendell," Dowdy recalls, "you get a contractor and get bids on fixing up the old building and take it to the board, to the membership, and that'll give them a choice." But there really wasn't any reasonable financial alternative. The club borrowed about $1.5 million from three members who were then operating or had sold successful businesses and were in position to aid the struggling club: Dowdy, Malcolm Tallmon and Bob Ellis.

Tallmon, who joined Glen Garden in the late 1980s, was in commercial real estate. He had been around Glen Garden since he was eight years old, caddying in the late 1940s. He became an assistant pro at various clubs around Fort Worth, including River Crest, where he recalls caddying for Hogan on multiple occasions. "He was always pleasant there," Tallmon says. "He didn't expect the caddie to tell him how far it was or what club to hit. We were on the eighteenth hole, a par-5 then. I took the woods and did this [pulling them to the side] because it was a perfect 2-iron for him. He looked at me and grinned, shook his head, took out the 4-wood and hit it about two feet from the hole. I said, 'Mr. Hogan, you feathered that one in there nicely.' Made him laugh." Ellis, who left school after the ninth grade, made his money in trucking. He started driving a dump truck and moving dirt around the Trinity River. He built up an entire company, went broke in the late '80s, dusted off and built up the company again. "Bob should have been a politician," Dowdy says.

The members said goodbye to the original clubhouse with a "Last Dance" party in November 1999. Groundbreaking for the new structure took place in April 2000, with Nelson in attendance. "We're going to create an oasis out here," Dowdy told the *Star-Telegram*. Before construction of the clubhouse was completed, the bill increased to $2 million.

That same month, Nelson turned eighty-eight, and Peggy quietly found what she considered a fitting present while the two of them were at Pinehurst. She had the gift shipped at a later date to the home of family friend Marcia Baggs. (Eddie Baggs came to work for Nelson during the 1980s as a ranch hand, and the Baggs still live just down the street.) On the Saturday night before they celebrated, Peggy and Marcia deftly set up the surprise in the yard after dark without the birthday boy's knowledge. When the Nelsons got ready to leave for Sunday services the next morning, Byron was surprised and pleased to see his present – a bronze statue of a caddie. When he turned ninety in 2002, he told *The Dallas Morning News* a few days earlier, "I've had very few unpleasant things happen to me. My life has been a happy life."

When George W. Bush was inaugurated in January 2001 to begin his stay in the White House, his first dance with new First Lady Laura Bush was to the strains of Ernest Tubb's "Waltz Across Texas."

24

LOSS AND LEGACY

ON SEPTEMBER 26, 2006, Peggy Nelson returned home just past noon after teaching a ladies Bible study class to find Byron lying on the back porch. Fearing the worst, she placed a hand on one of his cheeks and said, "I'm so glad you're in heaven now." His memorial service five days later at North Richland Hills Church of Christ attracted more than 2,000 mourners, including a who's who from the golf world including Tom Watson, Phil Mickelson, Ben Crenshaw, and Justin Leonard. Among the speakers was Ken Venturi, the former golf star turned TV analyst: "The game of golf would not be what it is today without Byron – the greatest gentleman there ever was." Nelson was laid to rest at Roselawn Memorial Park in Denton. Less than a month later, Nelson was posthumously awarded the Congressional Medal of Honor – only the fifth athlete among 132 recipients at the time – through the efforts of the Congressman who represented the district where Nelson lived, Michael Burgess. Peggy accepted the award at a ceremony in Washington, D.C. in June 2007.

A few months earlier, the school district in which Nelson lived – Northwest Independent School District – was ready to choose a name for a new high school scheduled to be built in the town of Trophy Club (named for the development that Ben Hogan helped start in the 1970s) and open in 2009. Six communities would send students to the new school, with two towns sending all or almost all of their high school students there – Trophy Club and neighboring Roanoke, home of Fairway Ranch. Roanoke mayor Scooter Gierisch had previously pushed for the district to name one of its elementary schools after Nelson. Gierisch's association with Nelson went back many years, to when the mayor was an eight-year-old attending Sunday school classes taught by Nelson at Roanoke Church of Christ. "He was kind of a mentor to me," Gierisch says. "I'd go out to his wood shop, and we would talk. He'd say, 'Thank you' for what I was doing. He was always positive. I never heard a harsh word come out of his mouth. He made you feel good when you were talking to him."

At a public hearing to discuss potential names for the new high school, Gierisch presented the case for Byron Nelson High School: "I told the story of Byron. The school would be recognized locally, nationally, even worldwide. Who wouldn't want to go to Byron Nelson High School? Who wouldn't want to play on the golf team at Byron Nelson High School? Probably the biggest problem you'll have is finding a golf coach who would meet or exceed Byron's expectations."

In all, seventeen names were submitted to the board, including names honoring national figures (Gerald Ford, Martin Luther King Jr.) and those honoring local dignitaries (Clara Love, John M. Tidwell, Lewis B. "Chesty" Puller, Truett Wilson), and Byron Nelson Memorial High. At a meeting on Monday night, April 23, 2007, the board selected Byron Nelson High School by a vote of five to two. For anyone concerned about the name being awkward or cumbersome, principal Linda Parker notes that students, when asked where they go to school, will often say, "I go to Byron." A curious offshoot involves how the state's scholastic athletic governing body, the University Interscholastic League, codes school names into four-letter, all-caps abbreviations for certain competitions. For Byron Nelson High, the first two letters come from the name of the school district (Northwest) and the last two letters come from the last name of the person for whom the school is named (Nelson). Hence, NONE.

Peggy Nelson addresses the audience at the dedication of Byron Nelson High School on October 18, 2009. (Northwest Independent School District)

Having selected a name, the next task in terms of public recognition was choosing a mascot. A district committee selected the bobcat, primarily because the animal is indigenous to the area. After the fact, committee members learned Nelson made a connection between cats and winning when he was interviewed for an oral history of American golf written by Al Barkow in 1986: "Is there a psychology for winning? I don't understand the psychological function of the human mind sufficiently to answer that very well, except to say that winners are different. They're a different breed of cat." A paraphrasing of Nelson's sentiments is displayed on the wall of the school's main gymnasium.

Byron Nelson High School in Trophy Club, Texas opened in the fall of 2009 and graduated its first senior class in June 2012. (Northwest Independent School District)

The high school opened in fall 2009 with only ninth- and tenth-grade classes and reached a full four-class enrollment in 2011-12. The Bobcats' football team started playing a varsity schedule in 2010 and qualified for the Class 4A state playoffs in 2011, reaching the second round before losing to perennial state power Stephenville in a game played at the Dallas Cowboys' massive stadium in Arlington. The 2012 girls soccer team advanced to the state championship game, playing Highland Park to a scoreless draw before losing in the subsequent shootout by one goal. Coach Barry Hawkins' boys and girls golf teams both competed in the two-round 4A state tournament at Jimmy Clay Golf Course in Austin. The boys placed fourth. They were led by senior Major Monzingo, headed for Stephen F. Austin State University on a golf scholarship, who tied for fifth place in the individual standings. The girls finished second, as did junior Maty Monzingo in the individual competition.

25

PLAY CONTINUES

ONE OF THE primary reasons why the Byron Nelson Classic was able to attract enviable fields from the 1970s into the next century was the presence of the sedate gentleman waiting to warmly greet each player following a day's toil on the course. P.G.A. Tour pros might not have been terribly pleased with the conditions at Preston Trail or later at the TPC Four Seasons out in the upscale Irving development known as Las Colinas when the event moved there in 1983 – Lanny Wadkins welcomed the event there with an opening-round 67 and promptly blurted, "This is not my favorite golf course." – but they were more than happy to come play for "Mr. Nelson." Many pros were mentored by Nelson, none more so than Tom Watson; Watson repaid the informal tutoring by winning the event four times over a six-year period from the late 1970s into the early 1980s. Tiger Woods played in the 1997 Nelson Classic during his first full season on the Tour and, five weeks after collecting his first major title at the Masters, wowed the fans at Las Colinas with his next victory.

In 2005, the Nelson (while the school is often simply referred to by his first name, the tournament is regularly referred to by his last name) boasted seven of the ten top-ranked players on the P.G.A. Tour and all of the top five – Woods, Phil Mickelson, Ernie Els, Vijay Singh, and Retief Goosen. When the 2007 tournament was played for the first time following Nelson's death, only two of the top ten were in the field. Peggy Nelson assumed full responsibility of the hospitality duties to provide a measure of continuity. But there was a more tangible predicament; the course was in terrible shape, notably the greens. The explanation given was that the putting surfaces had been seeded with rye atop Bermuda, resulting in greens that played poorly and might have looked worse, including on television.

Not long after hometown favorite Scott Verplank scored his first Tour victory in almost six years at the 2007 tournament, overhaul of the course began in earnest under the watchful eye of former Tour pro and Texan-by-choice D.A. Weibring. There was also the thorny issue of the Nelson's new placement on the Tour schedule, following the Masters by only two weeks instead of the customary four or five. "I don't think that's the way you show respect to Byron Nelson or to the tournament that raises the most money for charity on Tour," Weibring said. "It's time for the players to step up and support the legacy Byron cared most about."

Weibring's earthmovers were able to reshape the course suitably before the pros returned in spring 2008, but the damage inflicted on the tournament's reputation because of multiple factors couldn't be reversed overnight. Woods wasn't present from 2006 through 2012. Mickelson's absence in 2008 had nothing to do with putting lines; he took leave from Tour play after wife Amy was diagnosed with breast cancer. But Mickelson, the 1996 Nelson champion, didn't return in 2009 or 2010 or 2011. Finally back at the Four Seasons five years later for the 2012 tournament, he coyly observed he'd been away longer than expected. The tournament enjoyed a measure of name recognition in its champions for 2008 (Adam Scott) and 2009 (Rory Sabbatini). The 2010 and '11 events produced first-time Tour winners in Jason Day and Keegan Bradley, the latter redefining his Nelson triumph as a springboard a few months later when he claimed the P.G.A. Championship.

A less visible cloud hung over the Nelson in the form of the financial struggles of the Four Seasons Resort and Club itself. The resort was sold in September 2006 by San Antonio-based USAA Real Estate to Los Angeles-based BentleyForbes Holdings LLC, a privately-owned commercial real estate company (that happens to also own the Watergate complex in Washington, D.C.). The hotel's appraised value at the time of the sale was $229 million. Slightly more than three years later, Four Seasons went delinquent on its $175 million secured mortgage when it couldn't produce enough cash flow to cover its interest costs. An attorney representing BentleyForbes, Stephen Meister, told *The Wall Street Journal*, "We're not walking away from the property. We're trying to work things out." *The Journal* was told by debt-rating company Realpoint LLC that the hotel's appraised value had likely dropped to as much as $117 million or as little as $68 million. In January 2010, BentleyForbes defaulted on the Four Seasons' mortgage to start a series of transactions that saw the property change hands multiple times. In April 2010, Capri Capital, holder of the $39 million mezzanine loan, foreclosed on the resort's equity to move BentleyForbes out of the picture. The Irving hotel wasn't the only property in the Four Seasons' Toronto-based chain to change hands. The chain's founder and chief executive, Isadore Sharp, said that wasn't unusual given the time's economic turbulence. A foreclosure auction followed in June 2010. *The Journal* reported the winning bid was $122 million by US Bank, acting on behalf of investors. As of mid-May 2012, the P.G.A. Tour's agreement with the Four Seasons in Irving runs through 2017 but either party can give a notice of non-renewal beginning in 2013.

Over in Fort Worth, the Crowne Plaza Invitational at Colonial (the event's fourth title sponsor since beginning the practice in 1989) faced its own set of challenges. Its issues centered on a layout that places a premium on shot-making, where the longest hitters on Tour often say they can't take full advantage of their emphasis. Mickelson won the event in 2008, didn't play in 2009 because of his wife's illness, then didn't make the cut in 2010 after the most recent wave of changes were made to the course. In telling the *Fort Worth Star-Telegram* that he wouldn't play at the 2012 Colonial, Mickelson said the course "doesn't really suit my game anymore" and couldn't be sure when he'd play in the Fort Worth event again. Woods, even before the infamous events and injuries of the early 2010s, had not played there since his initial stop in 1997.

The most attention showered upon the Fort Worth tournament took place at the 2003 Bank of America Colonial with the "crossover" participation of L.P.G.A. superstar Annika Sorenstam. It was the first appearance of a woman in a P.G.A. Tour event since Babe Zaharias in 1945. What proved to be a boost for ticket sales and television ratings wasn't as warmly welcomed by at least a couple of Tour pros who were willing to publicly express their opinions. "This thing has become a sideshow," Scott Hoch said weeks before, as the rumors swirled that Sorenstam would play in Fort Worth. Singh said he hoped she'd miss the cut "because she doesn't belong out there." Indeed, she missed the cut – by four shots, shooting a 5-over-par 145 that bettered only eleven others in the field. But Sorenstam was greeted mostly by cheers and finished her play on Friday afternoon amid tears of joy in what surely was the most publicized and scrutinized male-female athletic competition in the state – if not the nation – since Billie Jean King swept Bobby Riggs in straight sets at Houston's Astrodome in 1973. In her post-play remarks, maybe Sorenstam intended to provide something of a response to Singh's rebuke: "It's been fantastic. They have cheered me on from the first tee to the eighteenth hole.

I didn't want to let them down. It was a great week, but I've got to go back to my tour, where I belong. I'm glad I did it, but this is way over my head."

The Nelson enjoyed its own brand of offbeat intrigue thanks to a high school student at Dallas' Jesuit College Prep (alma mater of Bernard Smith, who caddied for Nelson at the 1944 Texas Victory Open!). Jordan Spieth received a sponsor's exemption to the 2010 tournament as a 16-year-old junior in high school having won the state high school championship as a sophomore. What first appeared to be a novelty grew into much more when Spieth not only made the cut but was banging elbows with the leaders well into Sunday afternoon. He finished sixteenth and returned in 2011 to finish thirty-second. A freshman at the University of Texas during the 2011-12 school year, his collegiate schedule prevented him from returning to the Four Seasons for a third consecutive year. A month later, Spieth finished as low amateur at the U.S. Open played at the Olympic Club in San Francisco.

26

BUILDING A MONUMENT

A LASTING TRIBUTE TO one of America's great athletes of the twentieth century got its start at an emporium called the Chicken House Flea Market, a complex of metal buildings located on Texas' Highway 377/67 between Stephenville and Dublin. That was where Karen Wright had hopes of finding antique-looking furnishings for her Victorian house that weren't necessarily as expensive as antiques. Wright had moved to Dublin in 1982 after a tornado blew a condo she was about to buy in suburban Dallas to bits. The good news for Wright was Mother Nature got her out of an eighteen-percent loan; the bad news was she had no place to live. With much of her family living in Hamilton, Texas, about two hours southwest of Dallas, Wright took something of a calculated risk by leaving her work in public relations and marketing and decided to see how things would work out if she moved to a town not far from Hamilton, Dublin.

Wright owned a journalism degree from Texas Tech and, not long after settling in, was busy starting the *Dublin Citizen*, a weekly newspaper to compete with the longtime *Dublin Progress*. She found support for a new voice in town and, after about four months in business, turned Dublin into a one-paper town again – the *Progress* shut down. Wright initially operated the newspaper out of her home. And when looking for furniture at the Chicken House on one of her trips in 2001, she was assisted by John and Sissy Jones, who lived just southwest of Fort Worth in the town of Granbury. Sissy not only helped Wright pick out items but also traveled the couple of miles to Dublin to admire Wright's home and interior decorating.

In August 2009, Wright was out of the newspaper business (therefore, the newspaper was out of her home) and running the town's economic development corporation. She received a call one Thursday afternoon and heard a voice that exceeded even Wright's usually frenetic manner – something of a rarity. "I'm so glad I finally found you!" Sissy Jones yelled into her cell phone from a few blocks away. "Come out and meet my son!" Jones' son is Robert Stennett, a Fort Worth resident since 1984 who left a career in the aerospace industry at Lockheed Martin to become executive director of the fledgling Ben Hogan Foundation in 2008.

Wright nearly fainted from excitement when she and Stennett met, but recovered her composure in time to tell him of Dublin's yet-undefined interest in doing something to pay tribute to Hogan's first boyhood home. Efforts to that point, she indicated, had somehow gone down the wrong road. Stennett provided encouragement: "Maybe we can help you find the right road. Come on up to Shady Oaks." Wright is never much on waiting, and the conversation went like this:

"We can come tomorrow!"

"Well, not tomorrow."

"How 'bout Monday?"

"No, I'll be out of town."

"Well, we're free on Tuesday!"

And they agreed to meet for lunch at Shady Oaks in five days. Wright and Stennett's meeting wasn't completely happenstance. Stennett and long-time Nike engineering manager Tom Stites, a Hogan Foundation board member whose career in the golf club industry began at the Ben Hogan Company in 1986, had both wondered months earlier why Dublin didn't contain any tribute to its unique link to American golf royalty. Stennett decided that on a future visit to see his mother, he would continue south-west down to Dublin.

Over lunch at Shady Oaks with Stennett, Wright was pleased to learn how much of the Dublin portion of the Hogan tale that Stennett was familiar with: the blacksmith shop, that he attended Sunday school at First Baptist Church, where he attended elementary school. Stennett told Wright the foundation would gladly help open doors if the good people of Dublin had plans to move forward. When Stennett and company traveled to Dublin in the coming months, they always scheduled their trips for Fridays, the day that Granny Clark's restaurant served its fried chicken special. Those plans eventually congealed into a vision to open a Hogan museum. While Dublin is no metropolis, it's one town that loves museums. There was already Dublin's Dr Pepper Museum, the Dublin Rodeo Heritage Museum, and the Dublin Historical Museum – all located within a few blocks. Wright and other town luminaries almost immediately identified the logical place in town to house the Hogan shrine – the former Lyon-Prim Building across the street from the Rotary Building. While it would be only a one-room museum, it would be large enough to display various photos and artifacts from Hogan's life and golf career.

The next challenge was funding the project. Wright ran across the off-beat activity of staging a cow pasture golf tournament, which fit Dublin's needs perfectly given that the former Dublin-DeLeon golf course located a couple of miles outside of town had become part of a rancher's property. Staging such an event was a topic of conversation when Wright, Dublin mayor Tom Gordon and local video businessman Mike Simpson were returning from Abilene, where they attended the annual heritage symposium for west Texas towns called the Texas Forts Trail. The ever-imaginative Wright delighted in how zany a cow pasture tournament could be. Without greens, the golfers really couldn't even putt. Chipping toward the holes would prove entertaining instead of infuriating as long as the conditions were accepted in the spirit of the event. Simpson agreed with Wright's musings, but he emphasized that history should be as important as hilarity. When the next planning meeting was held at the Rotary Building, Simpson articulated how the former Dublin-DeLeon layout should fit in Hogan's legacy as "the forgotten fairways."

Eight of the nine holes of the former Dublin-DeLeon course were on the 150 acres belonging to one of Dublin's understated entrepreneurs, Clay Estes. He grew up in the Fort Worth suburb of Haltom City and built a meat market business not far from there in Colleyville. Estes eventually sold his business and sought the more serene environment of rural Erath County between Dublin and Stephenville. He moved his family to its current property in 1989, and he and son Scott operate Clay's Deer Processing and Smoke House in downtown Dublin. Wright approached the Estes family with the idea of turning part of their cattle grazing land into a golf course – for only one day – in the name of earning contributions to open the Hogan museum. The Estes family was not only willing but enthusiastic. Clay and Scott were aware of the property's history and had located remnants of the old clubhouse's concrete foundation and some metal signs that were used to identify the holes.

What followed was soon an activity that Pat Leatherwood – vice-president of the First National Bank of Dublin, whose father and grandfather had each served as mayor of Dublin – likely never imagined he'd be involved in. Armed with notes and a GPS, he and an intrepid group that included wife Lisa Lee, daughter Amy, and family friend Slayton Miller (plus Mike Simpson, capturing the process on video), set out to map nine holes that might come somewhat close to resembling the long-gone Dublin-DeLeon course. Leatherwood wasn't entirely new to the property. When in the insurance business in the 1970s, he met a client out on the land. He spotted something then that he initially thought was a flower bed only to determine he'd stumbled across a tee box.

Back then, there were no cows on that land. This time, there were. And they apparently weren't pleased with the scouting party measuring "fairways," digging golf holes in the ground (larger-than-usually holes since the poor players couldn't putt) and placing a flag in each hole. "The cows would come behind us pulling up the marking flags and pushing over the poles," Leatherwood recalls, his twang tinged with frustration. "It was almost like the cows didn't want us on their turf. One day we pushed the cows to another pasture. Before we could get started back with the layout of the course, the cows found a hole in the fence and were right back pushing over everything we'd just finished erecting." One of the challenges was placing the "fairways" amid live oaks, post oaks, cedar elms, and a few Texas mesquites far enough apart given that shots were apt to bounce in any direction on the crusty turf. "We would hit balls from every tee box to judge the placement of the holes," Leatherwood says. "It didn't take long before we realized it didn't really matter. I hit a ball toward the pin and was so happy when it was about to land two feet from the hole. It hit the ground and shot off at a ninety-degree angle never to be found."

Some gallant souls battle the terrain – without the benefit of fairways or greens – during the 2010 Cow Pasture Open tournament at the site of the former Dublin-DeLeon Golf Course. (Ben Hogan Museum of Dublin)

Hazards? Carelessly backing into a yucca plant or Mexican cactus would be more painful than a penalty stroke. Tournament rules allowed for participants to tote shovels and weed whackers. The highlight of the course architecture was locating the no. 1 tee box in the only existing tee box that sort of remained from the original course, believed to be the no. 3 hole. The determined Leatherwood party, after a couple of excursions, managed to lay out nine holes in plenty of time for the August 2010 tournament. August was chosen because it was the month of Hogan's birth. August, like the rest of the summer of 2010 in most of Texas, was even hotter than usual. A field of about fifty golfers paying $100 each divided into scramble teams that ignored common sense in the name of community pride and boldly took to the course. They immediately discerned that putters and golf shoes should be left back in the car. Golf carts? All-terrain vehicles were the order of the day though some players brought their horses. And the Estes family could only coerce so many of their cattle to vacate the course. Golfers were urged to grant the bovine right of way when they interrupted play. And there was no clearing the course of the cows' residue.

The honor of striking the first tee shot went to the Hogan Foundation's Stennett, who preceded his drive with a short speech to his fellow golfers: "You're going to have a blast, and you're raising money to help build the Ben Hogan Museum. I hope that this fall, as you watch that museum coming together, you reflect back on today, think of the role that you played in making that a reality, take a little pride in what you've done in making the Ben Hogan Museum part of the Dublin community." Stennett then took his stance in the shadow of a lone oak and began the tournament on the 145-yard, par . . . well, there weren't really any pars established for the Cow Pasture Golf Classic. Leatherwood and the other organizers figured counting total strokes would be enough to keep up with given the terrain. Only two of the holes were doglegs, the other seven straight shots ranging from 115 yards to 239. So it could be said most were par-3s when figuring two putts. But, of course, there were no greens. Fortunately for the golfers, they never had to go over any water. The only water on the course was found near the first and fifth hole areas; that was the pond where the Estes' cattle drink and bathe.

DeLeon's new school superintendent, Ray Crass, teamed with Dublin superintendent Shawn Barnett. Crass had ranched and run cattle in his day, so the prospect of wandering cows wasn't all that much of a distraction to him. Most of the players came from around the area and made it a day trip. The winning team, with a score of 24, was a foursome that drove in from Weatherford (located about an hour back toward Fort Worth). Matt and Jay Martin and Bo and Jacob Finley edged out the team from Dublin's First National Bank by three strokes. Jay Martin, Matt's father, lives in Savannah, Georgia. Father and son are partners in the magazine publishing business. Matt publishes *Erath County Living* and heard about the tournament through business dealings with Wright. Father and son are also avid golfers. So when Matt (a five handicap) told his dad about the unique golfing opportunity, Jay scheduled a working trip to Texas to coincide with the tournament. Matt owns a golf cart and jacked it up with oversized mud tires in order to deal with the terrain of the Estes property. The team made a critical decision early on. Its replacement for the non-existent putting game would consist not of using irons to chip toward the hole but of drivers and 3-woods for skimming the ball toward the eight-inch pipes that served as holes. Indeed, the team whacked a couple of "putts" of between twenty and thirty feet right in and won by three shots.

A closest-to-the-pin competition was staged at the 145-yard no. 1 hole, three shots for $5. Among the contestants was 23-year-old Chase Churchill, an Abilene resident about to go into his senior year of business management at Abilene Christian University. At five-foot-eleven and 200 pounds, Churchill sent his first shot about twenty yards short of the hole. He more than adequately compensated on his second effort, sailing the green and landing fifty feet beyond the hole; at least he didn't find the pond or hit a cow. Churchill's third and final shot represented everything the Cow Pasture Open was supposed to be. It traveled far right but struck a rock, ricocheted left and came to rest about two feet from the hole – the clear winner. Churchill's prize was something that he couldn't use at Dublin-DeLeon that day, a new Ping putter. The first- and second-place teams received an oversized replica of a wooden golf tee, carved from an oak tree that guards the no. 6 tee box on the Estes property, by local artist Dannis Lozano.

The Estes family served barbeque along with iced tea and Dublin Dr Pepper (a virtual requirement for dining in Erath County then) beneath the welcome cover of a couple of huge temporary tents. The grub was excellent, but the related conditions made eating an uncomfortable activity. For one, it was so blasted hot. Second, the cow patties provided an unwelcome aroma. Third, you might recall some golfers brought their own four-legged golf carts. When play concluded, they tied up their horses near the tents. Horses – especially horses on a blast furnace of an afternoon – attract flies. And the flies invited themselves to the barbeque.

All indications are Dublin-DeLeon Country Club closed in 1942, a casualty of the early months of World War II. In August 1941, the *Dublin Progress* published a front-page story announcing the club had completed renovations to the golf course related to the relocation of the highway and was also looking to add a tennis court and a croquet ground. Warren Hughes, secretary of Dublin's Chamber of Commerce, pledged to work with the club to increase the membership. While folks through the years might have mentioned in passing the old course and the fact that Hogan played there in his youth, it took more than sixty years for anyone to consider bringing the nine holes back to any semblance of life.

27

PAST MEETS PRESENT

DUBLIN'S ROTARY BUILDING was built in 1909 on the corner of East Blackjack Street and North Grafton Avenue, directly across the street from what was called the Lyon-Prim Building. The Rotary Club meets there every Tuesday, when the members sing the club song with Nina Rae Schrader at the piano (plugging along undaunted despite the piano lacking a few of the black keys) and say the Pledge of Allegiance before hearing from a guest speaker. The ground floor of the two-story building features a spacious hardwood surface that could serve as a dance floor, and that's just what an executive with the ABC-TV mini-series *Dancing With the Stars* thought when she phoned the Dublin Chamber of Commerce one Friday morning in the fall of 2008 and was connected with the executive director at the time, Karen Wright.

Wright was only half paying attention until the ABC executive stated the network wanted to rent the Rotary Building for ten hours a day, seven days a week, six or seven weeks. Ty Murray, the rodeo star from nearby Stephenville, and his wife, Jewel, were in training to appear on the series' next season, and they were dissatisfied with their practice venue in Stephenville. Someone at a practice mentioned a building over in Dublin that had a dance floor, and the ABC suits were ready to make things happen.

The executive asked Wright if the main room also had a wall of mirrors. She said yes (it didn't), and then asked when the network would need the building. "Monday," was the reply. "Which Monday?" Wright asked. "Next Monday." "No problem!" she crowed. Wright and a passel of other civic-minded Dubliners spent the weekend searching high and low until they found a wall of mirrors (from a store in Stephenville that was going out of business) and then got it installed before the ABC armada arrived bright and early Monday at 8 a.m. Jewel suffered an injury early on and couldn't compete. Murray was matched with professional dancer Cheslie Hightower and lasted ten weeks before being eliminated just before the season's final episode. (When Murray was done training in Dublin, he signed one of the interior support columns, and added "Never Weaken.")

That same Rotary Building hosted the $100-a-plate fund-raising dinner on August 13, 2011 – to coincide with what would have been Hogan's ninety-ninth birthday – after which the Ben Hogan Museum of Dublin was opened to the public for the first time. Robert Stennett came down from Fort Worth and brought four gentlemen who'd spent time working with or for Hogan to tell their most entertaining Hogan tales, which focused on how accurate he could still hit a golf ball well after his Tour career had ended and how quiet and nearly obsessed Hogan was while practicing.

"We want to tell the story in a way that the foundation would be proud, that the Hogan family would be proud and that Ben Hogan himself would have been proud, " Wright told the dinner audience. "We want to tell the story with dignity and with honesty in all the color that it warrants. As you'll see when you go over to the museum tonight, they were very happy childhood memories for Ben Hogan in Dublin, Texas." Stennett was the evening's final speaker. He began his remarks as a group of town volunteers (including Miss Dublin, Whitney Brown) handed out pieces of crystal that featured the foundation's logo. "Henry David Thoreau once said if one advances confidently in the direction of his dreams and endeavors to live a life which he had imagined, he will meet a success expected in common hours," Stennett said. "I guess he was fifty, seventy-five years before Mr. Hogan, but you'd think he wrote that about Mr. Hogan. You'd also say he wrote that about Dublin, Texas with the dream that we are realizing tonight." And he closed with a toast: "Mr. Hogan, on the occasion of your ninety-ninth birthday, we announce the opening of the Ben Hogan Museum of Dublin. May the Ben Hogan Museum be a key instrument to preserving your precious legacy, and may it always make the great city of Dublin proud. Cheers."

The Ben Hogan Museum of Dublin opened in 2011 thanks to the combined efforts of Hogan devotees living in and around Dublin and the Fort Worth-based Ben Hogan Foundation. (Ben Hogan Museum of Dublin)

GROWN AT GLEN GARDEN

At almost the same time that Dublin puffed out its collective chest at the establishment of a shrine to a town boy done good, the unthinkable began to happen to its most well-known institution. In June 2011, the parent Dr Pepper company – which had moved from Dallas to Plano and became Dr Pepper Snapple – filed suit in federal court against the Dublin operation, which just happened to be its oldest and smallest. The charge was that the Dublin bottler had violated its licensing agreement by selling its product beyond its authorized area of distribution and had further run afoul by injecting the name of the town into the product's official logo. The legal wrangling continued for months, and some Dublin residents anticipated – and feared – what would happen next. In January 2012, the sides settled out of court with the Dublin company reluctantly agreeing to stop making the sugar-sweetened Dublin Dr Pepper after 121 years. As part of the agreement, the Dublin Dr Pepper operation would once again be named Dublin Bottling Works. Its flagship product would become Triple XXX Root Beer; first produced in 1895, the slogan that appears on the bottle reads: "Makes Thirst a Joy."

It didn't appear anyone in Dublin was joyful over the developments that stripped the town of 3,700 of its most familiar entity. At the First National Bank of Dublin, Vice President Pat Leatherwood abruptly halted the bank's longtime practice of providing customers with free Dr Pepper. "As of today, I will never drink another Dr Pepper," he told the *Fort Worth Star-Telegram* as print and electronic media descended on the town. Beyond the emotional toll to the majority of Dublin residents, fourteen employees of Dublin Dr Pepper – about half the work force – were immediately laid off. Like the bank run in *It's a Wonderful Life*, bottles of Dublin Dr Pepper that were present across the product's distribution area began flying off shelves and into the hands of desperate consumers. Thanks to the law of supply and demand, the Three Sisters of Dublin gift shop down the street from the plant advertised bottles of Dublin Dr Pepper at $5, a six-pack for $25, and included in the ad a melancholy but accurate coda: "When it's gone, it's gone forever!"

In November 2011, Wright drove down to a regional Economic Development Corporation meeting in Hamilton. It took place across the street from the county courthouse in a 100-year-old stone building storefront bought four years earlier by Ray Ramsey Jr., an art connoisseur who moved from northern California to the childhood home of his wife, Frances. Ramsey converted the space into a private gallery, home to about 400 original paintings (from Picasso to Andy Warhol), open only by appointment. Ramsey came to central Texas from the Pebble Beach area, where he started collecting art after operating a Ferrari dealership for twenty-five years – and running a celebrity road racing team headlined by Paul Newman, Gene Hackman, Clint Eastwood, James Brolin, and Burt Reynolds. "I'm so glad you have that museum in Dublin," Ramsey told Wright. "I knew Ben Hogan. I caddied for him." Wright naturally implored Ramsey to tell her all about it.

Ramsey grew up amid the wealth of the Monterey peninsula, his father owning the local Cadillac-Pontiac dealership. Young Ray grew up seemingly interested in only two things: golf and cars. When he was four years old, his father would entertain friends by driving them around the area and having his young son identify passing cars by model and year. At age fourteen, Ramsey reached the final round of the Monterey Country Club junior championship, losing to best friend Pete Geyer. Ramsey and Geyer couldn't be pried away from the course in mid-January 1949 when the Bing Crosby tournament was played over three courses.

On one of the Tour pros' practice days, Ramsey and Geyer stood by quietly as the biggest names in the game made themselves at home on their turf. That included Hogan, who learned only minutes before his round that his caddie didn't show. Cam Puget, the club pro, turned to Ramsey and said, "Ray, go caddie for Mr. Hogan." Standing in his cashmere sweater, creased slacks, and FootJoys, Ramsey considered the request a breach of the country club's unofficial caste system. Instead of jumping at the opportunity, he stared back at Puget with a look of disbelief and replied, "I beg your pardon." At that point, Peter Hay, a highly respected Pebble Beach golfing executive, interceded: "Young man, you heard what he said." Ramsey wanted to scream out, "I'm the club junior runner-up! I'm dressed better than most of these pros! Caddie? Me? *I* should have a caddie!" Instead, common sense – and maybe self-preservation – took over. He simply answered, "Yes, sir." And he picked up Hogan's bag and joined the practice foursome.

As the group walked down Monterey's first fairway, Hogan surprised young Ramsey by engaging in conversation. "You must be a successful caddie," Hogan said, having no idea his intended compliment was taken as an insult. Ramsey fought to keep his frustration bottled up and answered, "I am *not* a caddie. I'm the runner-up of the junior club championship of this country club." "Well, I'll be damned," Hogan said. "Well, that's interesting. Thank you, very much for caddying for me. I really got into a tough spot. This is really nice." And Hogan then patted Ramsey gently on the back, totally disarming the upstart.

On the second hole, Hogan resumed the conversation: "Well, club champion, let me see your swing." And he handed Ramsey his driver. Ramsey swung a couple times, prompting a little laugh from Hogan, who then surprised his young helper once again. "Tee up a ball, and hit it out there," Hogan said. Ramsey complied. "Oh, my gosh," Hogan observed. "No wonder you didn't win the championship, with that swing." The good will that Hogan had built up was quickly fading. Ramsey blurted, "I beg your pardon." Hogan told Ramsey to stand in front of him and instructed him on how to properly grip the club and take his stance: "Hold it this way. Put your arms in close to your side. Relax your knees." Thus began a mini-lesson that lasted about five minutes and, much to Ramsey's chagrin, made perfect golfing sense. Hogan told him to watch as he hit two balls down the second fairway. "Now," Hogan said, "you just do exactly what I did there." Ramsey tried his best to mimic the five-time Tour earnings leader, three-time Vardon Trophy winner and reigning player of the year; his results weren't quite the same. On the fifth hole, Hogan invited Ramsey to try another shot and was more pleased with his execution. "You've got it now!" Hogan exclaimed. "You've got the hang of it!" Hogan and Ramsey chatted more throughout the rest of the round, and Hogan then invited him to eat lunch with him back at the clubhouse. That was where Ray Ramsey Sr. joined them and was introduced to Hogan by his son. Hogan struck up a conversation with Ray Sr.

At that point in Ramsey's rambling tale, Wright was mildly entertained by her host's recollections and was aware that Hogan went on to win that Crosby tournament. "Mr. Hogan and my father must have seen each other a couple of times the rest of that week," Ramsey continued. "At some point, Mr. Hogan told my dad that if he won the tournament, he'd buy a new Cadillac from him." At that point, Wright stopped listening to Ramsey almost involuntarily. She suddenly realized what Ramsey was going to say next. "Mr. Hogan said he wanted a new car for his drive back home to Fort Worth. But he never made it." Wright, the words almost stuck in her throat, said, "I look at that Cadillac almost every day at the museum."

It was the new Cadillac that Hogan bought from Ray Ramsey Sr. that he was driving when he couldn't avoid the westbound Greyhound bus on U.S. Highway 80 outside Van Horn, Texas that foggy morning in February 1949 "When I was talking to Karen Wright about that," Ramsey says, "it was the first time I'd told that story in my life. I was amazed at how I remembered all the details. For years, it was so horrible; you put it out of your mind. All I remembered was caddying for him and he fixed my golf swing."

28

FOR THE KIDS

A **STURDY BREEZE BLEW** right into the face of Hugh Prescott Bumpas as he prepared to take his stance in the no. 1 tee box at Rockwood Golf Course, staring down the par-5, 424-yard dogleg left that points southeast parallel to Jacksboro Highway in the direction of downtown Fort Worth off in the distance. All of four-feet tall and sixty-eight pounds, seven-year-old Hugh stood resplendent in shorts, well-worn sneakers, sky-blue golf shirt and his Westside All-Stars baseball cap. Such was standard garb for the day for the dozen or so boys and girls who were finishing a week's worth of instruction and spring break fun in March 2012 at the Ben Hogan Learning Center operated by The First Tee of Fort Worth.

Hugh and the other boys in his threesome were growing concerned as the group of girls ahead of them got ready to hit their second shots. The boys looked back occasionally from the red-tee area at the grown men who'd arrived a few minutes earlier at no. 1's back tees. Hugh and his friends were worried the men would grow impatient with the kids playing in front of them. "They'll wait," Donovan Solis said matter-of-factly, attempting to assuage any anxiety the boys might have. "That's part of the game." Solis is program director of

The First Tee of Fort Worth, joining the organization after eleven years as an assistant pro at Colonial and then two years as head pro at Northridge Country Club in Texarkana, Texas. Part coach, part referee, part guardian with the kids entrusted to his care, Solis would have looked much like any other golf instructor were it not for the bullhorn draped over his right shoulder.

"We're going to play a scramble today," Solis told the boys, then looking directly at Hugh adding, "Do you know what that is?" Hugh pondered for a few seconds then shook his head. "We're going to have scrambled eggs!" Solis replied. Hugh and the other boys said nothing, but the expressions on their faces indicated it was a little late in the day for having breakfast. Solis laughed and explained the golfing definition of scramble, about the same time the girls up ahead were safely out of range to allow the boys to finally tee off.

Hugh, a second grader at the Alice Carlson Applied Learning Center across the street from the TCU campus in southwest Fort Worth, likes to play baseball (hence the all-star cap) and also can't get enough of wakeboarding and mountain biking. But his parents, David and Angela, wanted Hugh and his older brother, William, to get an early foundation in golf. They believe their boys are less likely to be involved in baseball, wakeboarding, or mountain biking well into adulthood. (Small world: David's great uncle, Jim Bell, was a member at Colonial and played with Ben Hogan a couple of times. Hogan, David was told, even gave Jim a set of Hogan clubs.) So the Bumpases were eager to enroll their sons in multiple programs offered by The First Tee.

The Fort Worth chapter of The First Tee began operations in 2004 as an extension of the golf foundation started by long-time Fort Worth golf figure Lindy Miller in 1996. Kevin Long, former athletic director at Fort Worth Country Day, who was earlier involved with First Tee in Augusta, Georgia, became Fort Worth's First Tee director in 2006. About the same time that Long was brought on, The First Tee began its connection with municipal course Rockwood, which allowed the group to use nine of the eighteen holes for youth practice, but also offered its site for the 6,000 square-foot learning center. The building opened in spring 2011 and was officially dedicated the following December, with Lisa Scott traveling from California to represent the Hogan family.

The Ben Hogan Learning Center, located at Rockwood Park in Fort Worth, was opened by The First Tee of Fort Worth in spring 2011 and officially dedicated the following December. (Ben Hogan Learning Center)

Scott had traveled to Fort Worth a few months earlier for the "hard hat" tour and assumed she wouldn't be very surprised by the finished project. She says she was. "I walked in and was really taken aback," Scott says. Then she participated in the dedication ceremony and says she came away with a heightened appreciation of the city's interest in the project. "As an outsider, I got a sense of community that was really amazing. It's special to be a part of that.

Robert Stennett worked so hard to get the foundation's contribution and the building named for him. That golf could reach so many kids and teaches life lessons and core values – that walks side by side with him."

The center includes classrooms for golf instruction, hitting bays with computer analysis, a library, museums that detail both Hogan's career and the history of golf in the city plus a game room sponsored by J.J. Henry (the P.G.A. Tour pro who has played out of Fort Worth since playing for TCU in the late 1990s). One side of the structure's façade displays The First Tee's nine core values (honesty, integrity, sportsmanship, respect, confidence, responsibility, perseverance, courtesy, and judgment) and includes a nine-panel stone etching breaking down the famed Hogan swing.

29

HAPPY DAYS RETURN

THE FATE OF Glen Garden was bolstered indirectly in April 2012 when Fort Worth's city council voted to close the municipal Z Boaz Golf Course. The course opened in 1937, dug from the soil of southern Fort Worth as a W.P.A. project. It has often shown up on the list of worst golf courses in the country. When Dan Jenkins' beloved Worth Hills – affectionately called Goat Hills when he played it regularly from the mid-1940s through the late '50s – was dismantled in the early 1960s, Jenkins organized a "Goat Hills Glory Game Reprise" staged at Z Boaz as the next-best (or next-worst) option. Pulling the plug on Z Boaz would likely steer many a Cowtown golfer seeking an inexpensive round to Glen Garden.

Not terribly many Glen Garden members must have noticed in the March 2012 newsletter that the club's annual meeting was scheduled for Thursday evening, March 22, in the clubhouse dining room. Fewer than a dozen members attended and chowed down on the buffet of chicken fried steak, mashed potatoes, mixed vegetables, and tossed salad provided by general manager Sam Shafeeq, who came to the United States in 1966 as a young man from Pakistan and has been in restaurant-related businesses for most of his time in America. On the wall behind the desk in his office are photos of him taken with President Ronald Reagan and Speaker of the House Carl Albert from Shafeeq's time working at the Petroleum Club in Oklahoma City. He took the Glen Garden position in 2000, which meant no longer enduring a four-and-a-half hour drive from nearby Arlington out to a club in San Angelo; he usually stayed there a couple of days in an apartment, away from his family.

Shafeeq was charged with maximizing Glen Garden's revenue wherever possible. That means making the course available to outside groups to rent for tournaments, sometimes during peak hours on weekends. That also means providing a Sunday brunch buffet open to the public in general, which is very popular with neighborhood families. Members aren't always pleased with the effects that these efforts have on their play or having outsiders in their dining room. But the members have made it known they want the club's pricing system to essentially stay the same – no initiation fee and monthly dues of only $144. Also now in the club's favor is the improved condition of the course – particularly installation of new MiniVerde Bermuda greens in 2009 – that began under head pro Alan Courtney and continued under Jason Rocha, who took over in 2011 when Courtney retired. For Rocha, it was the second tour of duty at Glen Garden. He was Courtney's assistant 1997-2002 and then spent time as the program director with Fort Worth's First Tee program and as the pro at Lost Creek Golf Club on the city's west side.

There was another revenue source that literally came out of the ground. Chesapeake Energy began drilling for natural gas in 2009, setting up its equipment on the east side of the fence that runs down Glen Garden's no. 3 hole. (At one point, Chesapeake wanted to set up its equipment *on* Glen Garden's property, which would have meant altering the course.) For a time, the club was receiving healthy monthly checks from Chesapeake in exchange for the mineral rights beneath the club's property, essentially keeping Glen Garden afloat. But the checks aren't as big anymore, one of the messages in the club's state of the union message that night. The board members took their seats at the head table – co-owners Tallmon and Dowdy (Bob Ellis passed away three years earlier), club president Bill Nelms, and board member Jim Wurzbach. The message was one of tepid optimism. First, Nelms emphasized the need for members to bring new members into the fold. Dowdy then got into hard numbers of how much the club had lost each of the past two years.

"The gas wells have kept this thing open, but that money's gone," Dowdy said. "The good news is I think we can make this club work. I worked with Jason – if we can get thirty-five new members – and I think that's very achievable because I think we've already picked up seven or eight. We need about 3,178 more rounds of golf, which is nine more rounds a day. We think that's very achievable. Last year, Jason had a twenty-seven-percent increase in rounds of golf. It's like they said, we need more members." Tallmon was next to speak and began by hailing Dowdy's persistence in trying to fashion a financial plan that could help keep Glen Garden afloat. "Dowdy, he's a bulldog. He keeps chewing. I think he feels we're over the hump. It's only because Dowdy has sat in there almost every day of the week for several hours every day trying to make that work. I think all of us really need to appreciate the amount of work he's done in that office." Nelms closed the meeting with, "Thanks for coming. This was a very important meeting. Perhaps we didn't do our due diligence in promoting it correctly. Thank you very much, and let's have a lot of good years at Glen Garden." To which Wurzbach added, "Everybody tell somebody and have them tell somebody."

Glen Garden's centennial celebration was staged in early May 2012 with a full week of festivities, pieced together over a period of months by Shafeeq,

Rocha, and a committee of members, including club president Don "Scooter" Gault and Waddle. The highlights would be Friday night's banquet in the clubhouse dining room and a Saturday shotgun tournament in which players would pay homage to the past by using hickory shaft clubs. Much of the heavy lifting in securing adequate sponsorship and stumping for tournament registrations at clubs across Fort Worth was done by a non-member in the last weeks before the celebration took place. Ridglea's Bob Primm had played regularly at Glen Garden as a guest for years and was determined to help make sure the little club wouldn't fall short with a chance to enjoy a rare day in the sun.

The dining room filled quickly even with extra rental tables brought in, causing one member to quip: "Dowdy didn't build it big enough." The roll call of guest speakers at the dinner included Peggy Nelson, Jackie Towery, and Marty Leonard (daughter of Marvin Leonard). Glen Garden was fortunate its schedule of events took place the week before Nelson would assume her role as the hostess of the HP Byron Nelson Championship at the Four Seasons Resort and Country Club. There was also a parade of dignitaries representing assorted segments of local government. Kathleen Hicks, who represents Glen Garden's area on the Fort Worth city council, noted she grew up just around the corner on Robert Burns Street. "I have to tell you, I'm so pleased this organization is still around and they continue to do such wonderful things. This is really and truly a wonderful celebration. I hope you're around another hundred years. There's so much history in this room. Onward and upward!" Tarrant County commissioner Roy C. Brooks curiously pointed out that he doesn't play golf and that his son who does has played every major course in Fort Worth – except Glen Garden. "We'll have to correct that," Brooks added.

Peggy Nelson had the honors among the three headliner ladies and identified Glen Garden as the site not only where Byron learned the game but also where he recorded his eighteenth and final victory of 1945. "Byron had so many wonderful memories about Glen Garden and growing up here, becoming a caddie, learning to play the game and love the game and getting infected with the love of golf as he said. He didn't think he would have become as good a golfer as he was if it hadn't been for the support of the members here and all they did for him."

Peggy Nelson poses in front of an ice sculpture of Glen Garden Country Club's centennial logo before the celebration dinner in the clubhouse dining room on May 11, 2012. (Jeff Miller)

Peggy brought impressive hardware, including the championship trophy from Byron's 1945 victory in Toronto for the eleventh and final victory of his astonishing streak. She brought the Congressional Gold Medal that Byron was awarded in 2007 ("We're going to pass it around the room, and I do expect to get it back! I think we can do this because you look like a pretty reputable crowd.") She also passed around the 1937 Masters medal that Byron made into a pendant for her. "It used to be out on display at Preston Trail in Dallas," she explained. "Unbeknownst to me, he went to Preston Trail and negotiated to substitute another medal, took this one to our jeweler and had it made into a pendant and gave it to me." The ladies in the dining room let out a collective sigh. "And I did cry," she added. "This was the tournament that meant the most to him of all the ones that he had won because it showed him that he could compete with the big boys. I'm passing this one around on *this* side of the room, and I'm *definitely* expecting to get this one back." Jackie Towery spoke mostly about her father, Royal, and mentioned he bought a house a few blocks east of Glen Garden on Childress Street. That enabled him to conveniently stop at the club after work to hit a few balls or play a few holes. She said Royal didn't initially share her Uncle Ben's adoration for the game. "My dad really thought it was kind of silly to chase that little white ball around," Towery recalled. "But Ben came on and wouldn't quit. 'Just to keep you quiet and for you to get off my back, I'm going one time.' Dad came out here, and the rest is history." (He won the city championship three times in four years.)

Marty Leonard brought her own piece of jewelry related to Glen Garden's celebration. "It's a pin with a club head, and it says 'From BH to ML,'" she said, holding it out from her red pants suit jacket. "Valerie told me he picked it out for me." She went on to try to answer the frequent question of whether Hogan considered her father to be his surrogate father. "Ben's first instructional book, in the '40s, *Power Golf* – in it, it says 'To Marvin Leonard, the best friend I will ever have. If my father had lived, I would have wanted him to be just like you.' What more can you say?"

Glen Garden general manager Sam Shafeeq is flanked by club co-owners Clarence Dowdy [left] and Malcolm Tallmon following the centennial celebration dinner on May 11, 2012. (Jeff Miller)

The dinner gathering was barely aware of the thunderstorm that raged outside but had moved east by the time the program ended around 9 p.m. The heavy rain left the greens somewhat soft for the following day's hickory shaft tournament. Many of the 120 players gladly complied with the request that, in concert with the centennial theme, they dress in 1912-style golf attire. There was a wide array of argyle socks and knickers; some of the pants were actual knickers, but most were regular trousers tucked into the high socks and folded over. Many men wore ties (and so did longtime member Sally Underwood, along with a long skirt). Dowdy probably sported the loudest outfit – apple red cap and knickers, canary yellow golf shirt, and red-and-yellow socks. One observer deftly noted he could spill either ketchup or mustard in the lunch buffet line and no one would be the wiser. Primm took his costuming to another level. In addition to the tie, knickers, and plaid Scottish tam, Primm's head gear included scruffy red hair splaying out in all directions. And when asked to pose for pictures, he added an upper bridge of false teeth that looked like they might have been put together in 1912. "He looks like the superintendent in *Caddyshack*!" someone said.

The clubs were rented from Stirling's Hickory Club run by Brandon Clay from nearby Arlington. Glen Garden decided to rent only one set per foursome. Minutes before the shotgun start, Clay advised the participants that they should swing smoothly and not as hard as they would regular clubs. "Each set costs $1,700, so be careful," he said. "But I want you to have fun. We're going to have three or four broken; that always happens. If it does, just pick up both pieces and bring them back. I can get them reshafted." Turned out only four clubs were broken that day. The winning team was Rocha, his son, Cain, plus Don and Sally Underwood. Sally said she was unaffected by wearing the long skirt.

And no one struck the electrical tower.

BIBLIOGRAPHY

Awbrey, Jon Anthony and the *Dublin Citizen*. *Legends of Dublin: Personalities of the Irish Capital of Texas*. Dublin, Texas: Dublin Citizen. 2006.

Barkow, Al. *Getting' to the Dance Floor: An Oral History of American Golf*. New York: Atheneum. 1986.

Barkow, Al. *Golf's Golden Grind: The History of the Tour*. New York and London: Harcourt Brace Jovanovich. 1974.

Barrett, David. *Miracle at Merion: The Inspiring Story of Ben Hogan's Amazing Comeback and Victory at the 1950 U.S. Open*. New York: Skyhorse Publishing. 2010.

Bradley, Jon. *Quotable Byron: Words of Wisdom, Faith, and Success for Life and Golf by and about Byron Nelson, Golf's Great Ambassador*. Nashville, Tennessee: TowleHouse Publishing. 2002.

Companiotte, John. *Byron Nelson: The Most Remarkable Year in the History of Golf*. Chicago, Illinois: Triumph Books. 2006.

Davis, Martin. *Ben Hogan: The Man Behind the Mystique*. Greenwich, Connecticut: The American Golfer. 2002.

Davis, Martin. *Byron Nelson: The Story of Golf's Finest Gentleman and the Greatest Winning Streak in Golf History*. Greenwich, Connecticut: The American Golfer. 1997.

Davis, Martin. *The Hogan Mystique: Classic Photographs of the Great Ben Hogan by Jules Alexander: Essays by Dave Anderson, Ben Crenshaw and Dan Jenkins: Commentary by Ken Venturi*. Greenwich, Connecticut: The American Golfer. 1994.

Dodson, James. *American Triumvirate: Sam Snead, Byron Nelson, Ben Hogan, and the Modern Age of Golf*. New York: Alfred A. Knopt. 2012.

Dodson, James. *Ben Hogan: An American Life*. New York: Random House. 2004.

Editors of GOLF Magazine. *GOLF Magazine's Encyclopedia of Golf, second edition*. New York: Harper Collins Publishers. 1993.

Frost, Mark. *The Match: The Day the Game of Golf Changed Forever*. New York: Hyperion. 2007.

Gregston, Gene. *Hogan: The Man Who Played for Glory*. Grass Valley, California: The Booklegger. 1978.

Hauser, Melanie, editor. *Under the Lone Star Flagstick*. New York: Simon & Schuster. 1997.

Hogan, Ben with Wind, Herbert Warren, and Ravielli, Anthony. *Ben Hogan's Five Lessons: The Modern Fundamentals of Golf*. New York: Golf Digest Classic. 1957 and 1985.

Hogan, Ben. *Power Golf: Championship Secrets from a Golf Legend*. New York: Gallery Books. 1948.

Meyers, Reid E. *The Ghosts of Old Brack: A Pictorial History of the Brackenridge Park Golf Course, the Birthplace of Public Golf in Texas*. Dallas, Texas: Padgett Printing. 2010

Nelson, Byron. *How I Played the Game: Byron Nelson: An Autobiography*. Dallas, Texas: Taylor Publishing Company. 1993.

Nelson, Charles Wade. *As I Remember: Memoirs*. Abilene, Texas: self-published. 2001.

Nelson, Peggy. *Life With Lord Byron: Laughter, Romance and Lessons Learned from Golf's Greatest Gentleman*. Fort Worth, Texas: Creative Enterprise Studio. 2010.

Newberry, Kevin. *Texas Golf: The Best of the Lone Star State*. Houston, Texas: Gulf Publishing. 1998.

Sampson, Curt. *A Dallas Classic: A Club History of Lakewood Country Club*. Dallas, Texas: Lakewood Country Club. 2011.

Sampson, Curt. *Hogan*. Nashville, Tennessee: Rutledge Hill Press. 1996.

Sampson, Curt. *The Eternal Summer: Palmer, Nicklaus and Hogan in 1960, Golf's Golden Year*. Dallas, Texas: Taylor Publishing Company. 1992.

Sampson, Curt, and Milosevich, Paul. *Texas Golf Legends*. Lubbock, Texas: Texas Tech University. 1993.

Stricklin, Art. *A History of Northwood Club 1946-2002: Thanks for the Memories*. Virginia Beach, Virginia: The Donning Publishers. 2002.

Trimble, Frances. *Colonial Country Club: The Diamond Jubilee*. Fort Worth, Texas: Colonial Country Club. 2010.

Tschetter, Kris, with Eubanks, Steve. *Mr. Hogan: the Man I Knew: An LPGA Player Looks Back on an Amazing Friendship and Lessons She Learned from Golf's Greatest Legend*. New York: Gotham Books. 2010.

Vasquez, Jody. *Afternoons with Mr. Hogan: A Boy, a Golf Legend and the Lessons of a Lifetime*. New York: Gotham Books. 2004.

Voorhees, Randy. *As Hogan Said: the 389 Best Things Ever Said About How to Play Golf*. New York: Mountain Lion Books. 2000.

Wade, Don, editor. *One Week in April: The Masters*. New York: Sterling Innovation. 2007.

Wright, Karen. *The Road to Dr Pepper, Texas: The Story of Dublin Dr Pepper*. Abilene, Texas: State House Press. 2006.

ADDITIONAL SOURCES

Associated Press, Atlanta Journal, Augusta Chronicle, Golf Digest, GolfChannel. com, Dallas Morning News, Dallas Times Herald, Dublin Citizen, Dublin Progress, ESPN.com, *Fort Worth Press, Fort Worth Record, Fort Worth Record-Telegram, Fort Worth Star-Telegram, Fort Worth Weekly, Los Angeles Herald-Examiner, Los Angeles Times, Philadelphia Evening Bulletin, Philadelphia Inquirer,* Portland's *Oregonian, Richmond News Leader, New York Herald Tribune, New York Times, Seattle Post-Intelligencer, Seattle Times, Shreveport Journal, Shreveport Times, Sports Illustrated, Texarkana Gazette, Texarkana Press, Toledo Blade, Toledo Times, Wall Street Journal*

ACKNOWLEDGMENTS

Thanks so much to the many people who helped with this book:

Former Skyhorse Publishing editor Mark Weinstein; current Skyhorse editor Jay Cassell; the copyediting genius of Tom McCarthy; the members and staff of Glen Garden Country Club, particularly Dirty Dozen "commissioner" Wendell Waddle, Sam Shafeeq, and Jason Rocha; Karen Wright; Robert Stennett and Lisa Scott of the Ben Hogan Foundation; Charles Nelson; Jon Anthony Awbrey; Jon Bradley; Peggy Nelson; Marty Leonard; Cathy Spitzenberger of the University of Texas at Arlington; Curt Sampson; Jeff Rude; Martin Davis; Verne Lundquist; Reid Meyers; Jerhea Nail and Lesley Weaver of Northwest Independent School District; Byron Nelson High School principal Lesley Weaver; Kevin Long and Donovan Solis of the Ben Hogan Learning Center; Ron Hadfield, Lance Fleming, and Chris Macaluso of Abilene Christian University; Sharon Taylor of LSU-Shreveport's Noel Memorial Library; Ray Ramsey Jr.; Mary Yantis; Roy Housewright of Fort Worth ISD; Art Romero of Texarkana Country Club; Bob Elliott of Northwood Club; Gilbert Freeman of Lakewood Country Club; Nancy Stulack of the U.S.G.A.; Dylan Rogers.

Wendell Waddle, a regular at Glen Garden since he worked part-time in the golf shop while attending Poly High in the 1940s, poses in his 1912-style golfing garb before teeing off in the club's hickory shaft tournament on May 12, 2012. (Jeff Miller)